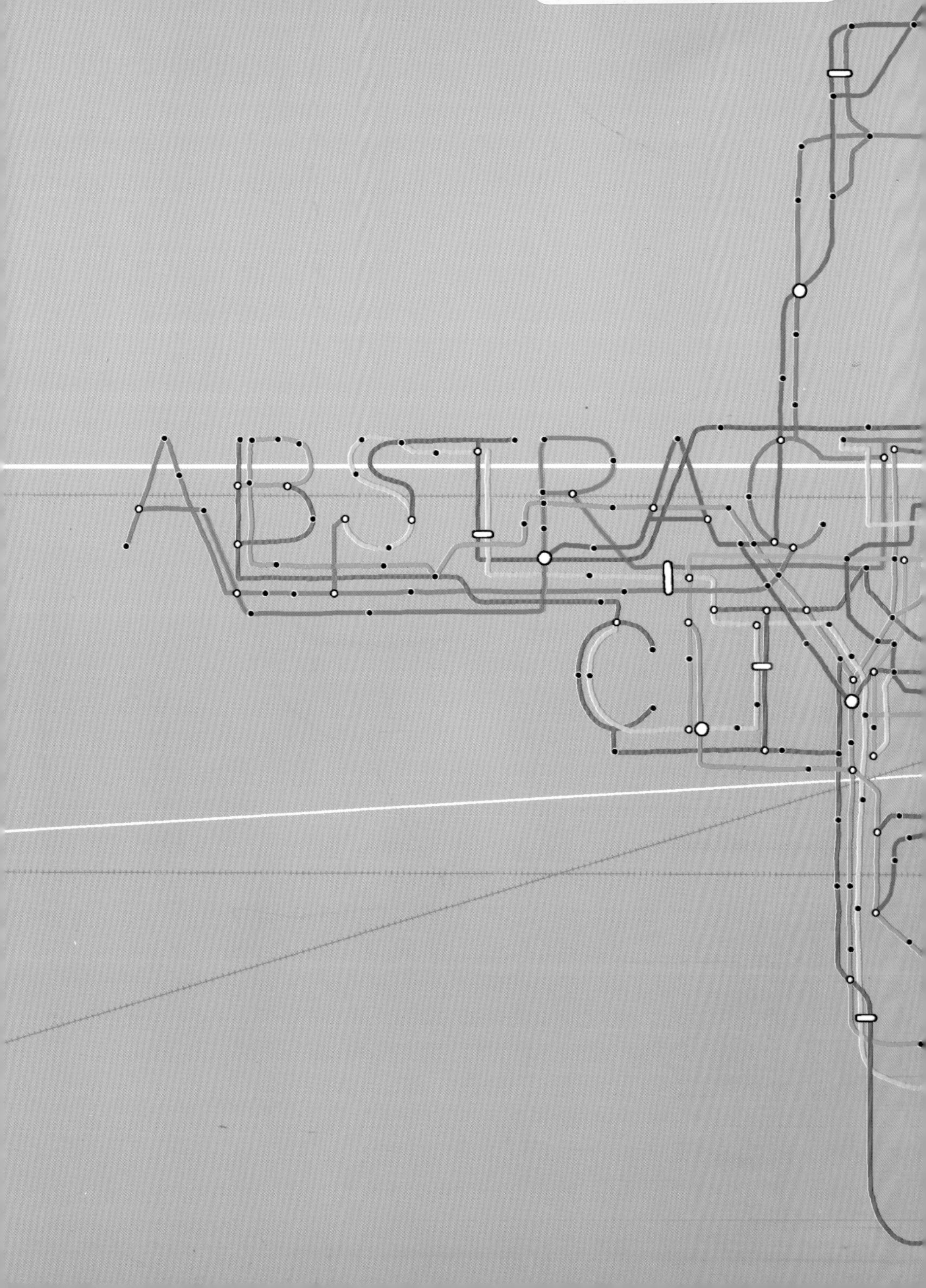
ABSTRACT
CITY

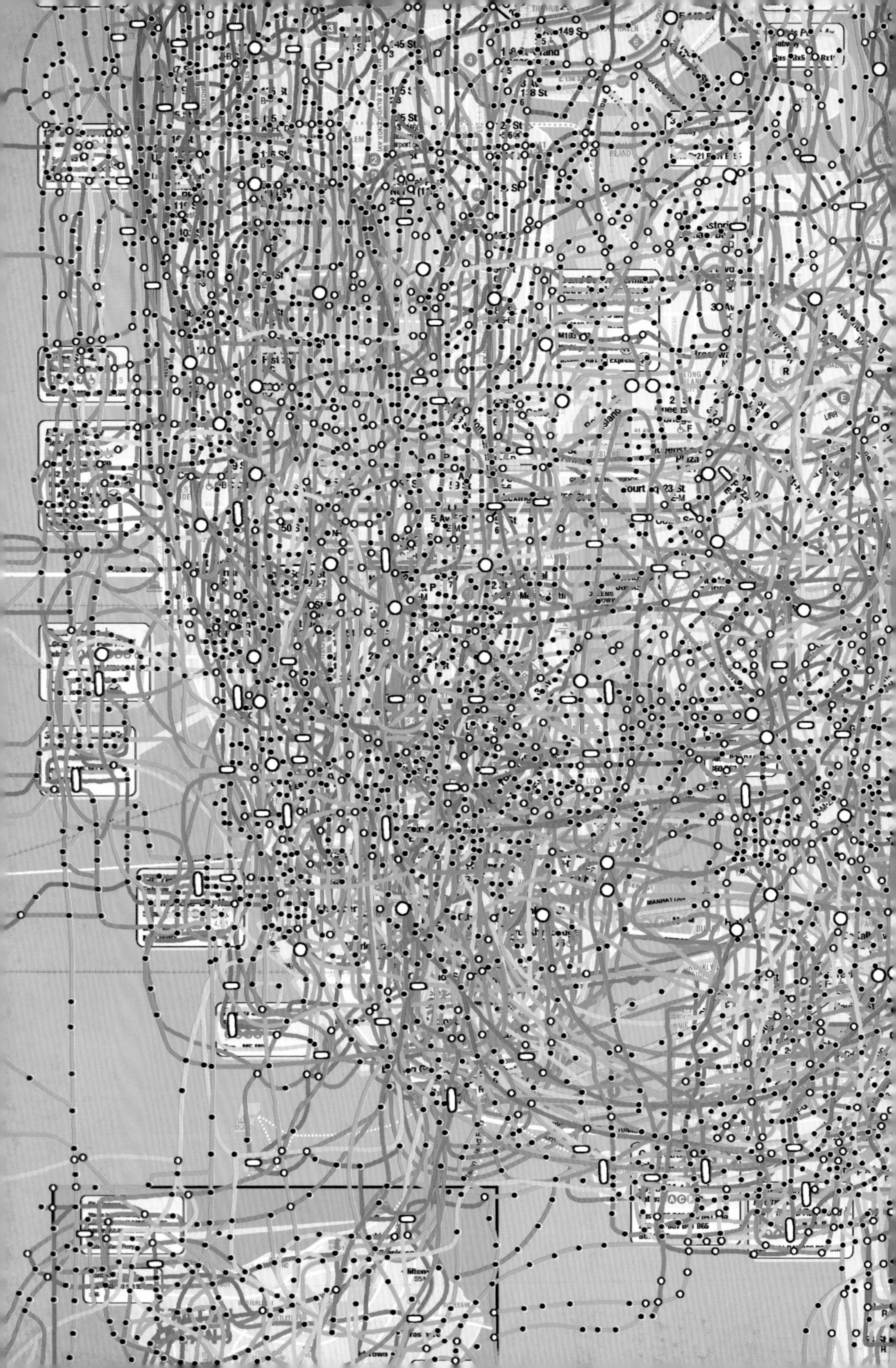

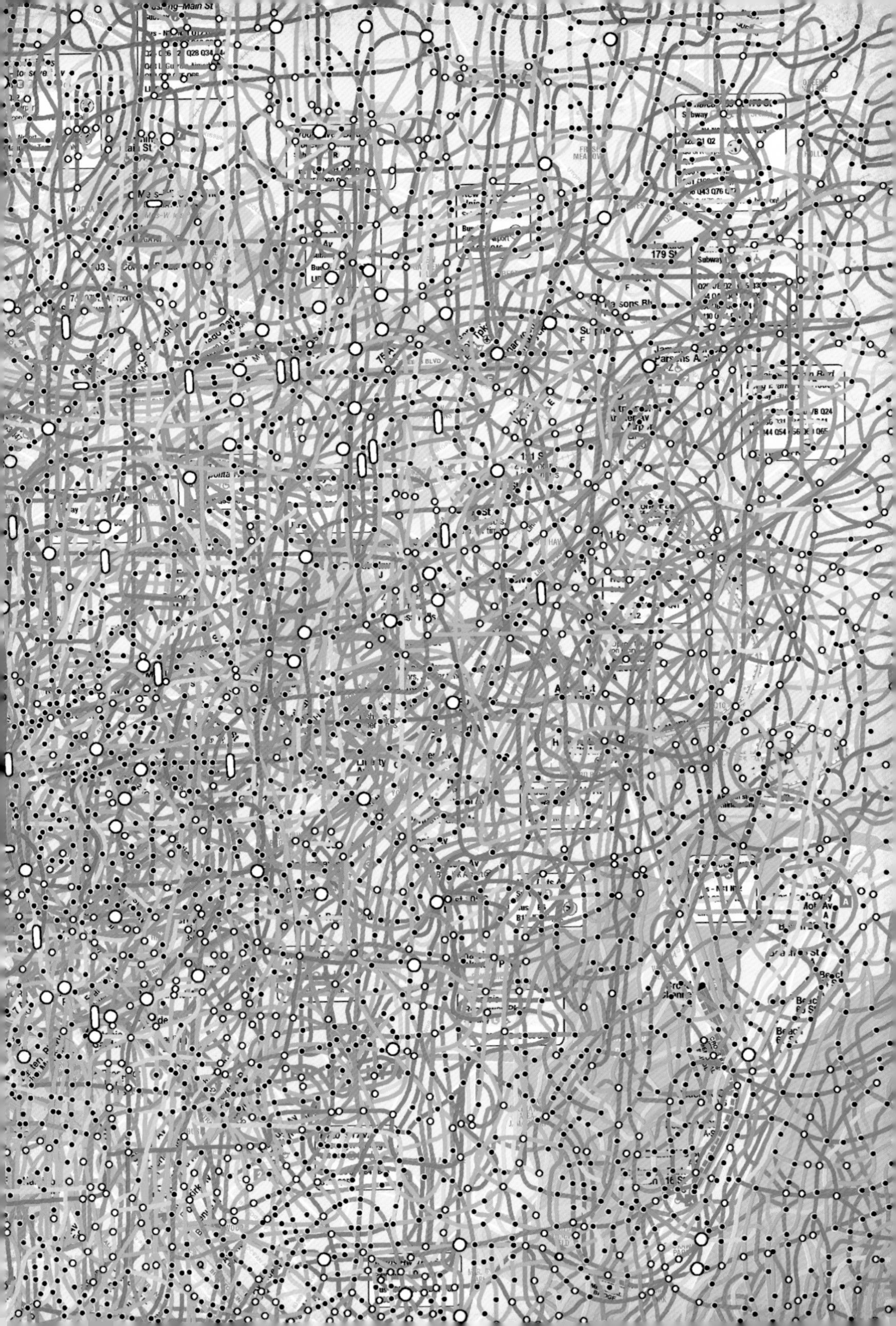
179 St
Subway

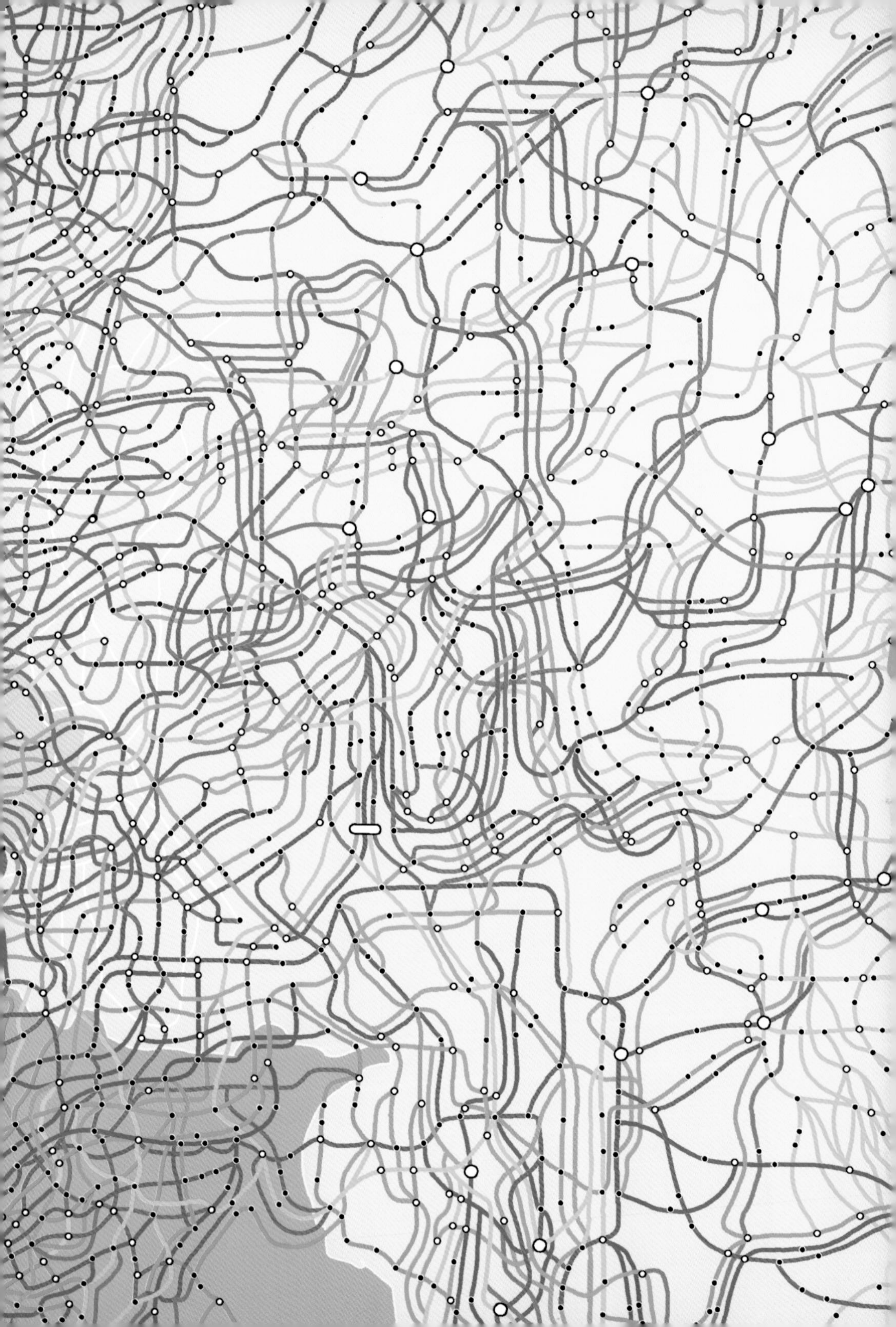

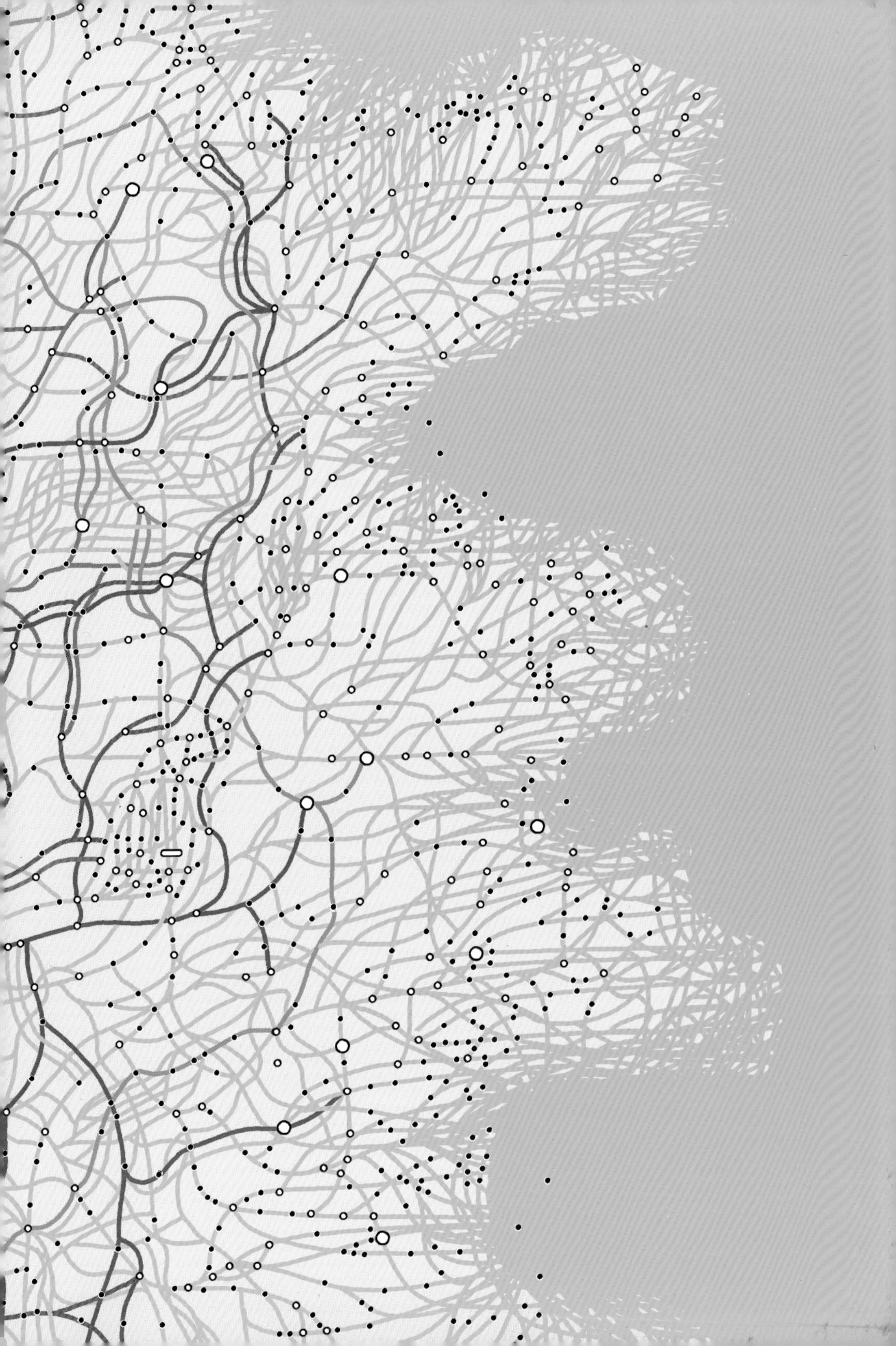

Abstract

Christoph

Niemann

City

Abrams, New York

Contents:

1. The Boys and the Subway

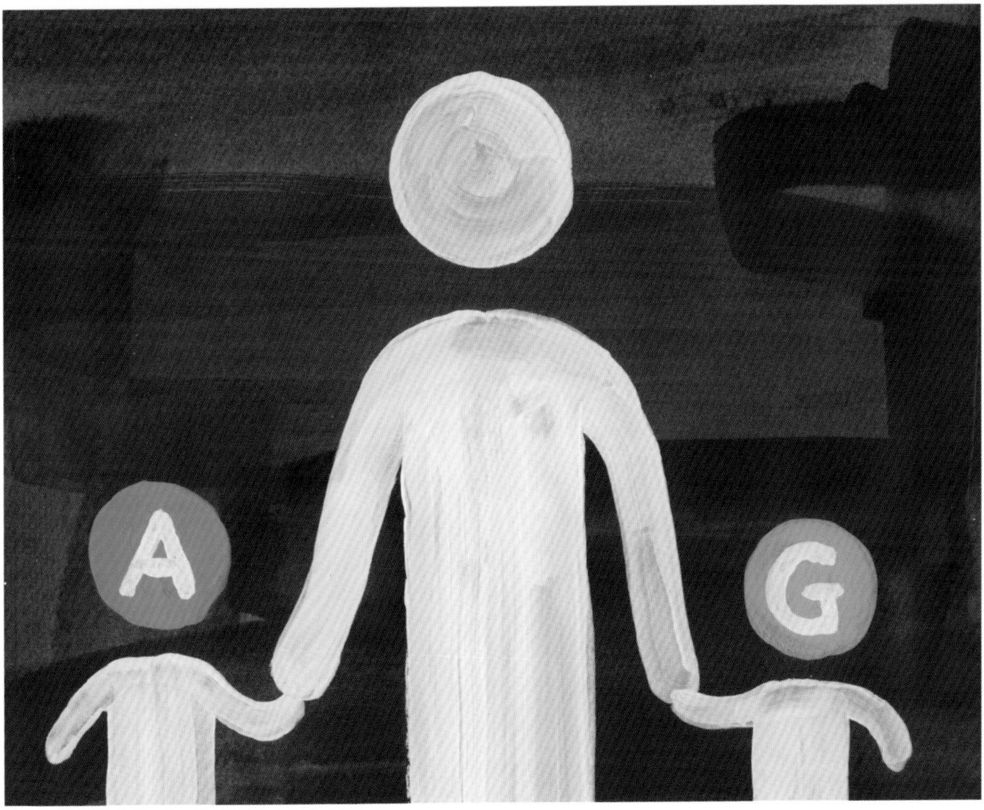
A
G

My sons Arthur, five, and Gustav, three, are obsessed with the New York City subway system.

They can barely sit through an episode of *Sesame Street*. But when we go for aimless subway joyrides on the weekends, they sit like little angels, devoutly calling out the names of every station for hours.

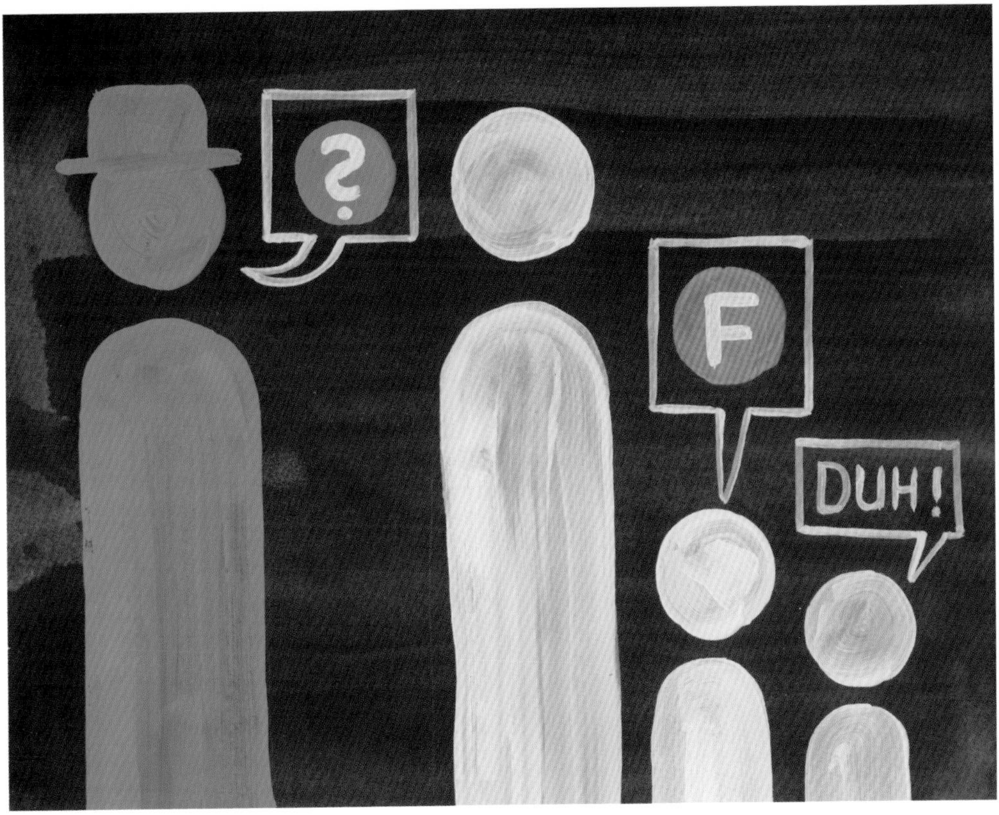
?
F
DUH!

People often ask me for directions in the subway. Even though I know my way around rather well, I still have to defer to Arthur very often. Yet it seems people don't trust the advice of a preschooler. They should.

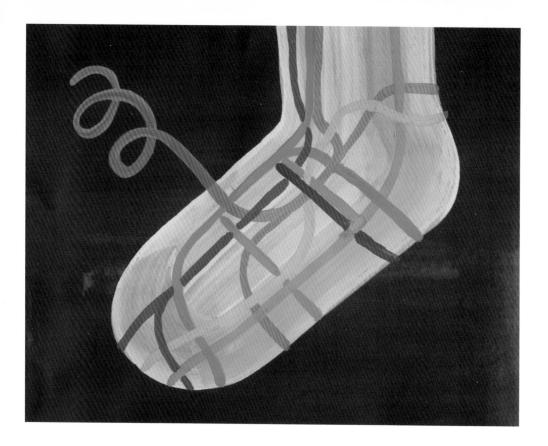

Arthur knows the map so well that when he got his first pair of subway-map socks, he pointed out with a chuckle that it had the Q still running as an orange line.

SKERMERON
SCHKERMERMON
SHKERMORON
SCHMERMERON

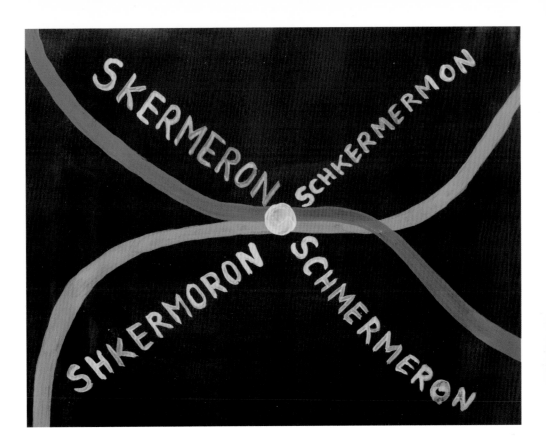

Arthur spends hours studying the subway map. He laughs at his mother when she suggests taking the B on a weekend. The only questions he has are about the pronunciation of some station names.

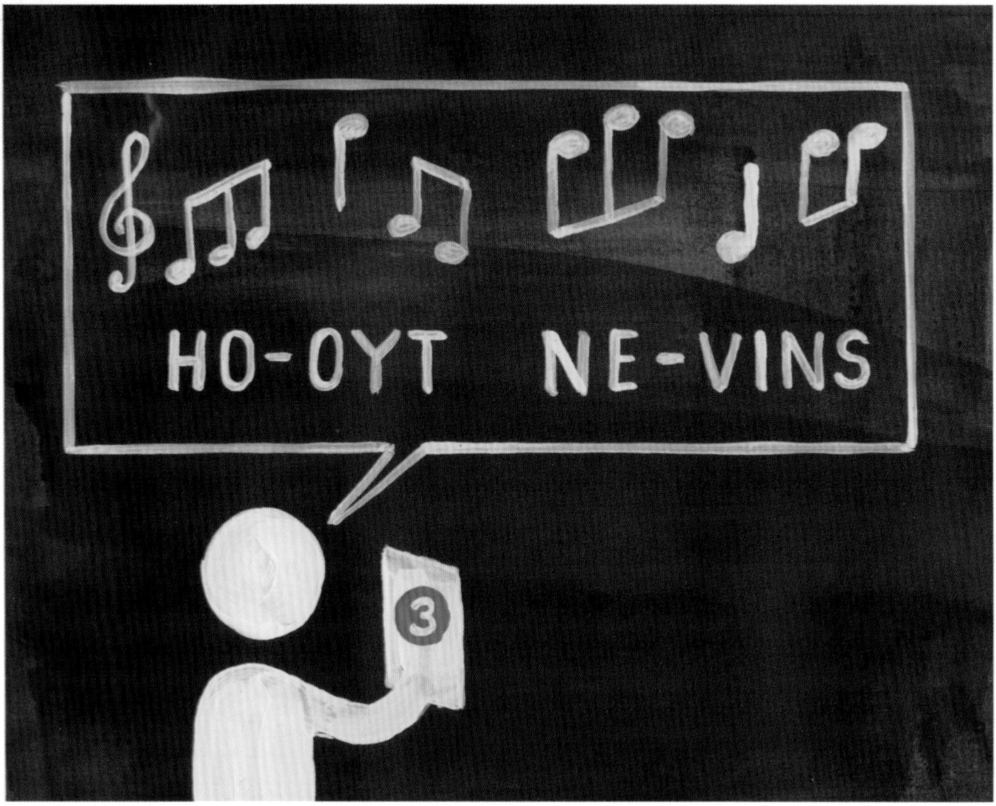
HO-OYT NE-VINS
3

This morning he read the timetable for the number 3 train and sang the stations to the tune of "Shalom Aleichem."

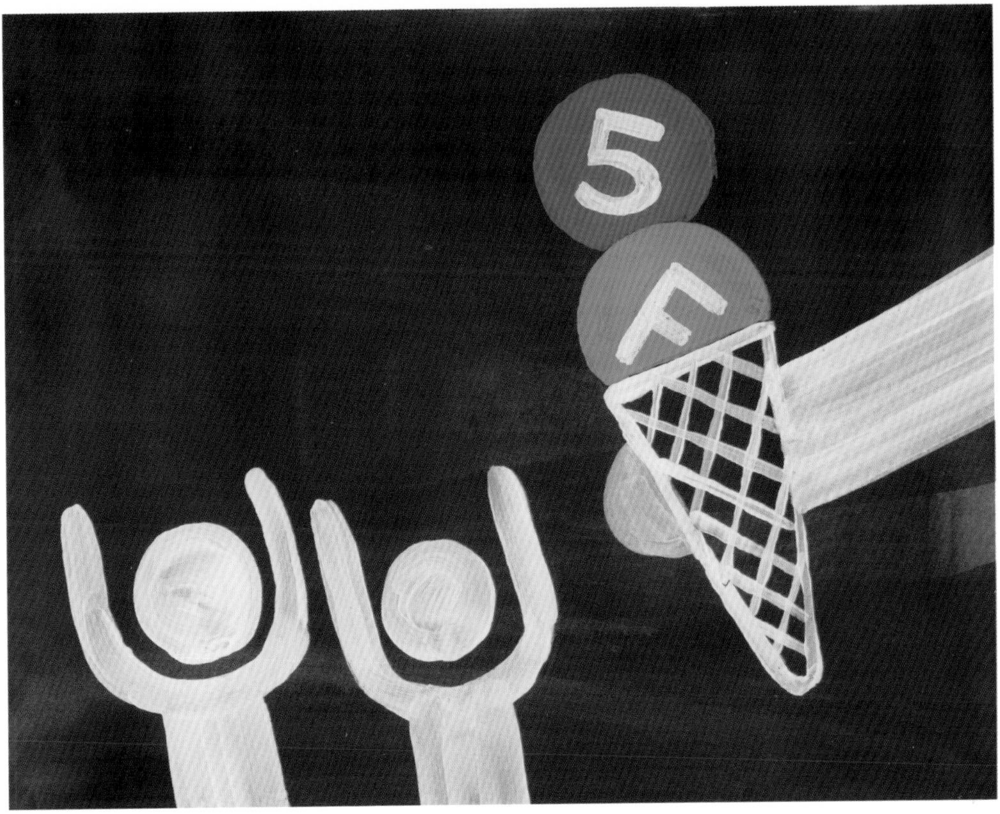
5
F

The two happiest words Arthur and Gustav can hope to hear are "service changes."

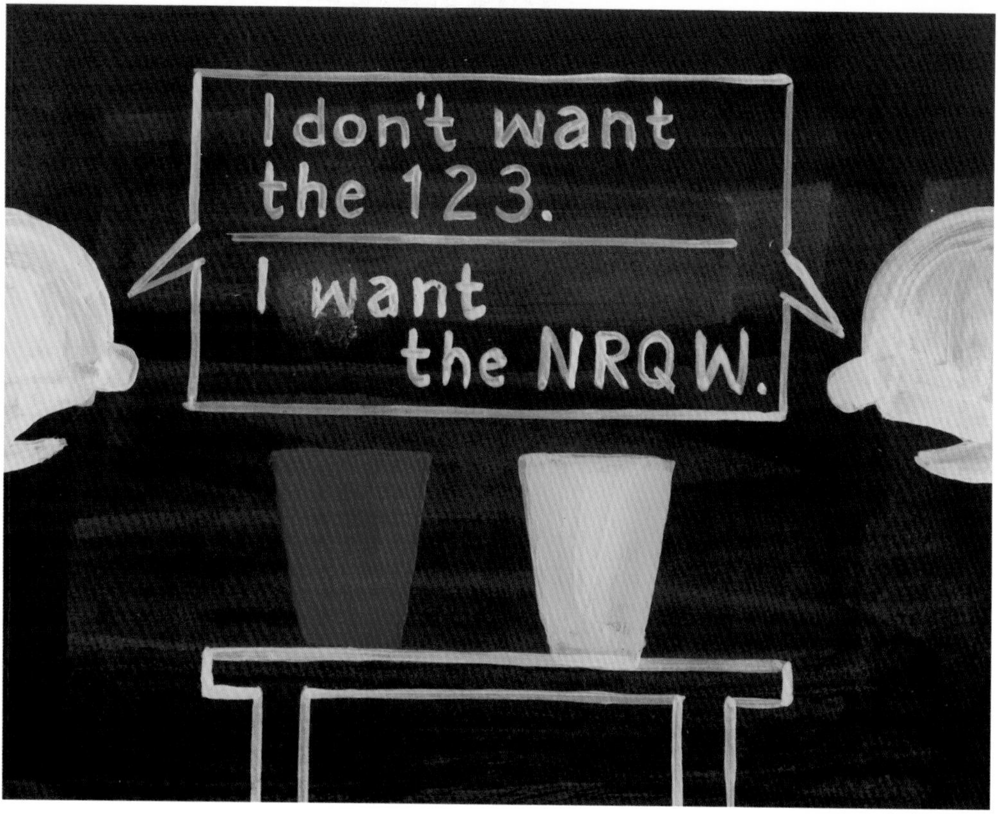
I don't want the 123.
I want the NRQW.

They see everything through a subway lens. When they fight about who gets which cup for their apple juice, they don't refer to them by color.

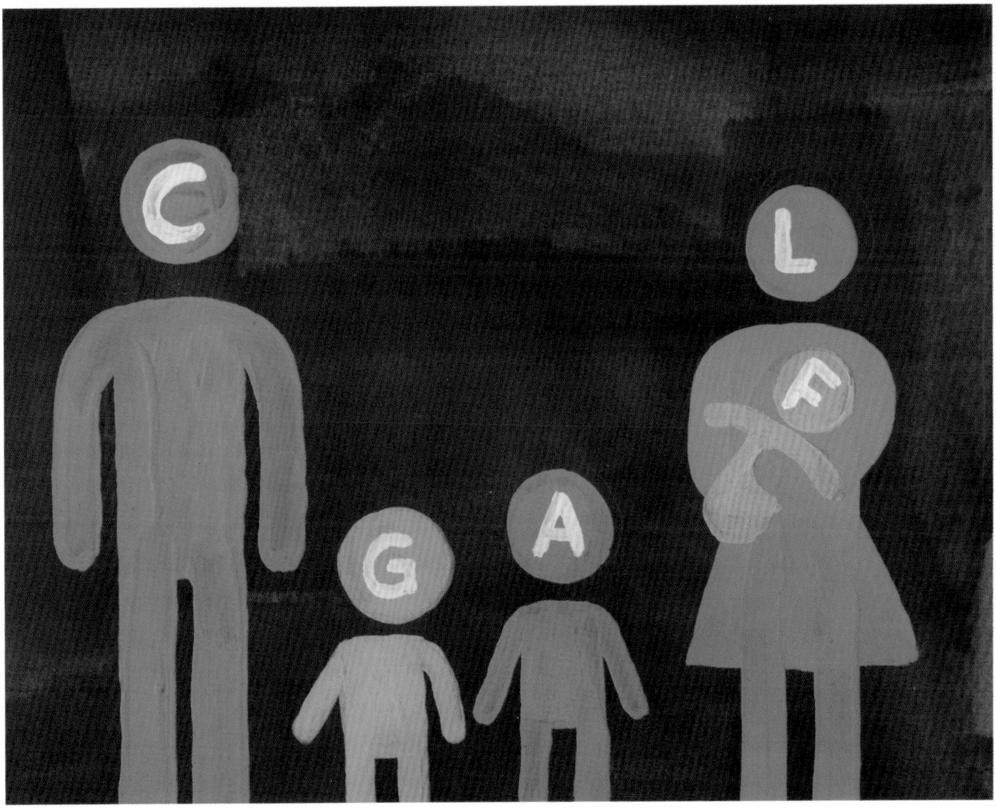
C
L
F
G
A

When we had our third son recently, my wife, Lisa, and I knew that we could not name him anything like Ivan, Keith, Otto, Pierre, Toby, Ulysses, or Xavier. We decided to go with Fritz.

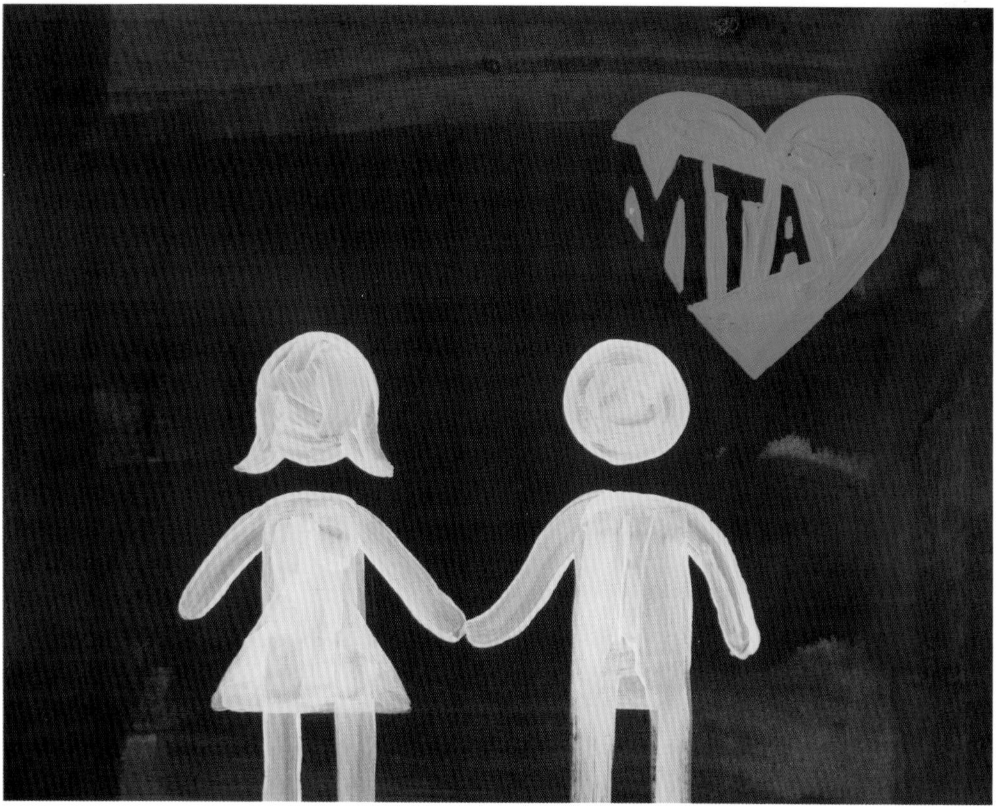
MTA

A chaperone on one of Arthur's school trips told me something he overheard when all the kids were neatly lined up in rows of two. The girl holding Arthur's hand asked him, "Have you heard of Peter Pan?" "No," he replied. "Have you heard of Metro-North?"

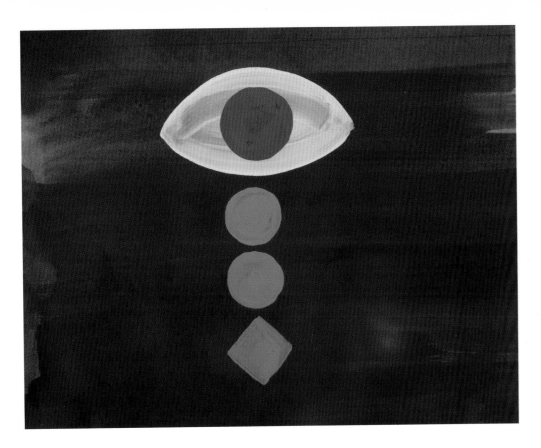

When your child cries in public, it is usually an uncomfortable situation. Once, we needed to get home quickly from Chambers Street, and I told Gustav that we had to take whichever blue train came next. The A train pulled in, and Gustav (who had been hoping for the C) started throwing a fit. However, the other passengers in the car gave me warm smiles. I guess they hadn't seen that many three-year-olds sobbing, "Local . . . I want the local."

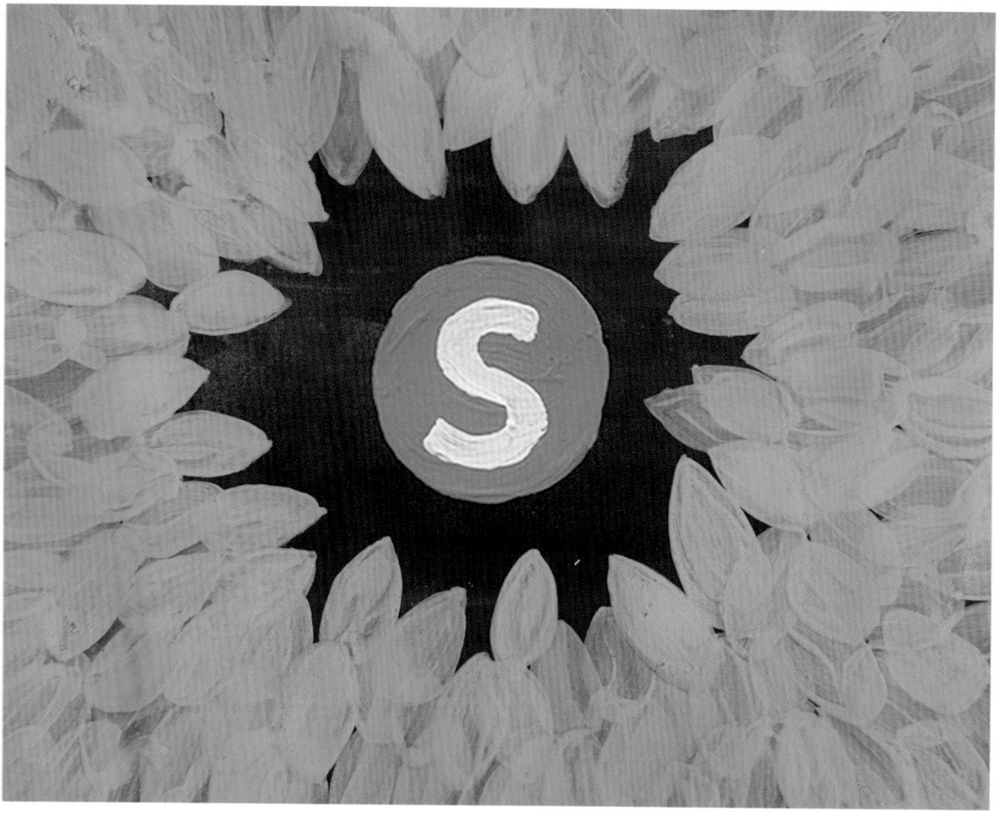
S

We often go to the Brooklyn Botanic Garden. They have a little children's garden that the boys love. Arthur and Gustav's favorite spot is a little gap between some bushes, from which you can see the Franklin Avenue shuttle train go by.

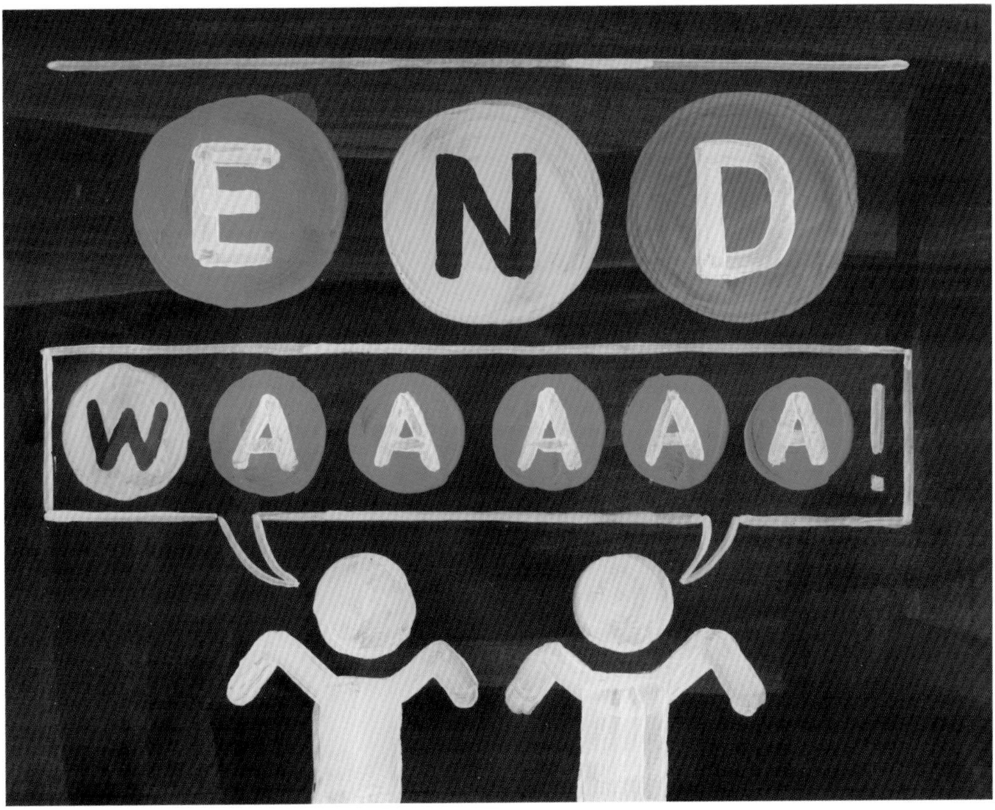
END
WAAAAA!

There is one place that's even better than the subway: the Transit Museum! One weekend, I promised them they could stay there as long as they wanted, just to find out how long they could possibly last. After four hours, I heard the announcement that the museum would close in ten minutes. Arthur and Gustav cried as I dragged them out.

2. Bathroom Art

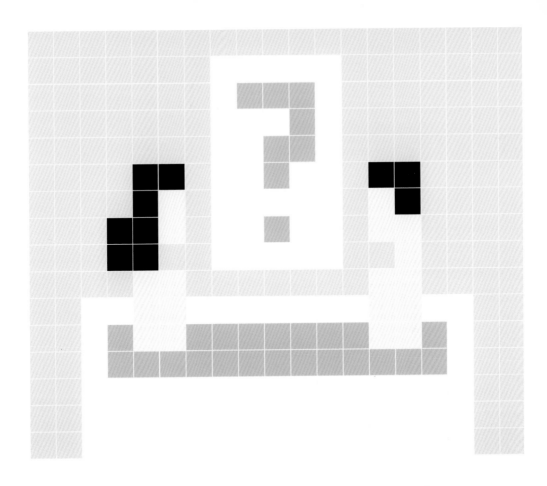

My wife, Lisa, and I just finished renovating our new home in Berlin. I took this as an opportunity to realize one of my old artistic dreams: designing the bathrooms with pixel drawings made of classic 4-by-4-inch colored tiles.

I don't like to surround myself with my own drawings (I stare at them all day long when I work). So we decided to take a famous piece of art and turn it into an abstract mosaic.

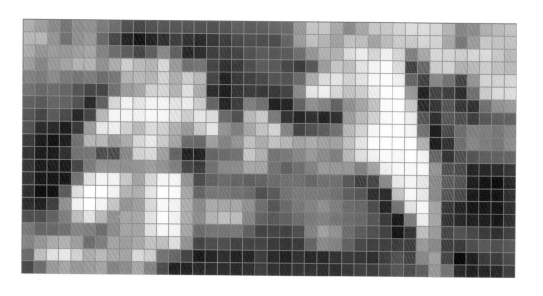

Done!
Or so we thought... until we found out that the tile maker didn't have that many shades of color.

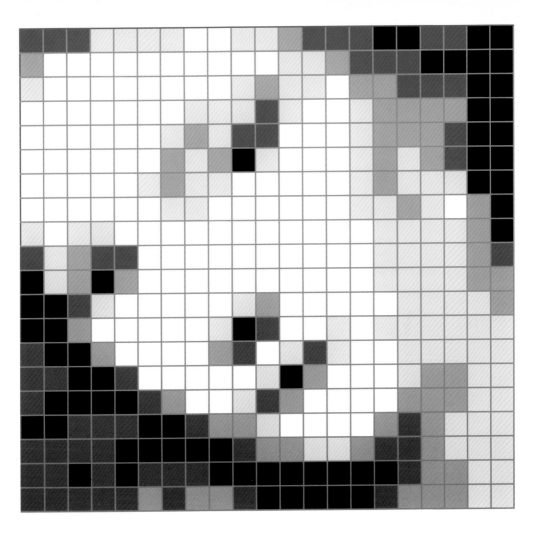

A detail of the "Venus of Urbino" might have worked in black and white, but this made the 1530s feel too much like the 1980s.

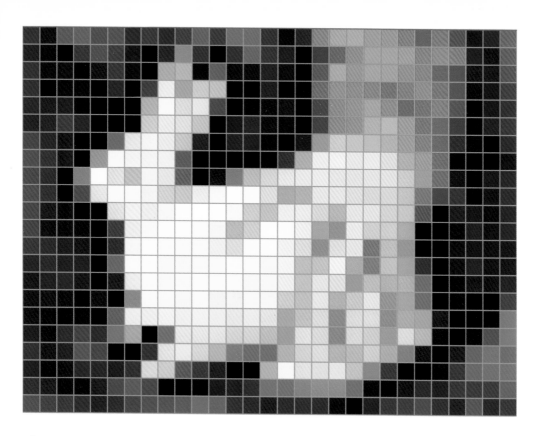

"The Madonna of the Rabbit" (1530), minus the
Madonna, was pushing it for Lisa, who wrote her
dissertation on Titian and takes these things
more seriously than I.

Clearly, we had to move forward a couple of hundred years. And the second half of the 20th century turned out to be much more suitable.

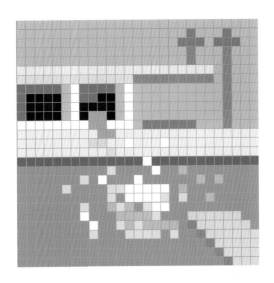

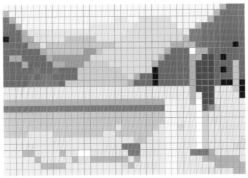

Hockney, at first, seemed like a good choice but proved a tad too Californian for Berlin.

Lisa proposed Gerhard Richter. However, as much as we adore his art, taking a calming bath underneath a fighter plane just wasn't going to do the trick.

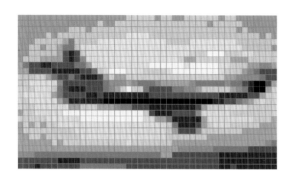 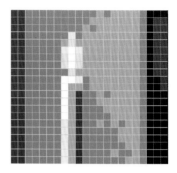

"Kerze" ("Candle"), from 1988, worked graphically but somehow wasn't chipper enough.

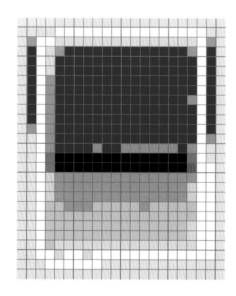

I countered with Rothko's "Red, Orange, Tan and Purple" (1949). We concurred that neither purple, tan, orange, nor red would be soothing enough.

I realized that I didn't just want to rip off a piece of art but, rather, create a visual pun to illustrate our love of art. Maybe a little pop quiz that would take us through recent art history?

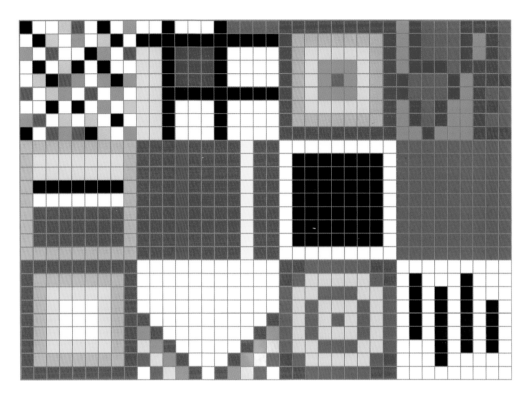

From top left:
Jackson Pollock, Piet Mondrian, Frank Stella, Robert Indiana
Mark Rothko, Barnett Newman, Kasimir Malevich, Yves Klein
Josef Albers, Morris Louis, Jasper Johns, Lucio Fontana

Finally we had an idea for the shower:
an appropriation of an appropriation.
Warhol's "Brillo Box"!

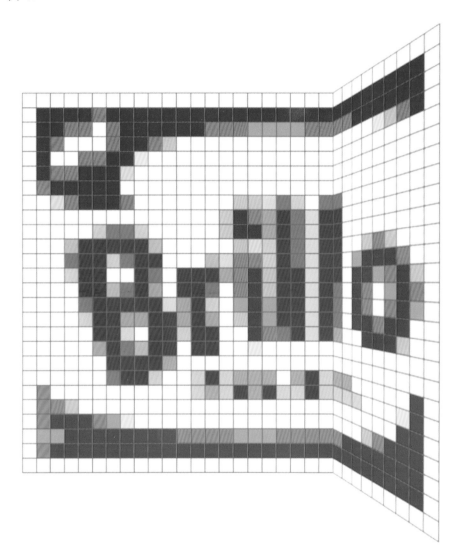

Here's a
photo:

But what to do with the bathtub?
Too much color would overwhelm a place that is
supposed to be quiet and peaceful.

Then I had a terrifyingly perfect idea.

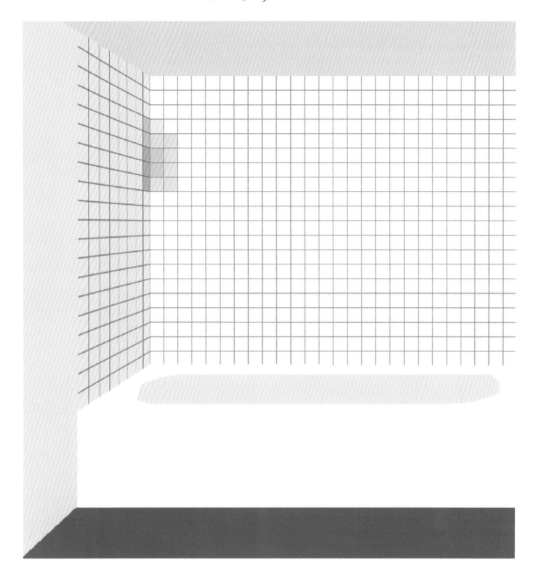

In 1982, Joseph Beuys took five kilograms of butter and stuck it up in a corner of his studio at the Art Academy in Düsseldorf. The "Fettecke" ("grease corner") became infamous after an overeager cleaning woman disposed of it in 1986.

"I wanted a Titian and all I got was a Lump of lard," Lisa gasped. But she had to admit that, conceptually, we had no choice.

P.S. The bathroom for our subway-obsessed kids, on the other hand, was much easier.

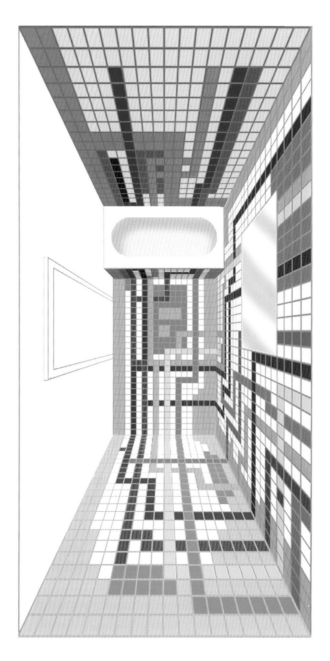

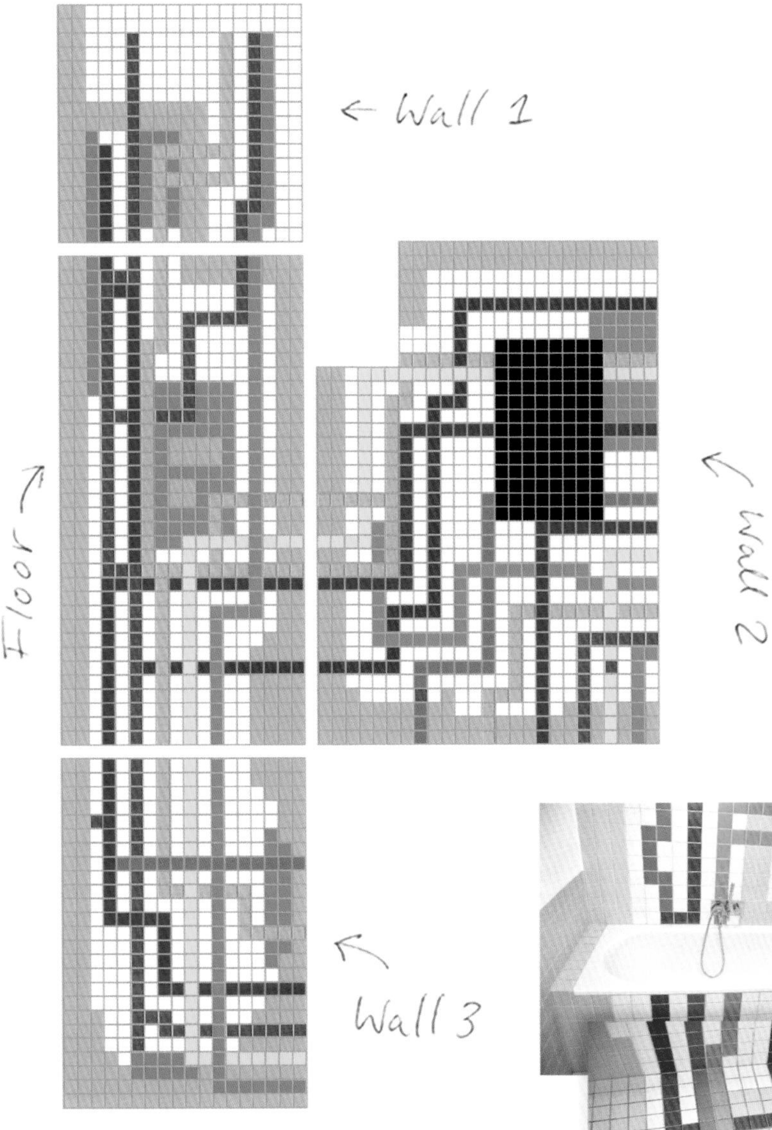
Wall 1
Floor
Wall 2
Wall 3

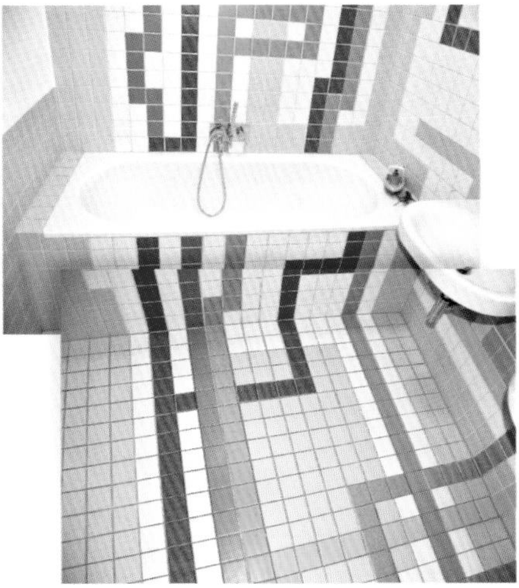

3. New York Cheat Sheets

All New Yorkers develop tricks that allow them to stay ahead of the pack in daily life. These are generally tightly guarded secrets, but now that I don't live in New York, I have generously decided to share some of mine.

What follows are a few handy charts that will help readers improve their lives.

Shopping at the crowded Fairway supermarket in Red Hook with an impatient toddler in your cart is not easy. (The first section—fruits and vegetables—is especially treacherous, as quick little hands can threaten the large pyramid of Fuji apples.)

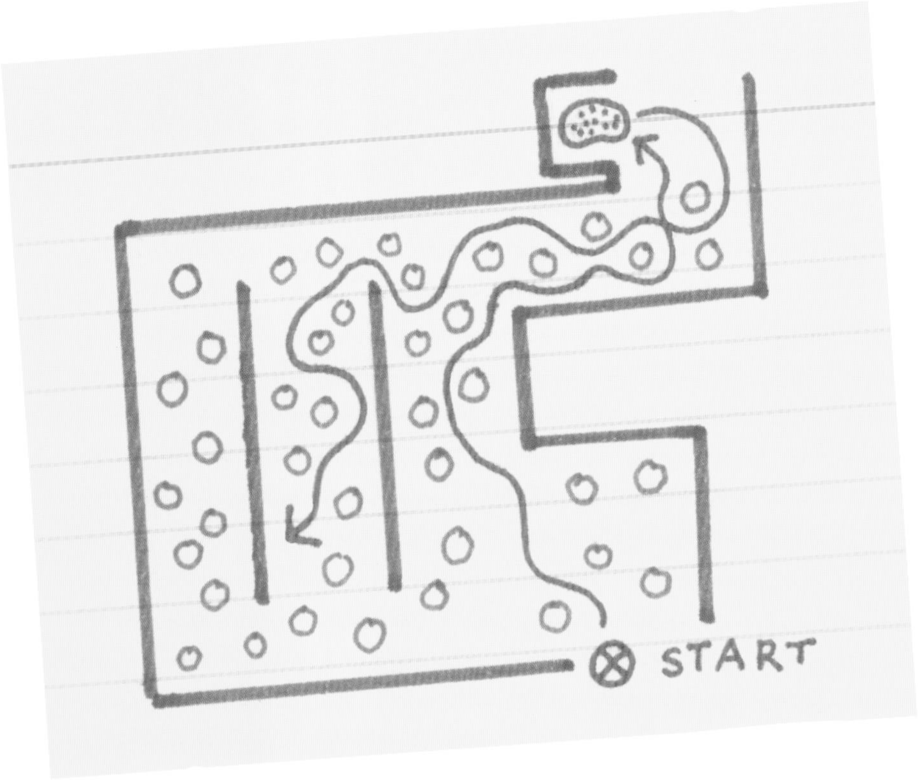
START

The solution: Try to make it to the olive-oil-tasting station (opposite the cheese counter) and stock up on sliced baguette. This will keep the young shoppers happy, at least for a while. The only downside: going against the stream in the narrow soup aisle on your way back to the produce.

Our building in the Williamsburg section of Brooklyn had no buzzer, and I would have to run downstairs to let friends in, accept deliveries, etc. After some training—and thanks to my six four height—I perfected a maneuver I like to refer to as "the Northside Eagle": Place your left foot in the middle of the vestibule, lower your upper body to precisely ninety degrees until you reach the front door, while sticking out your right foot to keep the vestibule door from closing shut.

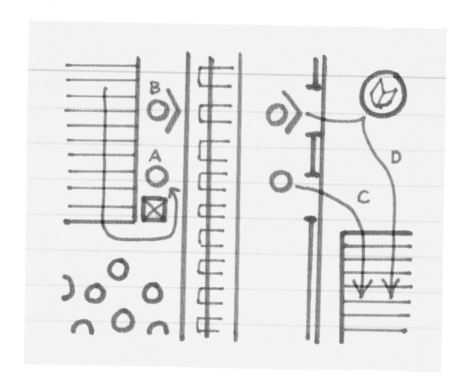

In the morning, I used to take the 2 or 3 train from Clark Street to get to my studio in Manhattan's Meatpacking District. Here's some advice, if you happen to make that commute, too: When you get off the elevator at the Clark Street station, go down the stairs to the left. On the platform, make a sharp left; this will position you directly behind a column (A). It's pretty close to the tracks, so there will be very few people around, thereby improving your chances of getting on, even at rush hour. If you happen to bring a newspaper, use one door farther up (B).

When you arrive the at Fourteenth Street station and step off, you'll be near the Thirteenth Street exit, and the door will open right in front of the stairs (C). If you chose the newspaper option mentioned above, the door will open in front of a convenient trash can, where you can discard your paper (D) before leaving the subway system.

Whenever I rode the subway with my two older boys, I tried to hold on to their hands at all times. In the process, I developed a special move. Anyone who saw it must have been impressed.

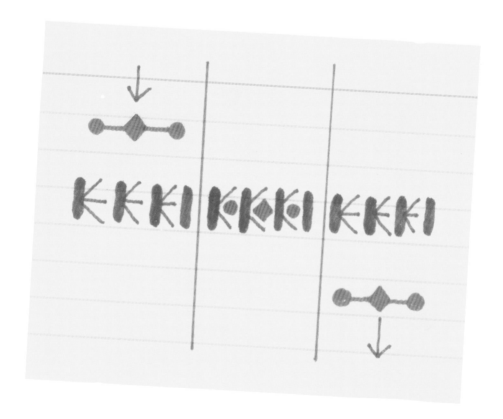

I would hold the boys' hands as we briskly made our way out of the station, then, just as we reached the turnstiles, I would let go. We would pass through the turnstiles simultaneously, and so smoothly that the boys' hands would still be up in the air when we got to the other side, where I would grab their little fingers again in one fluid motion. (Requires practice.)

One of our favorite playgrounds is in Brooklyn's Dumbo neighborhood. It comes with a big downside, though: There are three gates, and it's impossible to see all of them from a single vantage point. If you happen to go there with a free-spirited five-year-old and a two-year-old, you can find yourself in a tricky situation: The older one takes off suddenly and heads toward the river, and you have to leave the younger one by himself while you fetch the escapee. However, you can take advantage of a boat-shaped sandbox in the north part of the playground, whose sand level is so low that the kids are surrounded by an insurmountable three-foot wall.

(Disclaimer: I always made sure there was another grown-up at "the Grotto," as we liked to call it.)

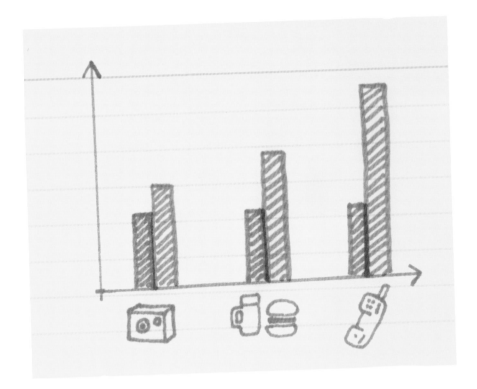

One of the most frustrating things in New York is that everything is always much more expensive than (a) you think and (b) what the price tag says. One way to come up with a reliable budget is to use the following Price-vs.-What-You-Actually-End-Up-Paying Ratios.

Digital camera: Add 30 percent. (Because the particular model you picked is out of stock, and the one that's left is more expensive. Plus sales tax.)

Burger and beer: Add 60 percent. (Tax and tip for you and for that friend from Europe who left early and "didn't know" that you have to pay tax and tip.)

Phone plans: Add 130 percent. (To cover FCC, USF, TRS, ABC, CIA, and LOL.)

Every parent knows that the surest way to get children to fall asleep is to roll them around in strollers on bumpy sidewalks. Since I spent a good chunk of the last several years pushing infants through New York, I have the following recommendations:

When our first son was born, we were living in Chelsea. Here you mostly find the standard four-by-four-foot concrete squares that result in roughly one bump per second. A perfectly fine starter surface for the new father.

With our second child, we graduated to the cobblestone streets of Dumbo, which have the bonus of being broken up by an occasional rail. Pushing a stroller here is physically challenging, but your little darling will be snoring within seconds.

With our third son, I discovered the Champs-Elysées for putting kids to sleep: the west sidewalk along Columbia Heights, in Brooklyn. Tree roots have rearranged the old granite slabs into a bizarre topography. Navigating a stroller through the jumps and jolts is not for the faint of heart, but to my amazement, I have never seen a baby fall asleep as peacefully.

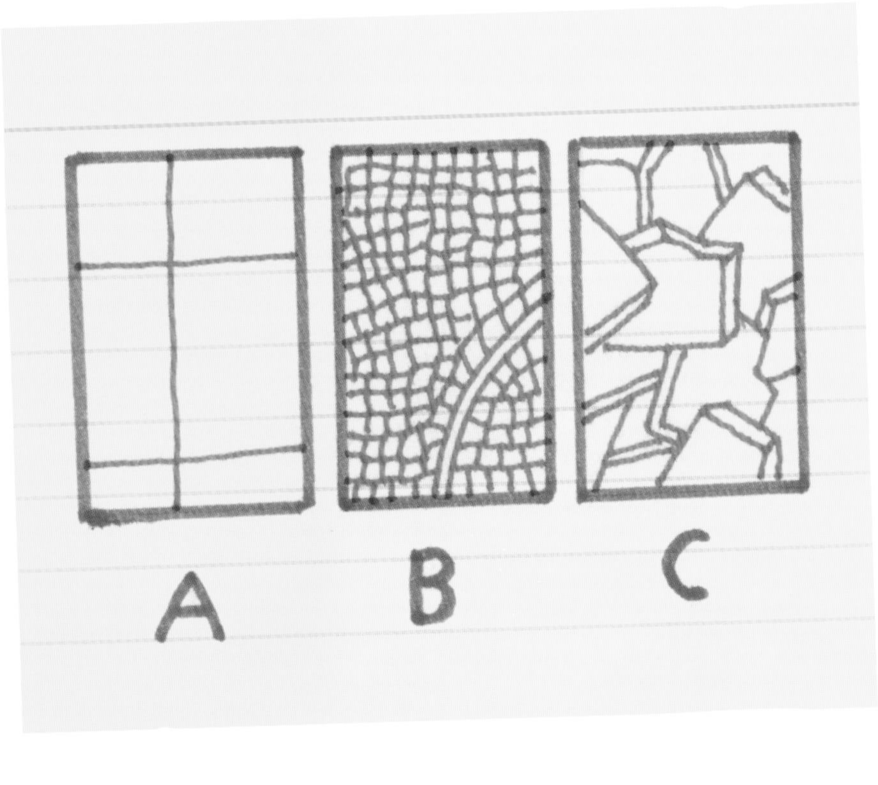
A
B
C

My favorite breakfast spot in New York is a little coffee shop on Eighth Avenue between Thirteenth and Fourteenth Streets. They have a lemon poppy muffin that is absolutely divine when fresh—and tastes like drywall when not. The easiest way to test for freshness, of course, is to poke the crust, which would be wrong.

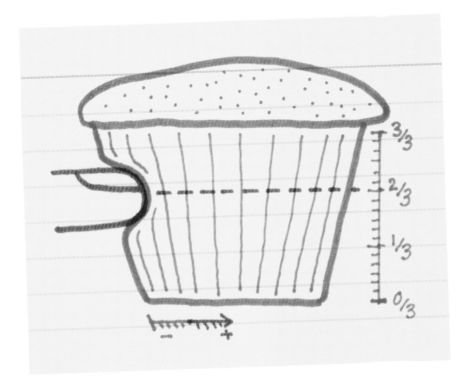

Fortunately, you can ethically conduct the freshness test by poking the paper muffin cup at one specific point, at about two-thirds of the height of the base. Lower or higher poking doesn't yield reliable results.

It is always great to visit the Museum of Modern Art, but I have pretty strong likes and dislikes, especially when it comes to paintings from the nineteenth and twentieth centuries. And I have a hard time enjoying a beloved painting while being irritated by another, less beloved piece of art. If you happen to share my preferences, I suggest the following:

In room 1 on the fifth floor, stand exactly in between Gauguin's *Seed of the Areoi* (1) and Braque's *Landscape at La Ciotat* (2). Turn east, facing room 5, and you will be able to enjoy two wonderful Klimts (*Hope II* and *The Park*) (3) without being annoyed by the pointless Kandinskys (4), to the left, and Chagall's disturbing cow (5), to the right.

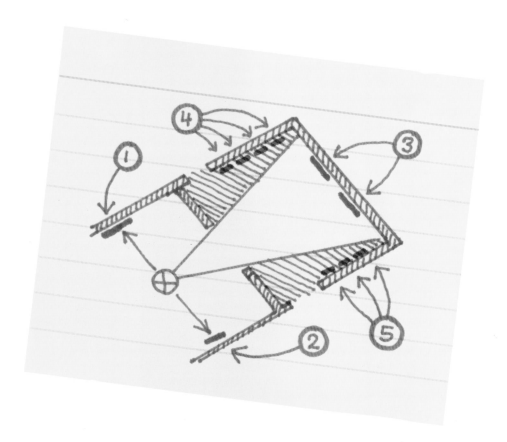

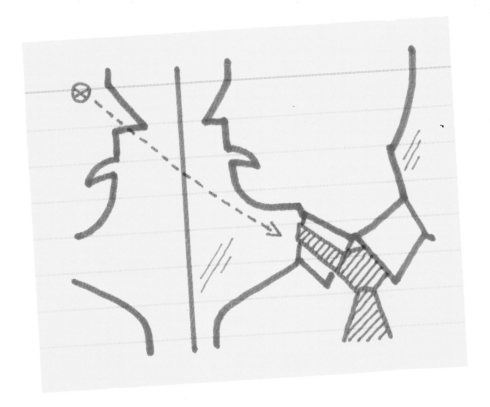

New York is the City of Vanities. There is nothing more embarrassing than leaving the house in a hurry, without realizing that your pant leg is stuck in a sock, or that a lump of shaving cream sits on your earlobe. Thankfully, Manhattan provides a plethora of shiny surfaces—from polished marble walls to spotless chrome door frames—that offer you ample opportunities to spot-check your appearance. I am especially grateful to the tinted windows of 101 Park Avenue, which once alerted me to a collar/tie mishap just minutes before an important meeting.

Ultimately, though, the mirrored exterior of 546 Fifth Avenue (at the corner of Forty-sixth) is second to none for anybody in midtown in need of an auto-once-over.

4. Coffee

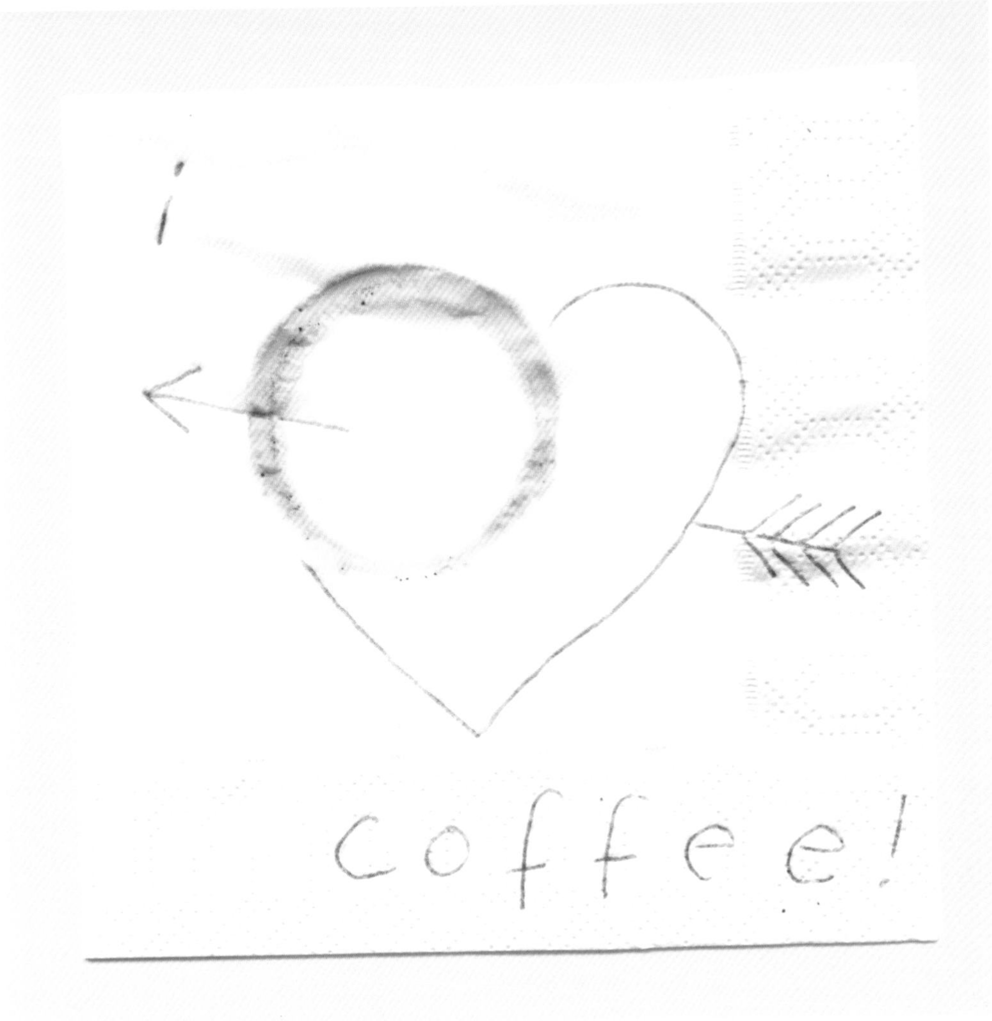
i
coffee!

I like coffee so much that I have tea for breakfast. The first cup of the day in particular is so good that I'm afraid I won't be able to properly appreciate it when I am half-asleep. Therefore, I celebrate it two hours later, when I am fully conscious.

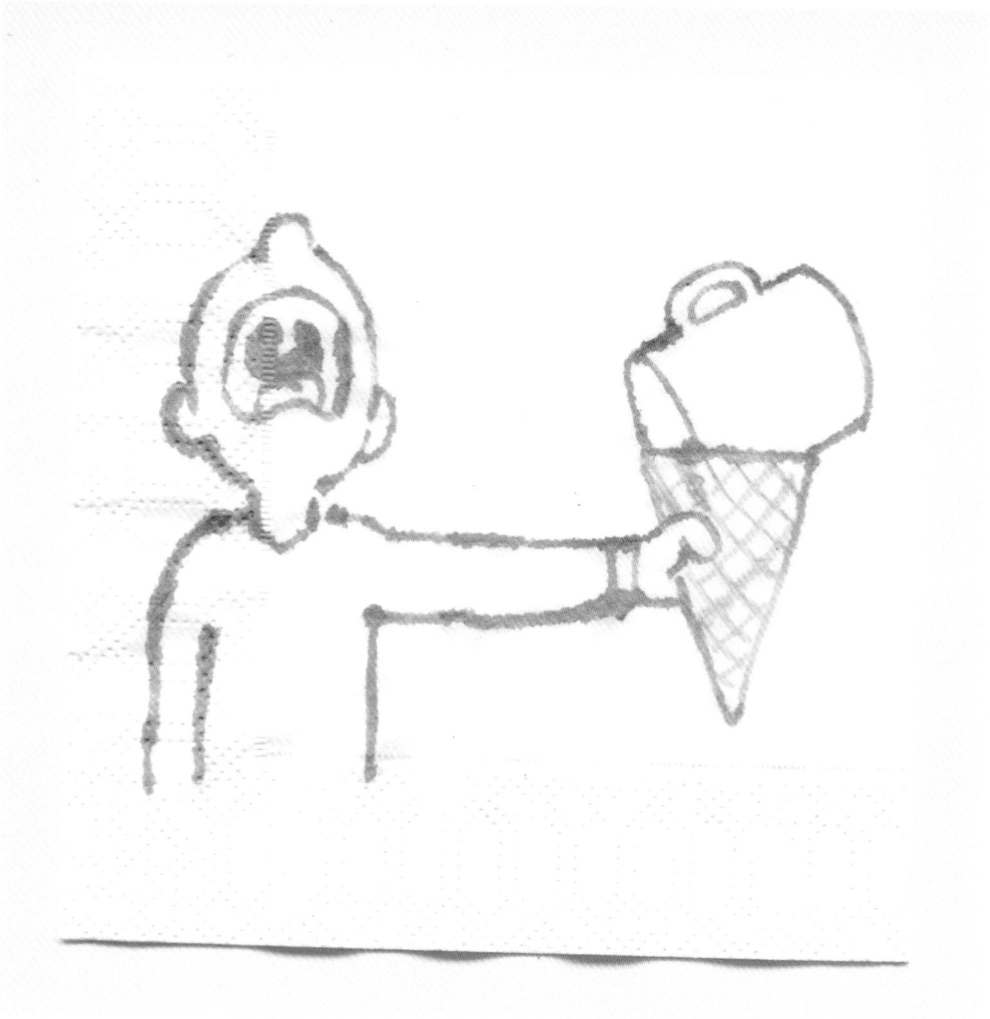

I must have been five when I first discovered the taste of coffee, when I was accidentally given a scoop of coffee ice cream. I was inconsolable: How could grown-ups ruin something as wonderful as ice cream with something as disgusting as coffee?

A few years later I was similarly devastated when my parents announced that for our big summer vacation we would go . . . hiking.

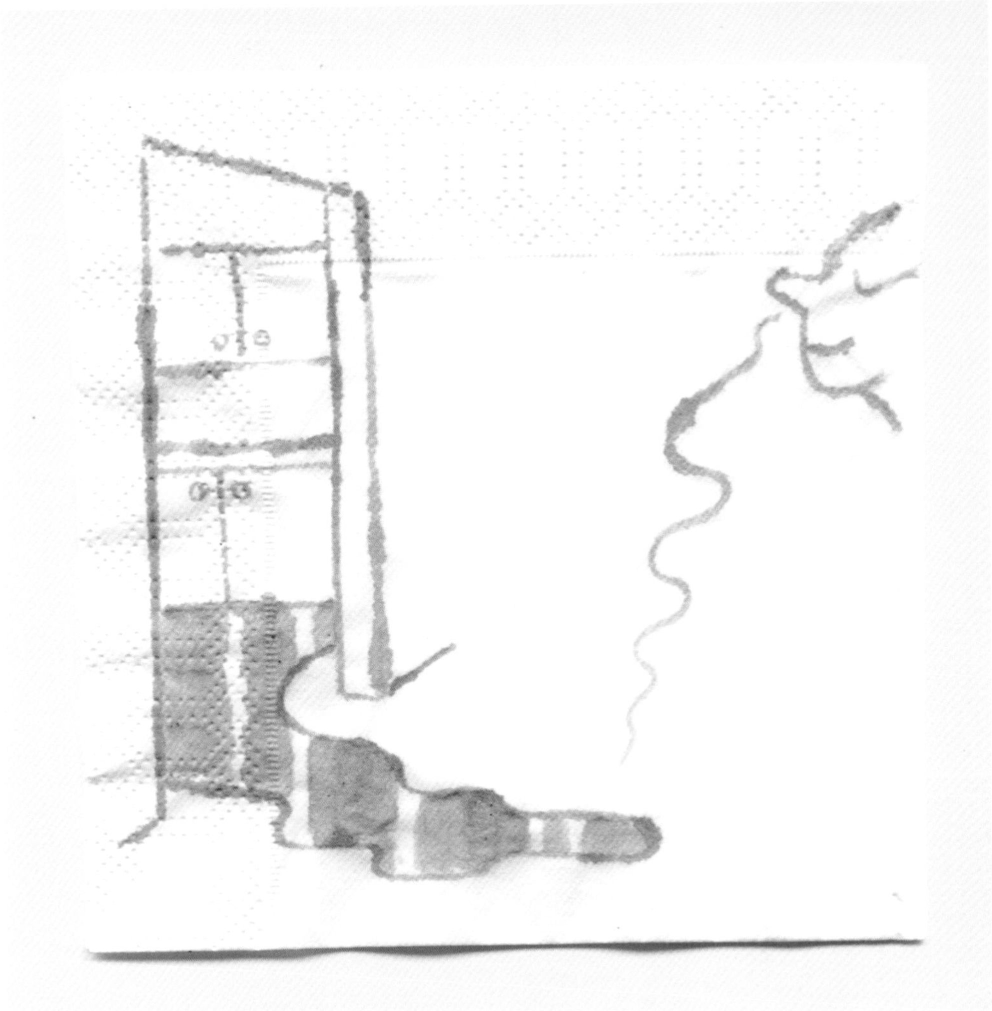

When I was ten I still hated coffee, but fell in love with the ritual of making coffee. My parents were thankful enough about me fixing them coffee every morning that they overlooked my first clashes with brewing technology.

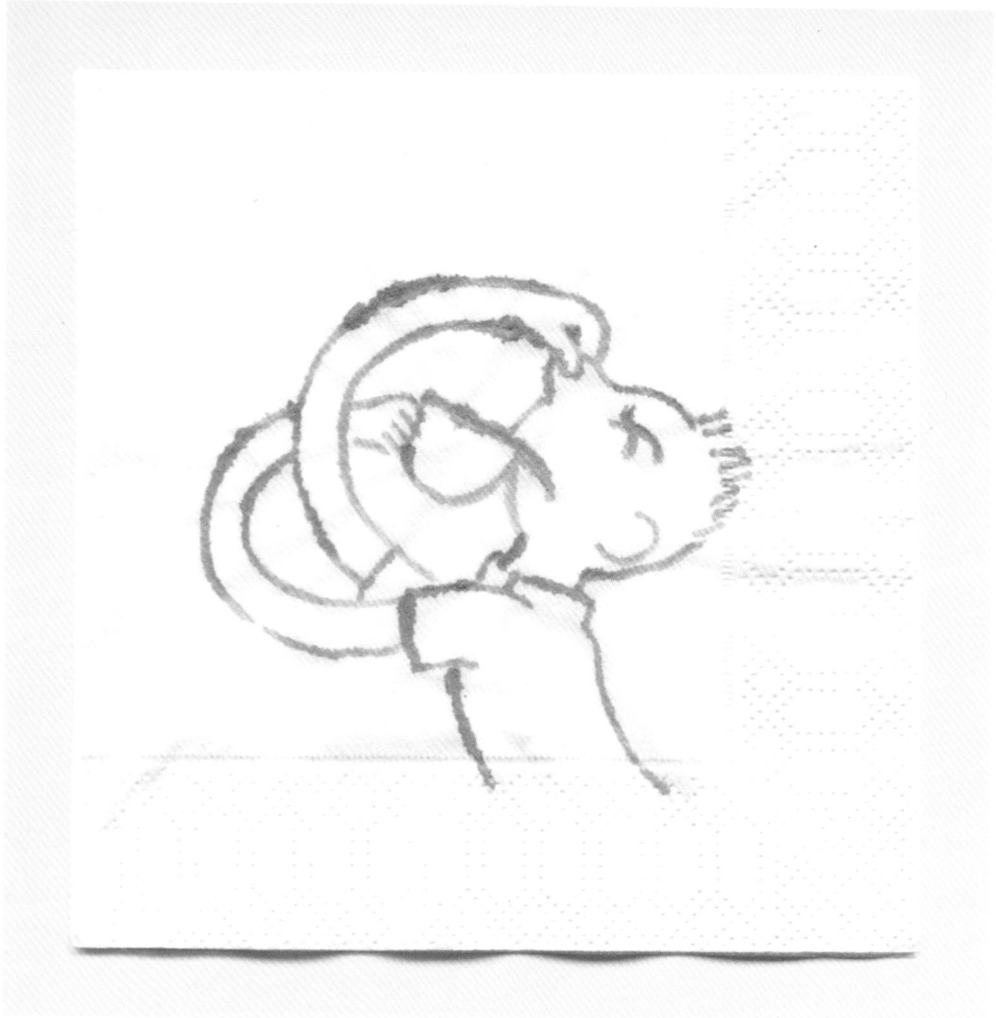

At seventeen I still suffered from coffee schizophrenia: I loved the concept of coffee, but resented the taste. I decided to cure myself through auto-hazing. Around that time, my parents took me on my first trip to Paris. We arrived by train early in the morning and went straight to a little café. I ordered a large café au lait and forced down the entire bowl.

It worked. Since then I have enjoyed coffee pretty much every day.

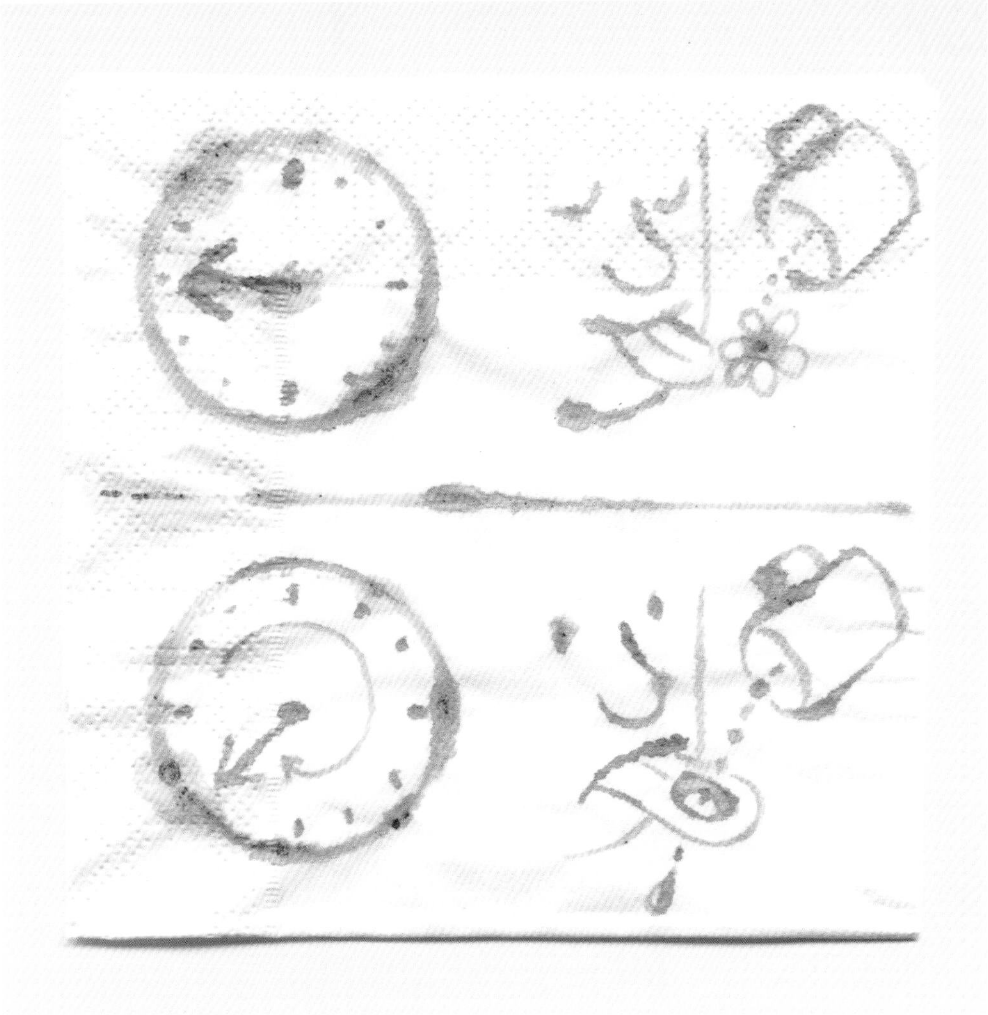

When I was twenty-one I worked as an intern at a magazine. The art director and I would brew a gigantic pot of coffee around 9:00 A.M. to help us get through the day. The pot would simmer in the coffeemaker, and through evaporation the coffee strengthened noticeably at lunchtime. In the evening hours, the remaining coffee had turned to a black concoction with a stinging smell and tar-like taste. We endured it without flinching.

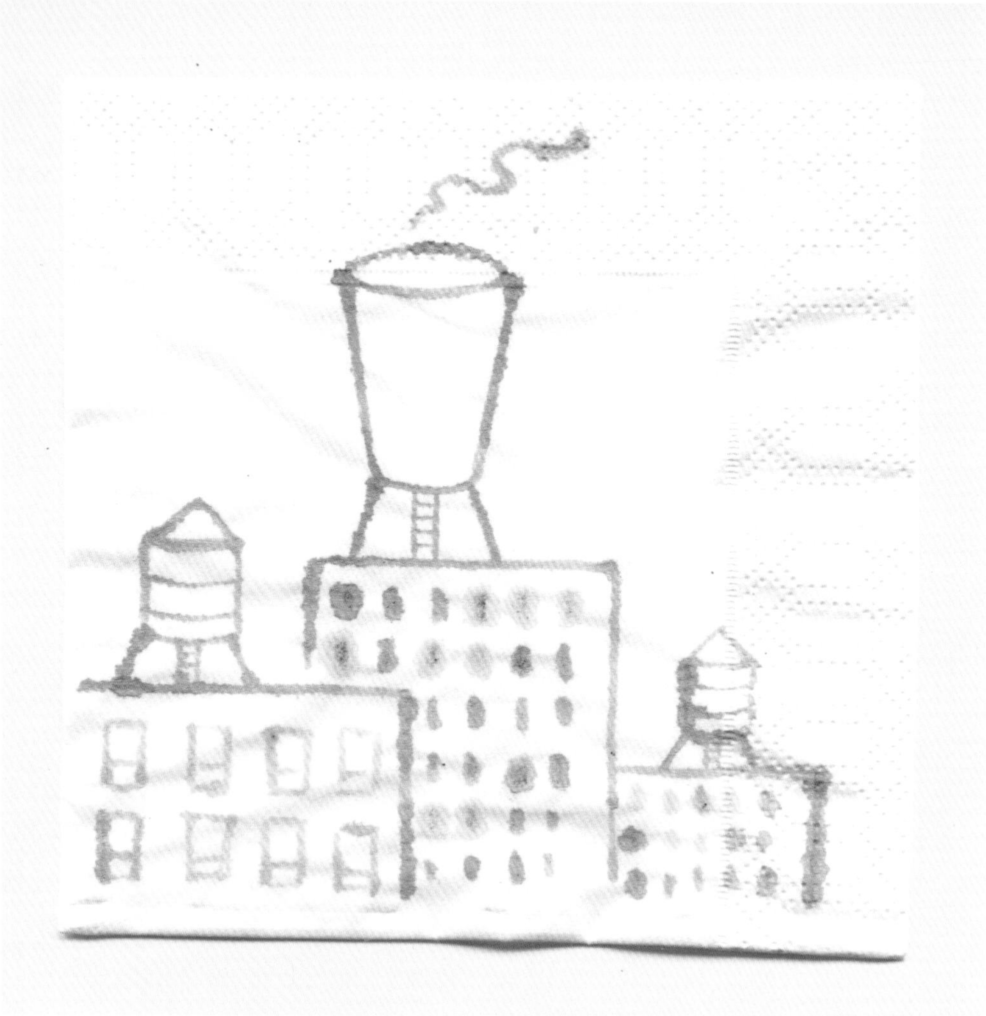

When I came to New York in 1995, I was delighted to discover deli coffee. At the time, I was focused less on taste and more on quantity and price. Thus, I was in caffeinated paradise.

In January 1999 a friend seduced me into switching to latte. Within weeks a considerable portion of my budget ended up at the L Cafe in Williamsburg.

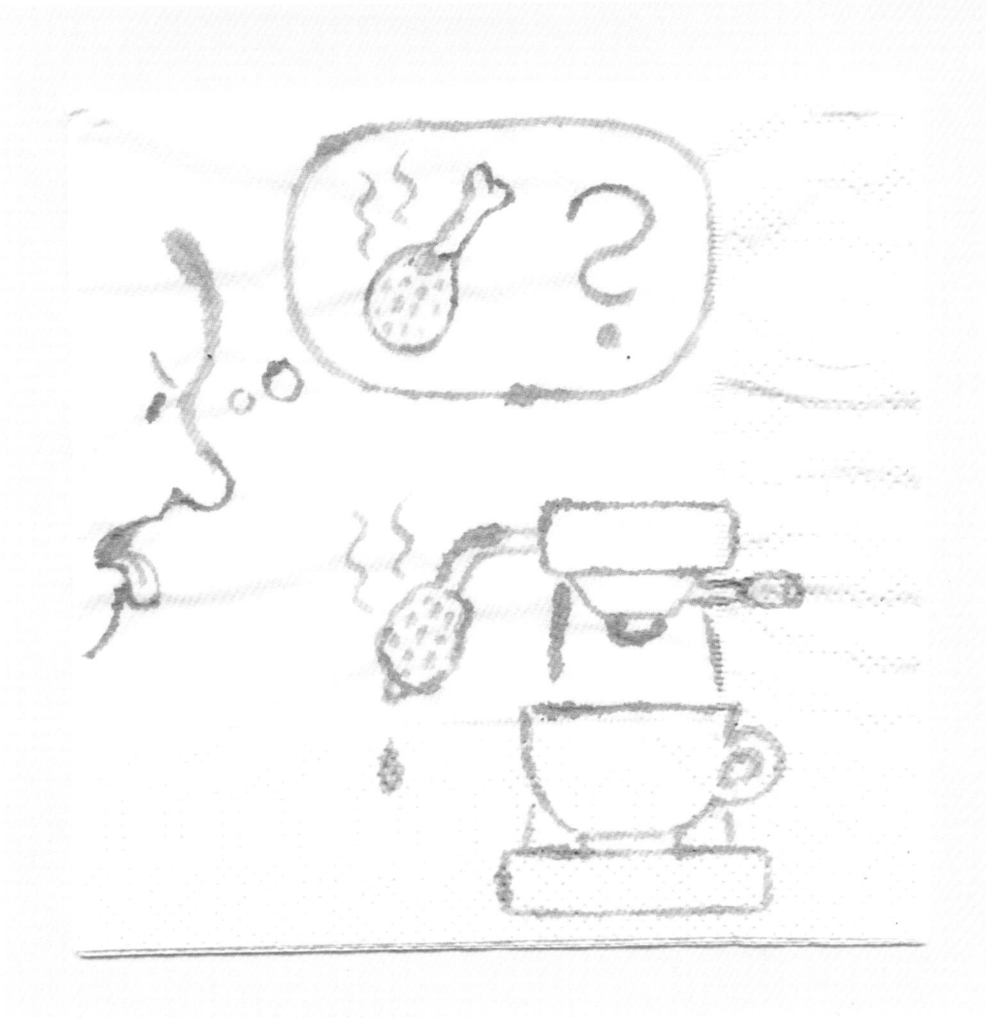

My inner accountant quickly convinced me to buy one of those little espresso machines (for the price of approximately ten tall lattes). It had a steam nozzle to heat milk, which one should clean very thoroughly after each use. I didn't have the patience to do so. Within a few uses, an unappetizing, dark brown, organic lump developed around the nozzle. A few days later it had become unremovable, and I reverted to getting my coffee outside.

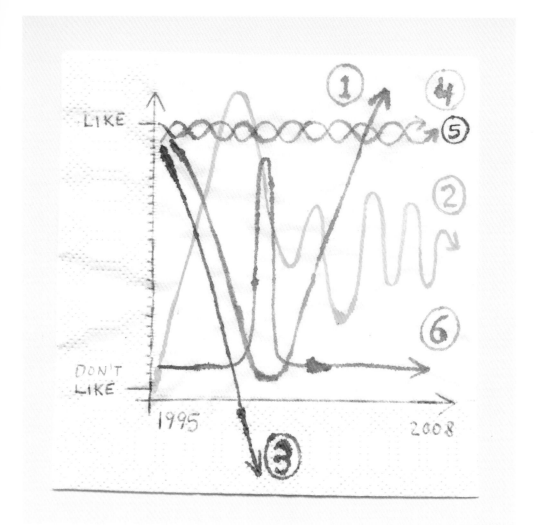

Here's a chart that shows my coffee bias over the years.

For good measure I have added my bagel preferences over the same period. (1) drip coffee, (2) Starbucks, (3) blueberry bagels, (4) sesame bagels, (5) poppy seed bagels, (6) everything bagels

Please don't hold my brief affair with blueberry bagels against me. I cured myself of this aberration.

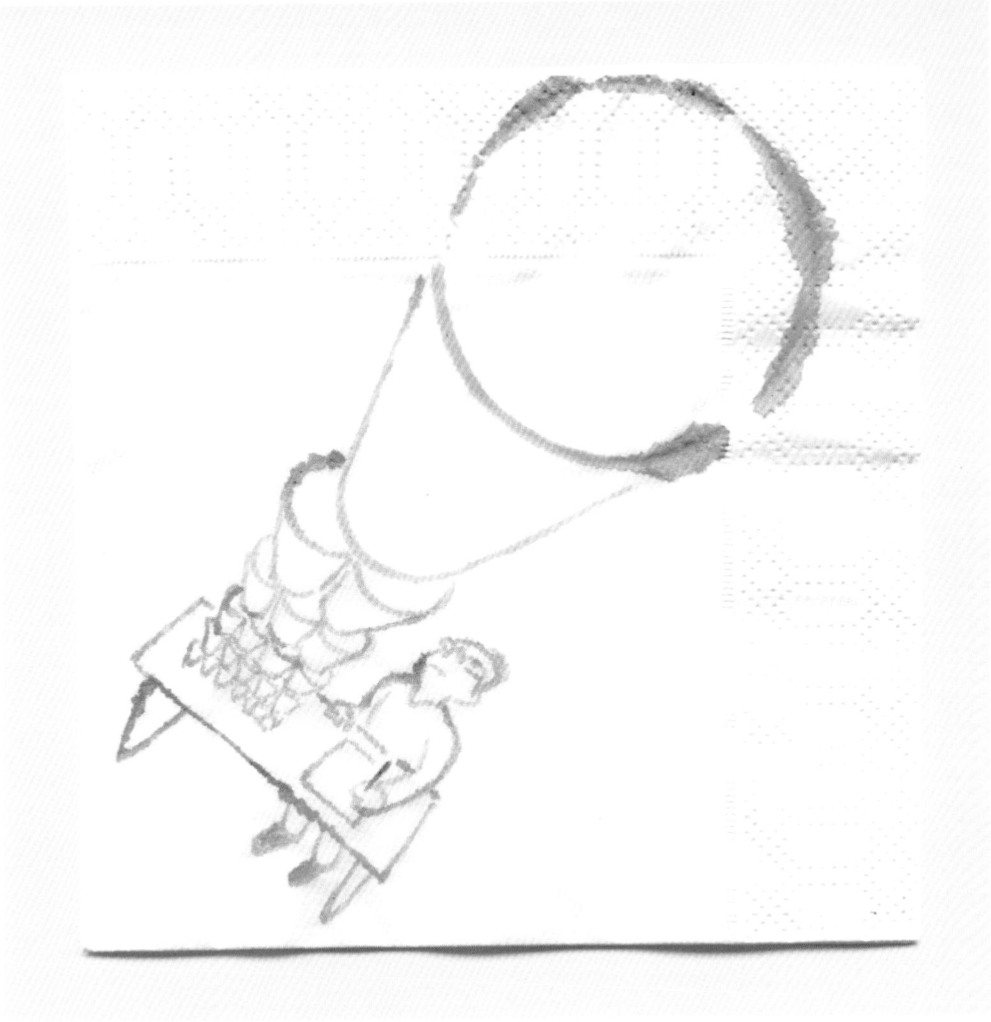

I order large coffees, but stop drinking when the coffee gets too cold. There's always a couple of ounces left in the cup, so I can't just toss it into my wastebasket. I dread the long haul to the bathroom to properly dispose of the coffee remains. Hence you will usually find a tower of paper cups on my desk.

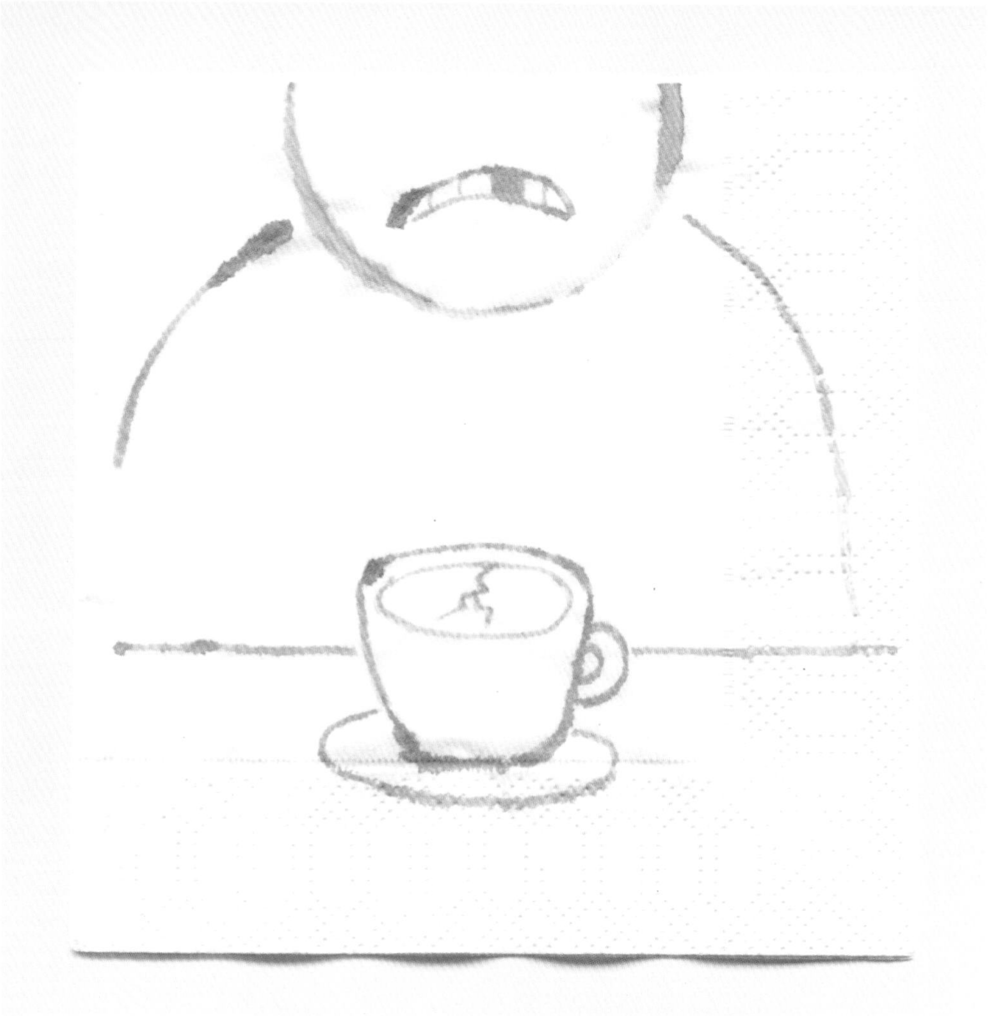

Hot milk greatly improves the taste of coffee, but I find milk foam useless and annoying.

My mother (who makes the most delicious coffee in the world) is obsessed with a particularly potent mechanical foam maker. The result is a layer of impenetrable foam, a kind of lacto-stucco. I have to gnaw my way through it before being able to get to the actual coffee. Apart from that, she really makes the best coffee in the world.

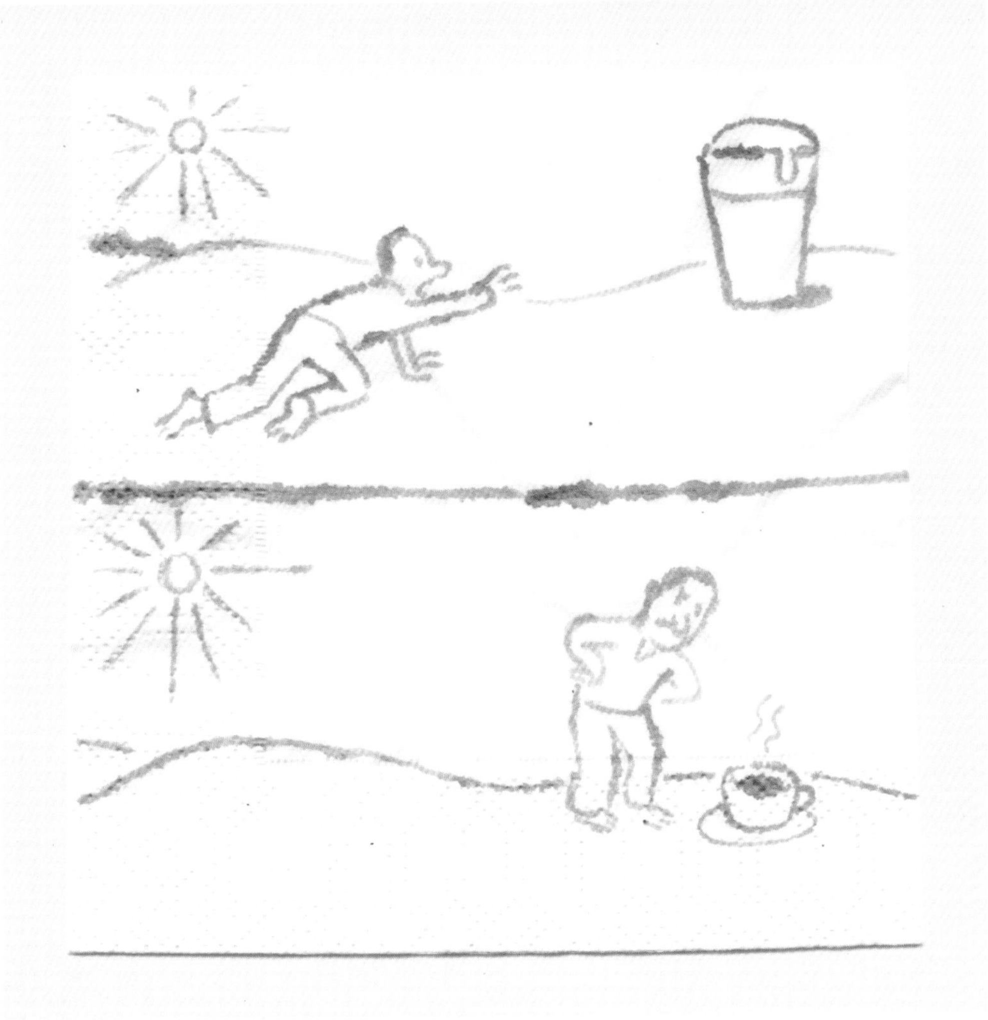

Once, after a grueling all-day design conference at a university, I was invited to dinner on campus. To go with the various delicious pastas, salads, and quiches, coffee was served.

When you are craving a beer, coffee is the most disgusting drink in the universe.

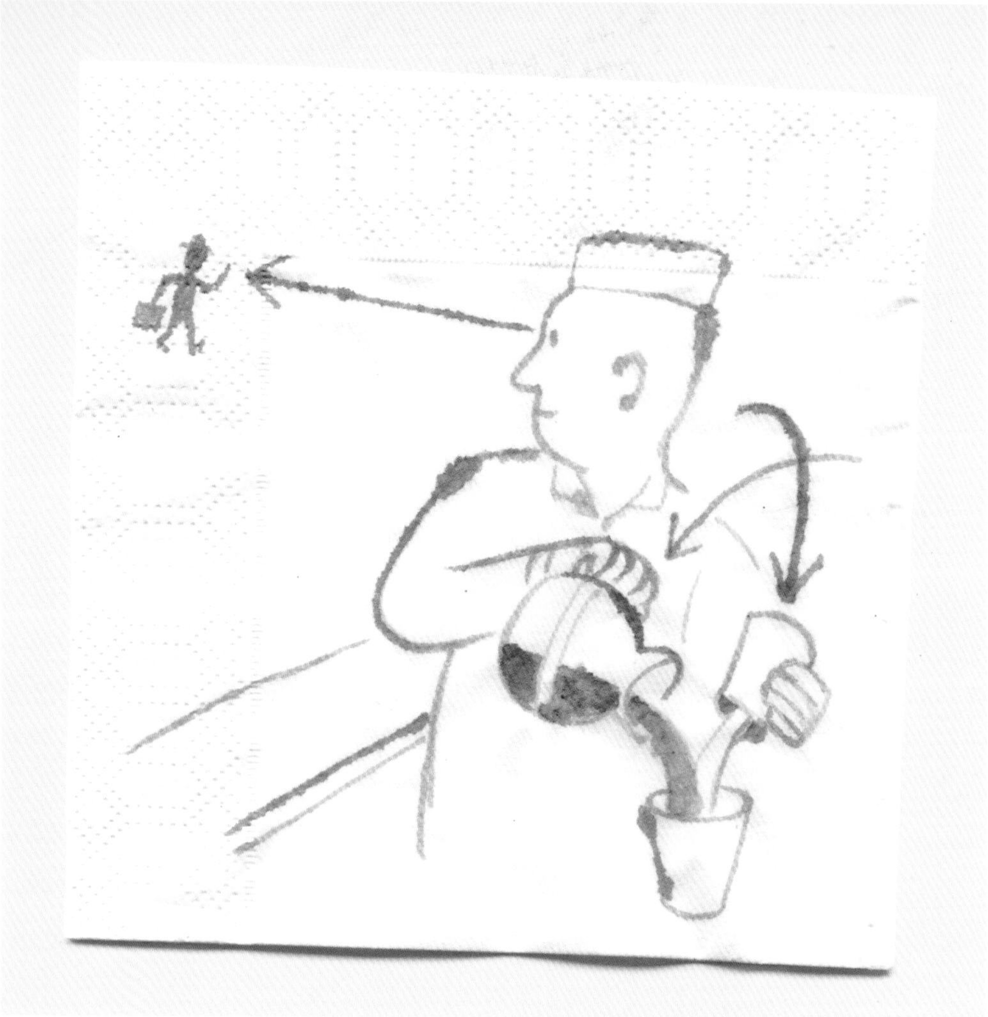

In New York, I was always envious of people who could walk into a coffee place and the guy behind the counter would know them so well he would just start fixing their order, without any exchange of words. It took me more than ten years to get to that stage, but at the very end of my tenure in New York I finally achieved it: I would enter my little spot on Eighth Avenue and, with nothing more than maybe a nod of acknowledgment, my buddy prepared my personal choice: drip coffee with steamed milk.

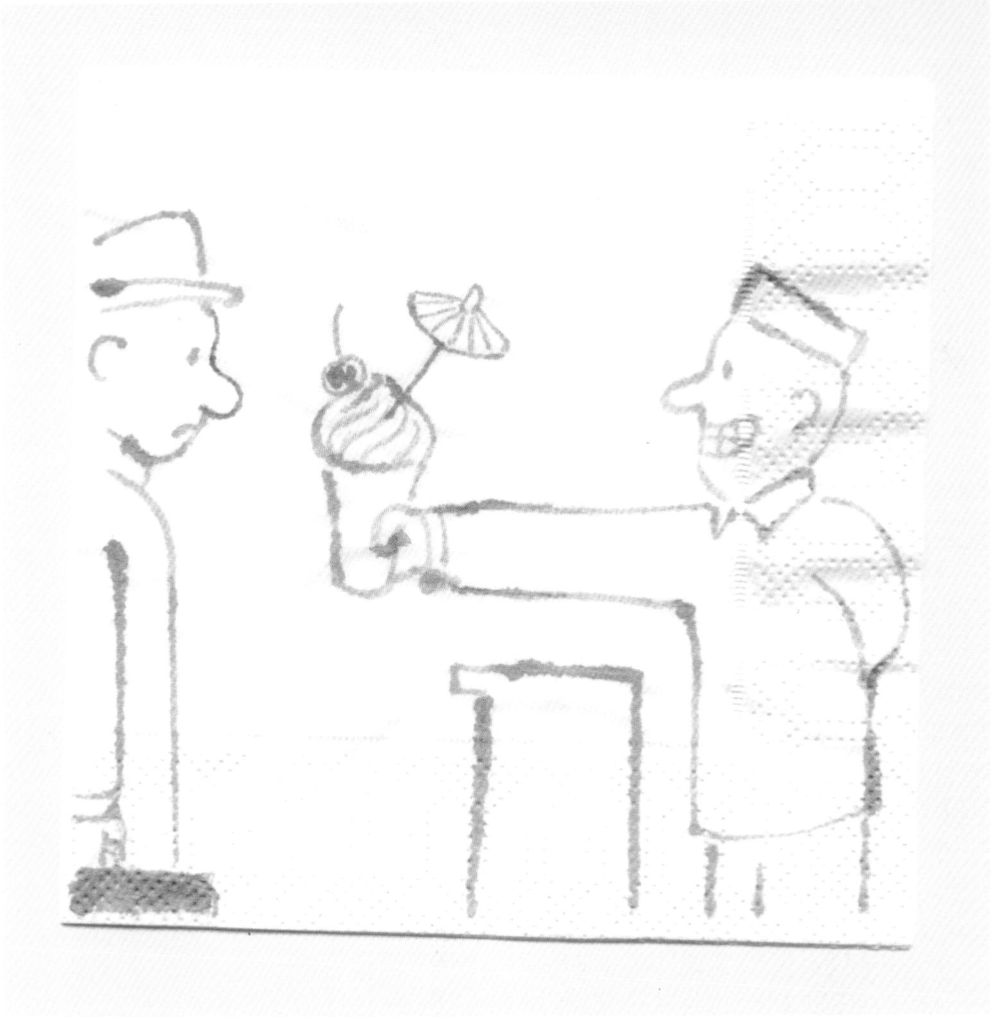

After a couple of blissful weeks, though, things took an unfortunate turn. For some reason he started making the wrong coffee (half-and-half, two sugars). I knew that if I corrected him, our mystic bond would be forever tarnished.

So I swallowed the coffee, instead of my pride.

5. I LEGO NY

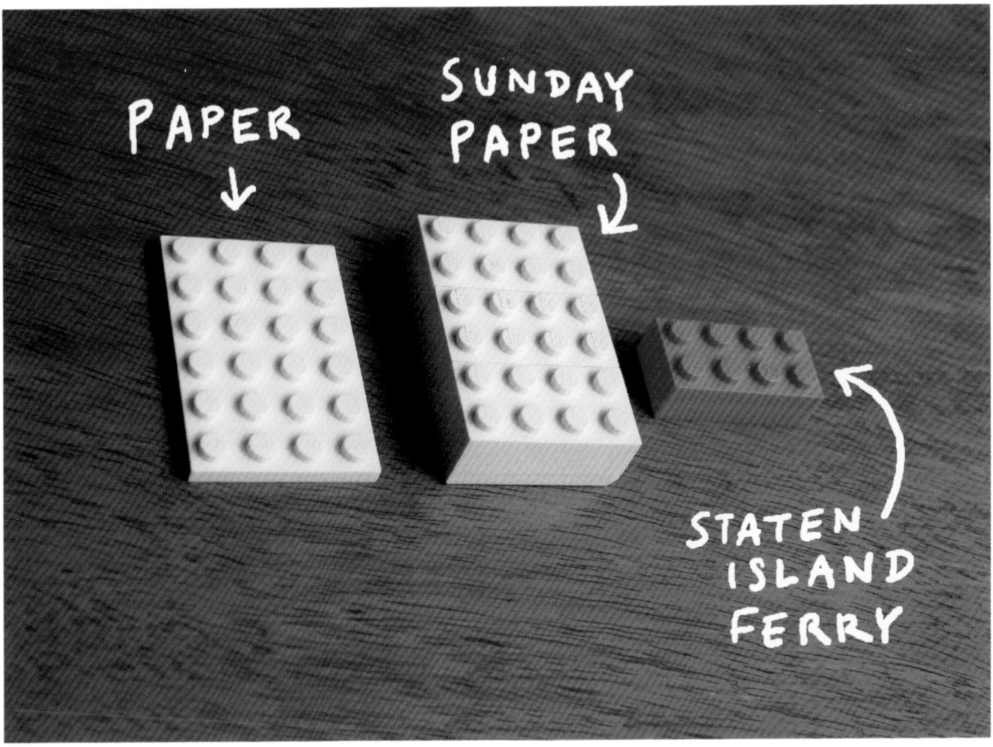
PAPER
SUNDAY PAPER
STATEN ISLAND FERRY

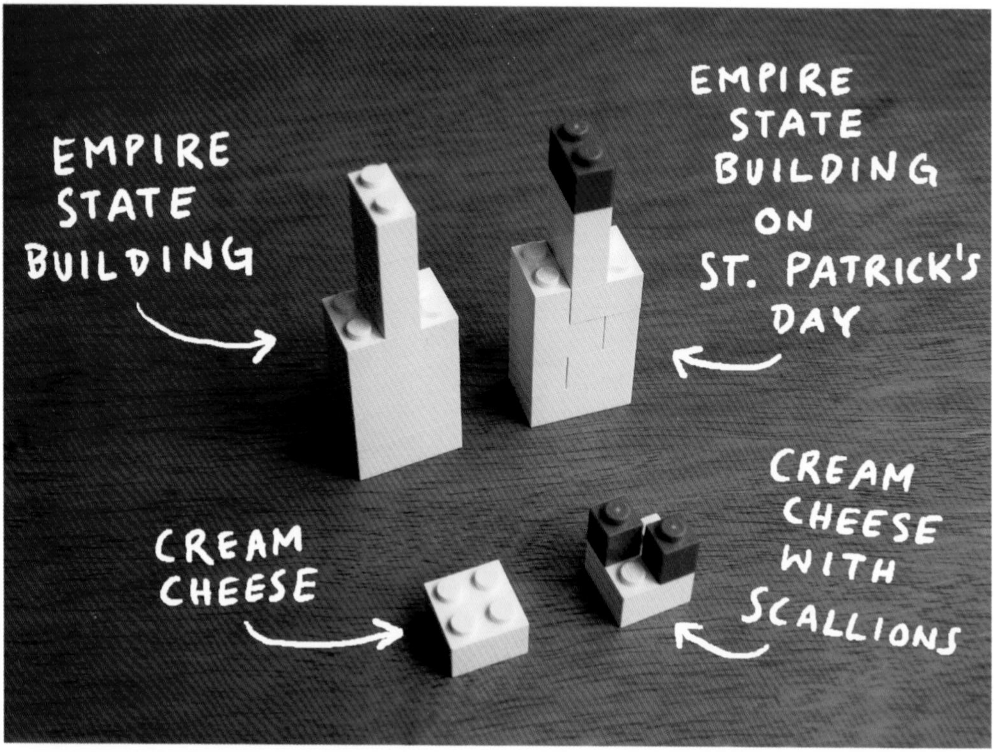
EMPIRE
STATE
BUILDING
EMPIRE
STATE
BUILDING
ON
ST. PATRICK'S
DAY
CREAM
CHEESE
CREAM
CHEESE
WITH
SCALLIONS

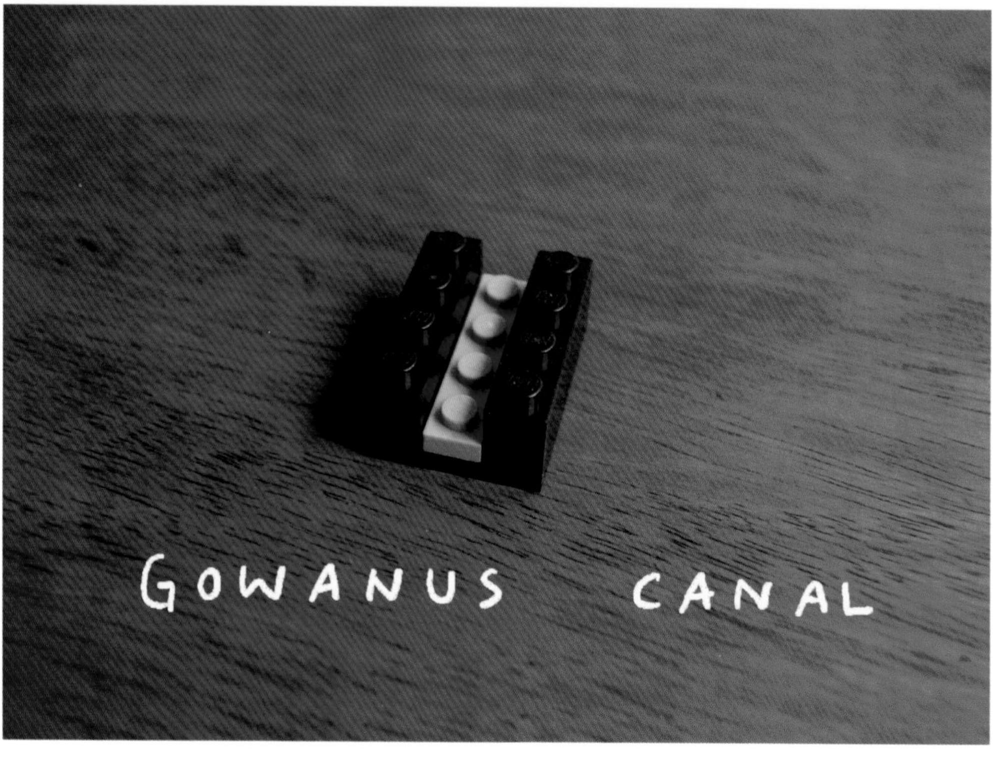
GOWANUS CANAL

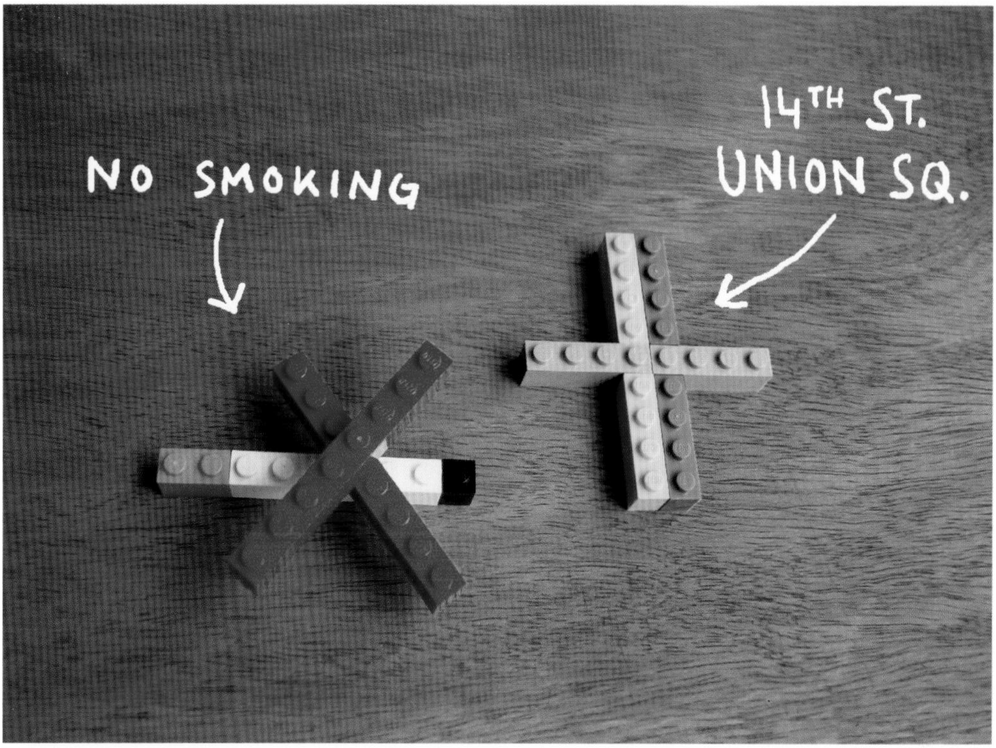
NO SMOKING
14TH ST. UNION SQ.

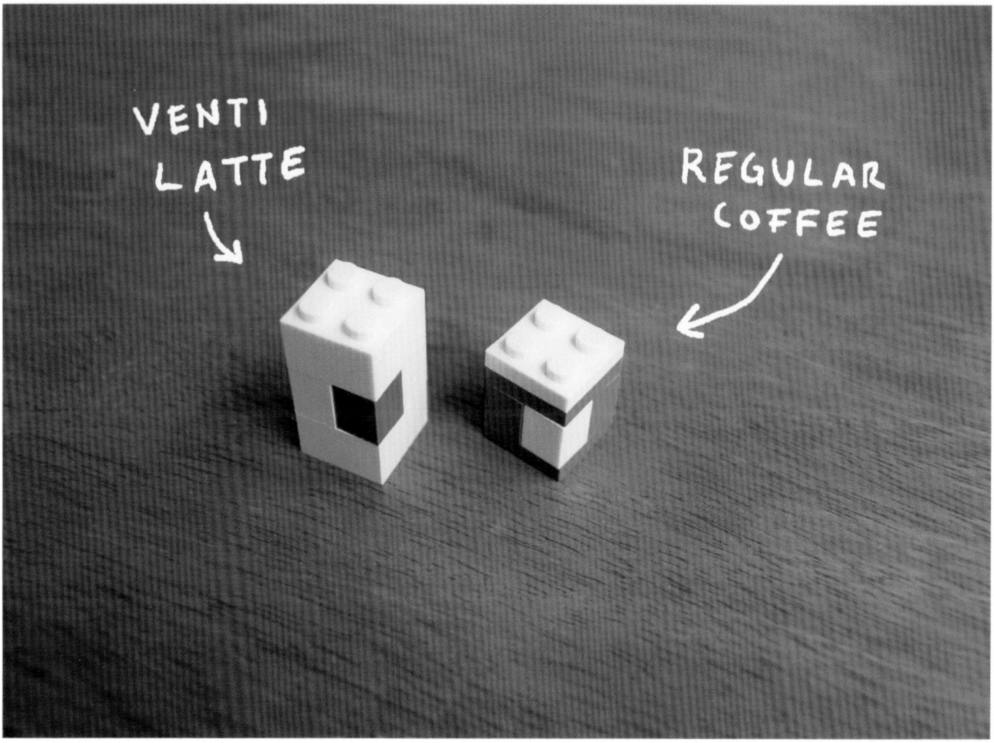
VENTI LATTE
REGULAR COFFEE

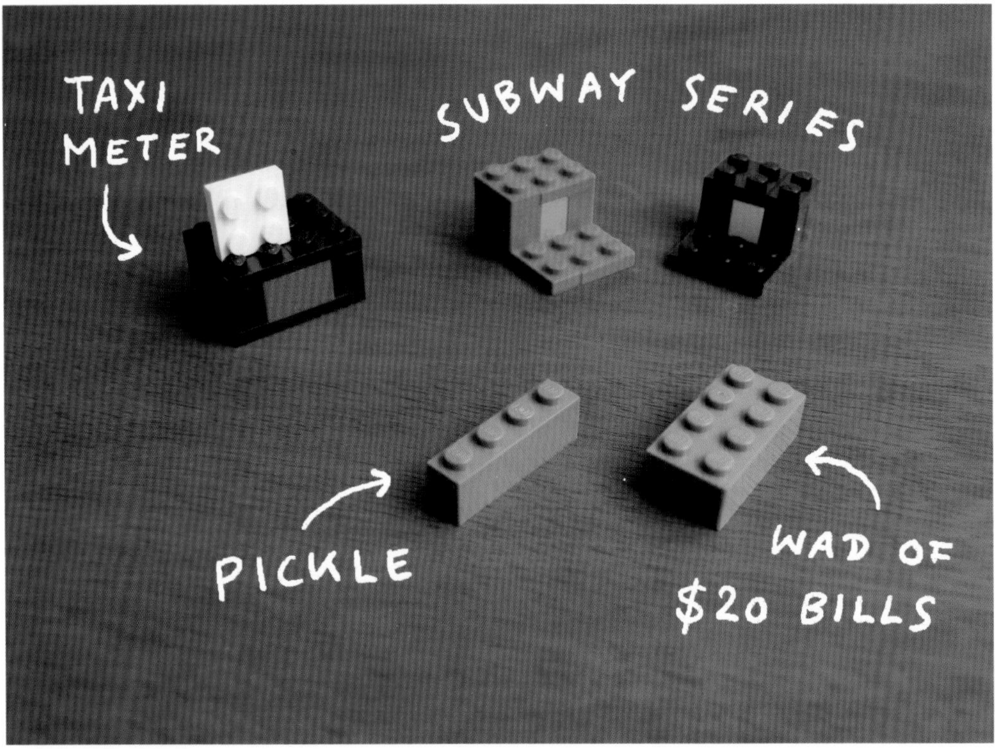
TAXI METER
SUBWAY SERIES
PICKLE
WAD OF $20 BILLS

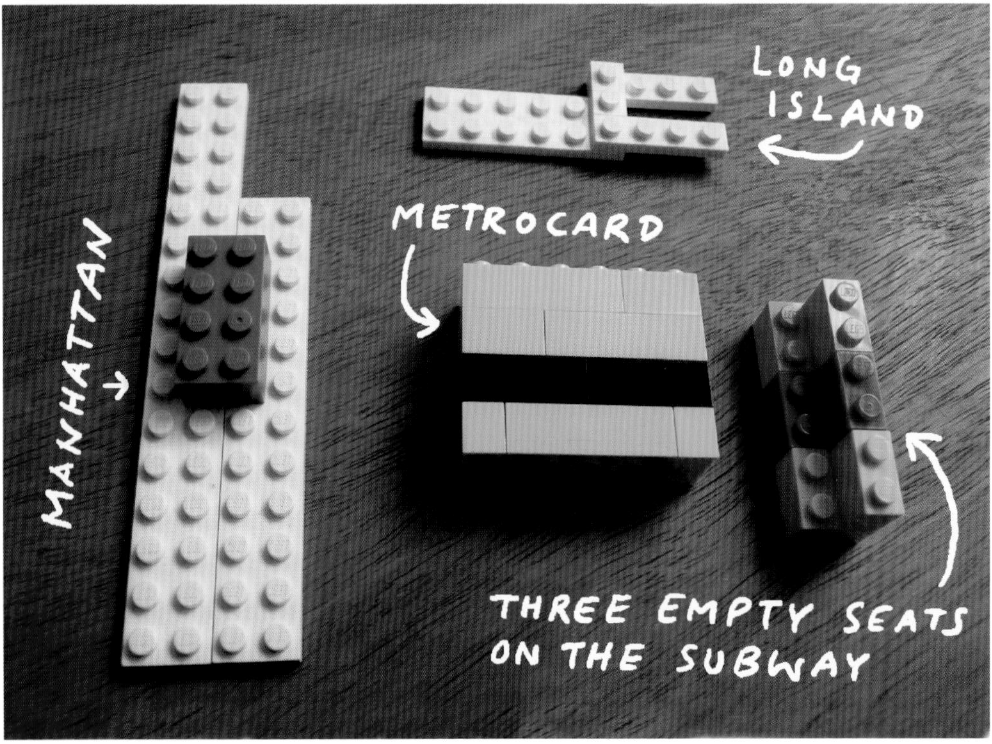
LONG ISLAND
METROCARD
MANHATTAN
THREE EMPTY SEATS ON THE SUBWAY

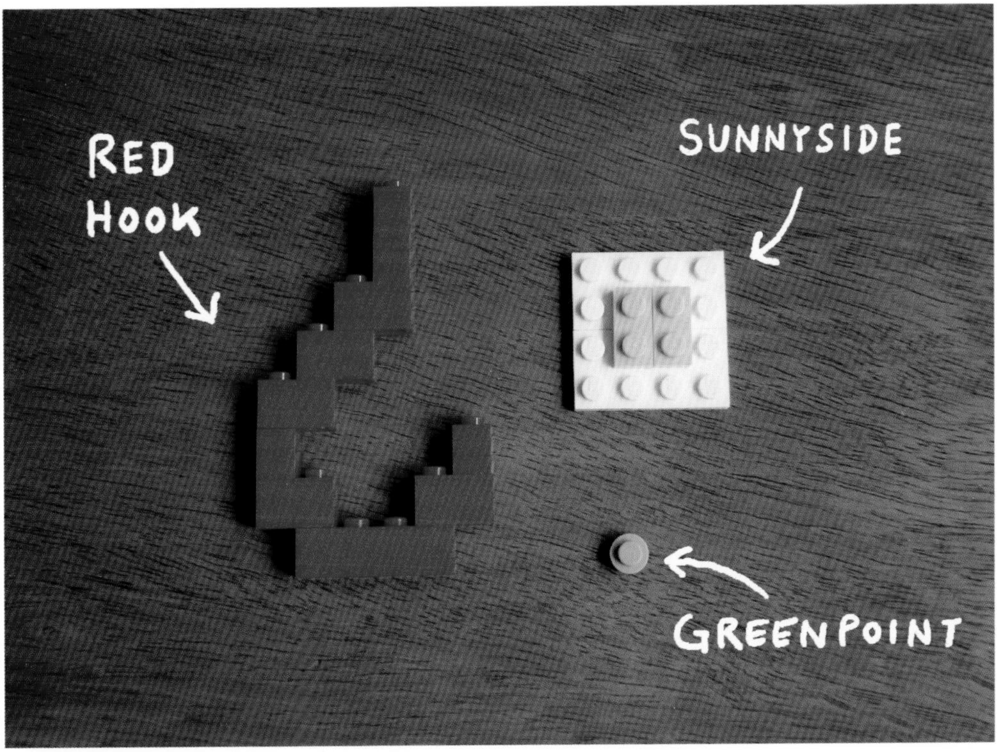
RED
HOOK
SUNNYSIDE
GREENPOINT

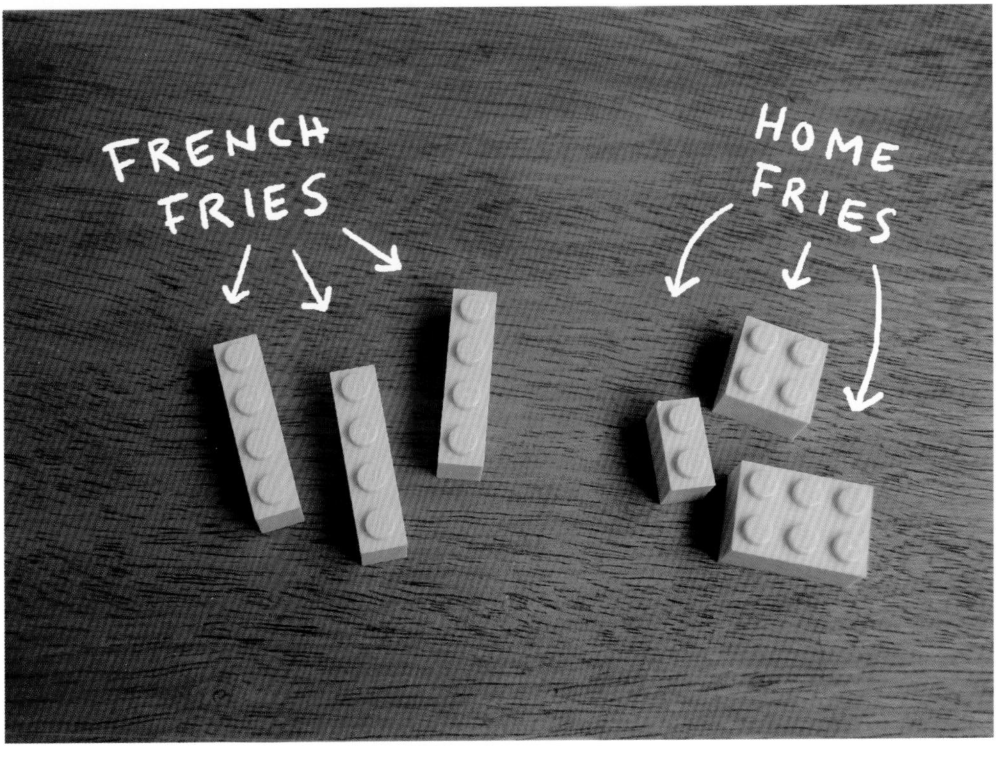
FRENCH
FRIES
HOME
FRIES

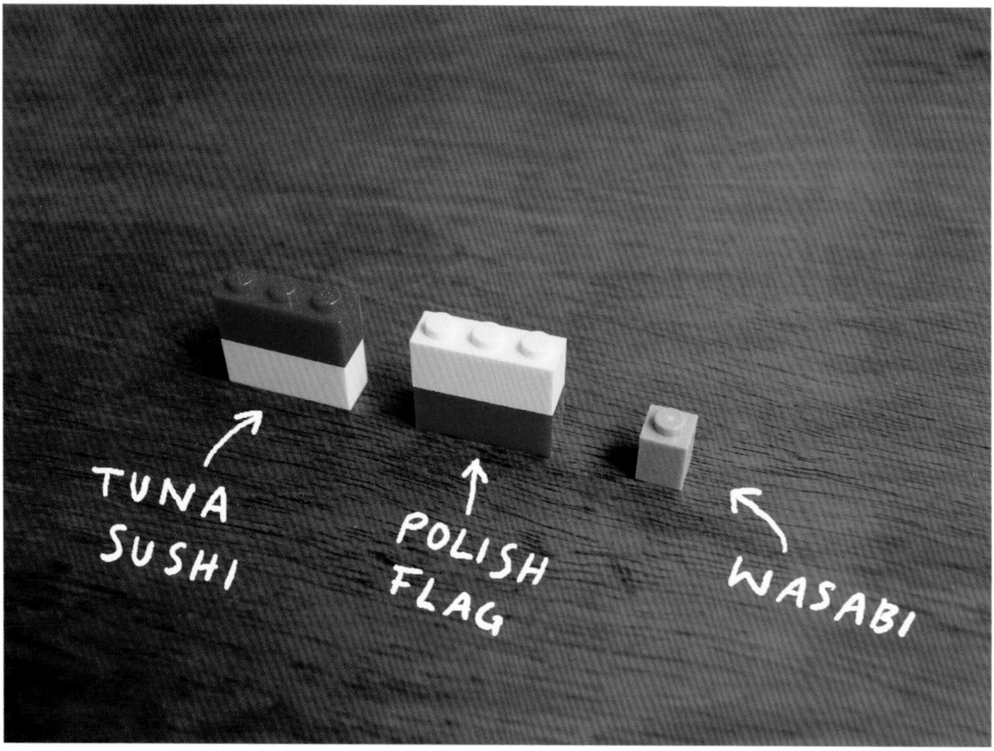
TUNA SUSHI
POLISH FLAG
WASABI

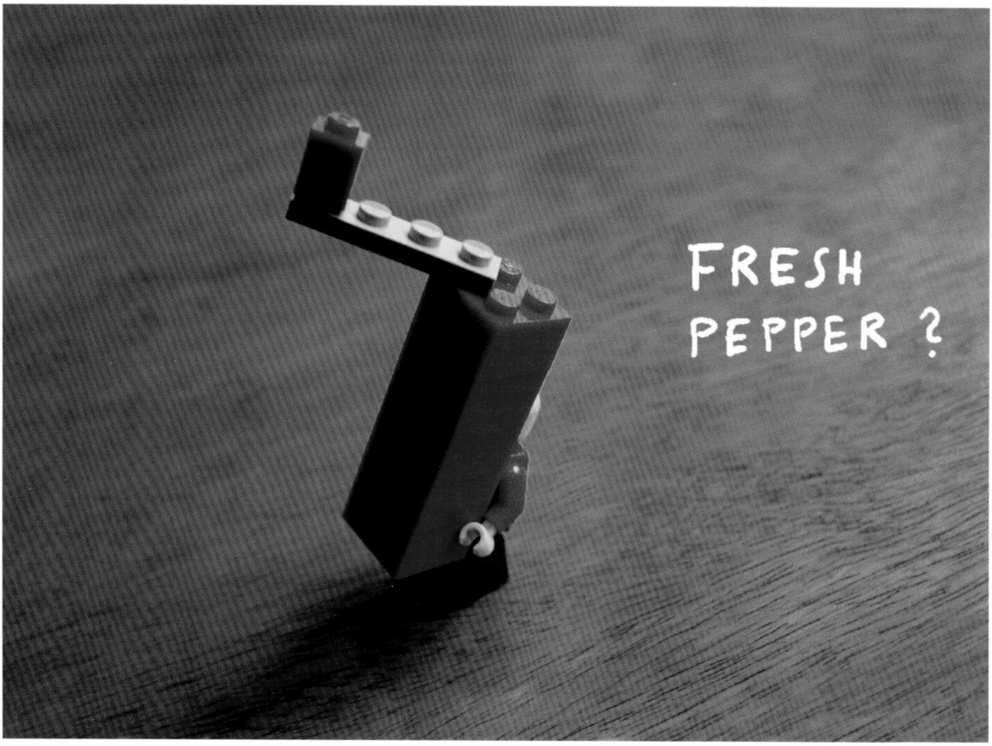
FRESH PEPPER ?

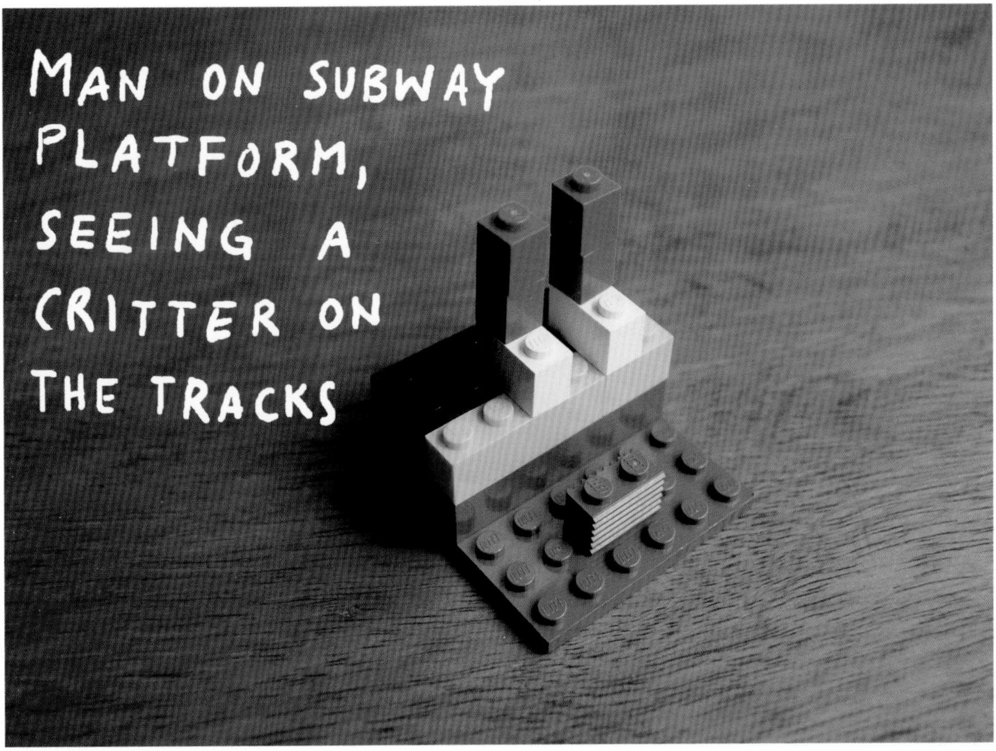
MAN ON SUBWAY PLATFORM, SEEING A CRITTER ON THE TRACKS

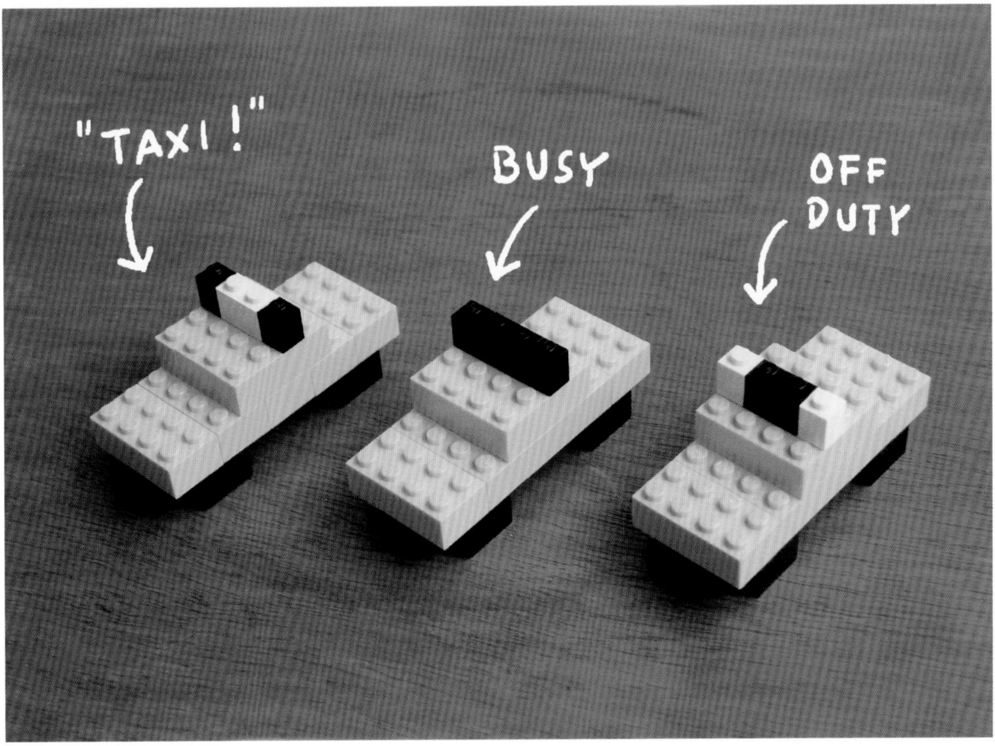
"TAXI!"
BUSY
OFF DUTY

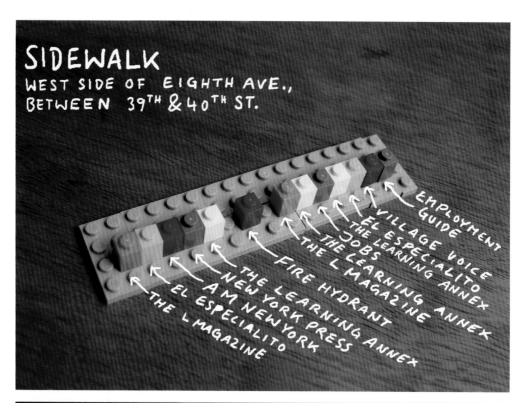

SIDEWALK
WEST SIDE OF EIGHTH AVE.,
BETWEEN 39TH & 40TH ST.

EMPLOYMENT GUIDE
VILLAGE VOICE
EL ESPECIALITO
THE LEARNING ANNEX
JOBS
THE LEARNING ANNEX
THE L MAGAZINE
FIRE HYDRANT
THE LEARNING ANNEX
NEW YORK PRESS
AM NEW YORK
EL ESPECIALITO
THE L MAGAZINE

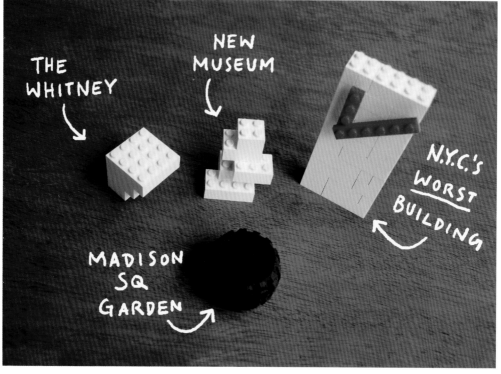

THE WHITNEY

NEW MUSEUM

N.Y.C.'S WORST BUILDING

MADISON SQ GARDEN

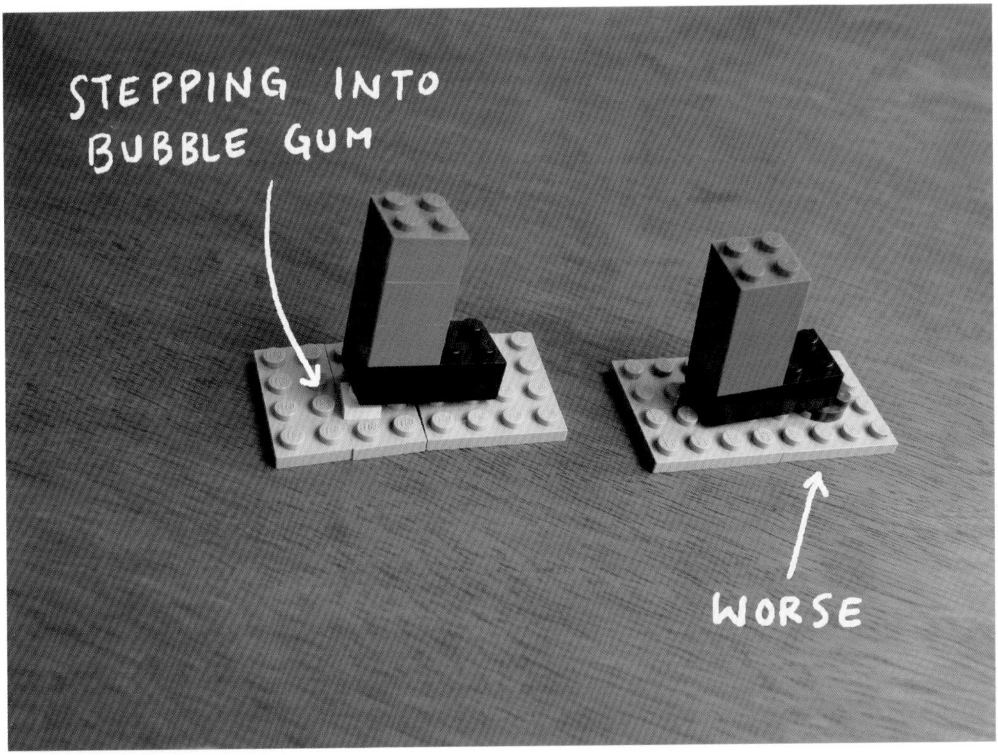
STEPPING INTO BUBBLE GUM
WORSE

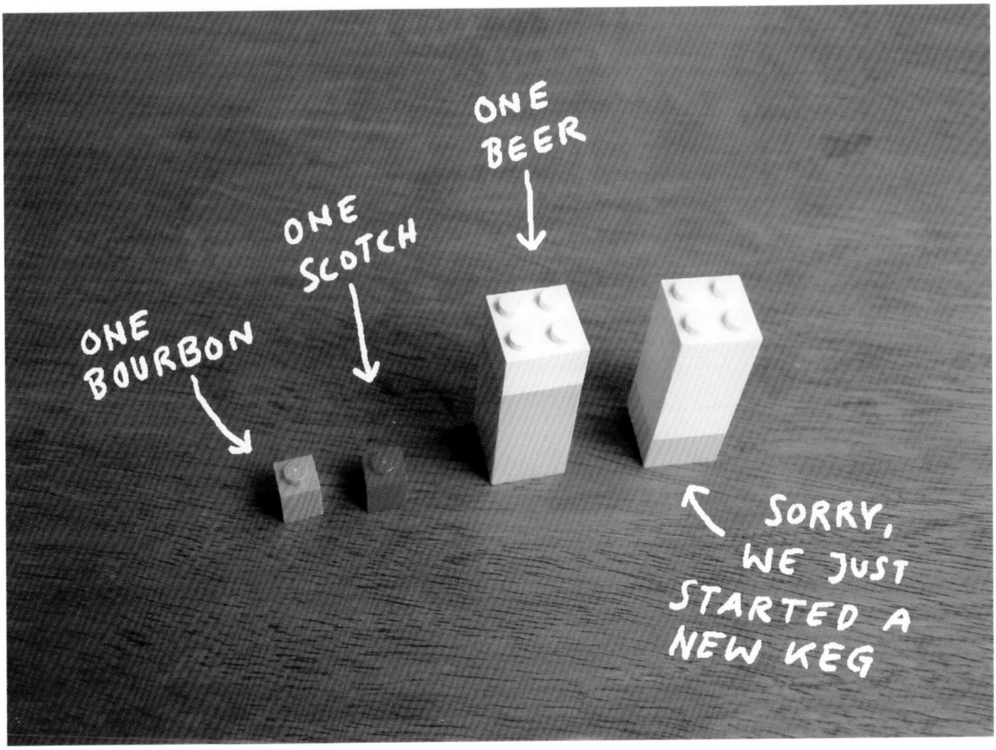
ONE BEER
ONE SCOTCH
ONE BOURBON
SORRY, WE JUST STARTED A NEW KEG

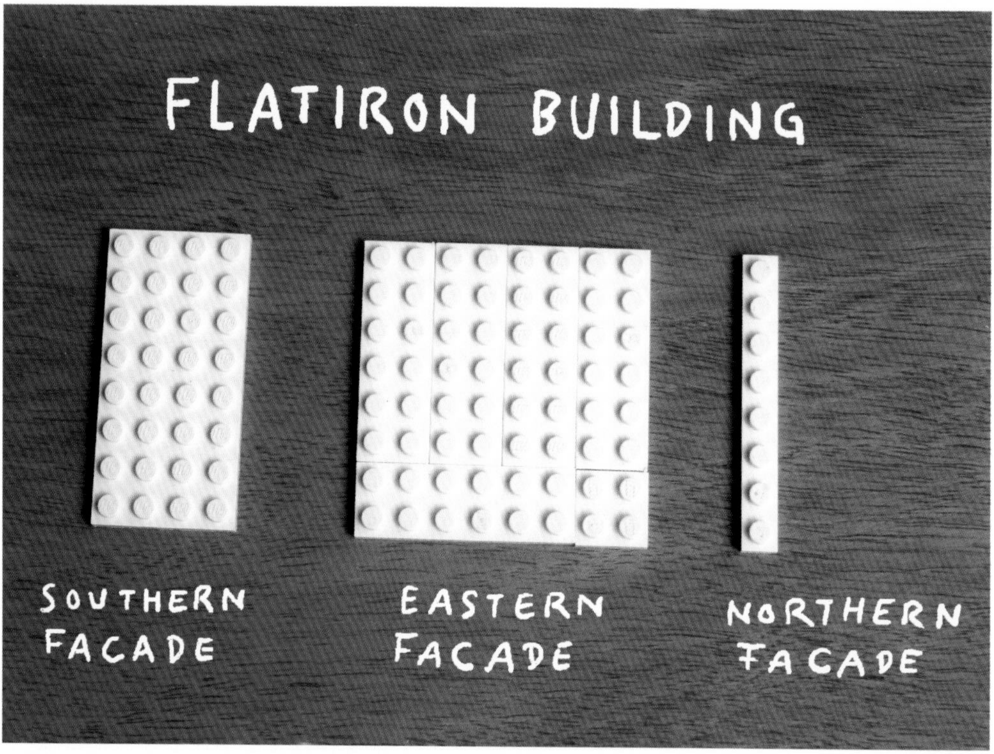
FLATIRON BUILDING
SOUTHERN FACADE
EASTERN FACADE
NORTHERN FACADE

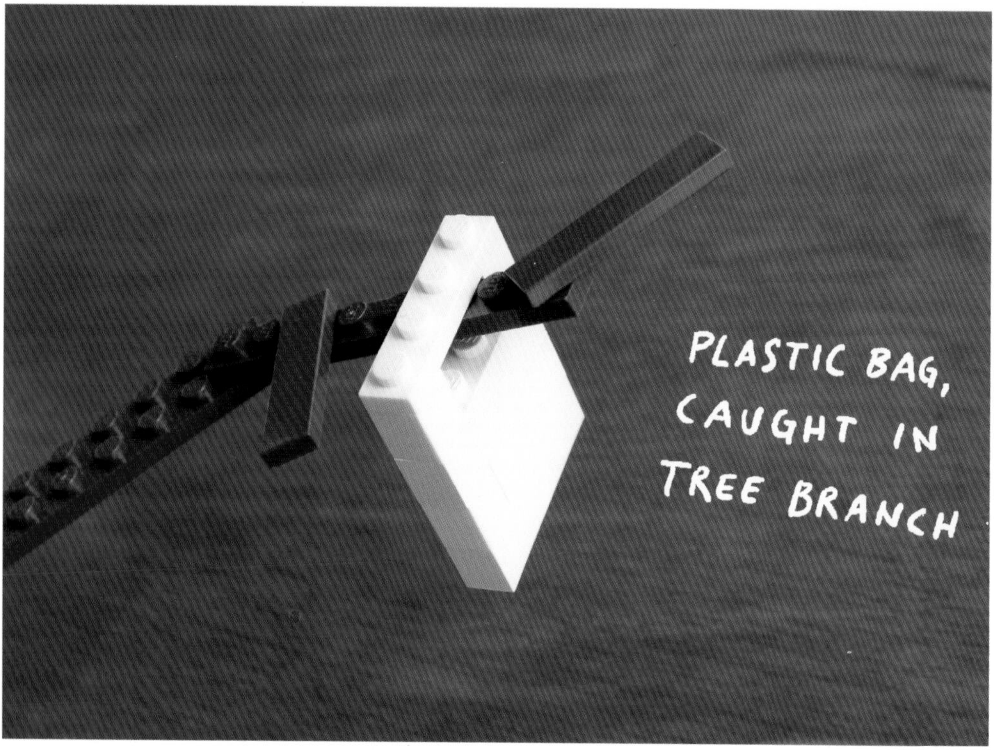
PLASTIC BAG, CAUGHT IN TREE BRANCH

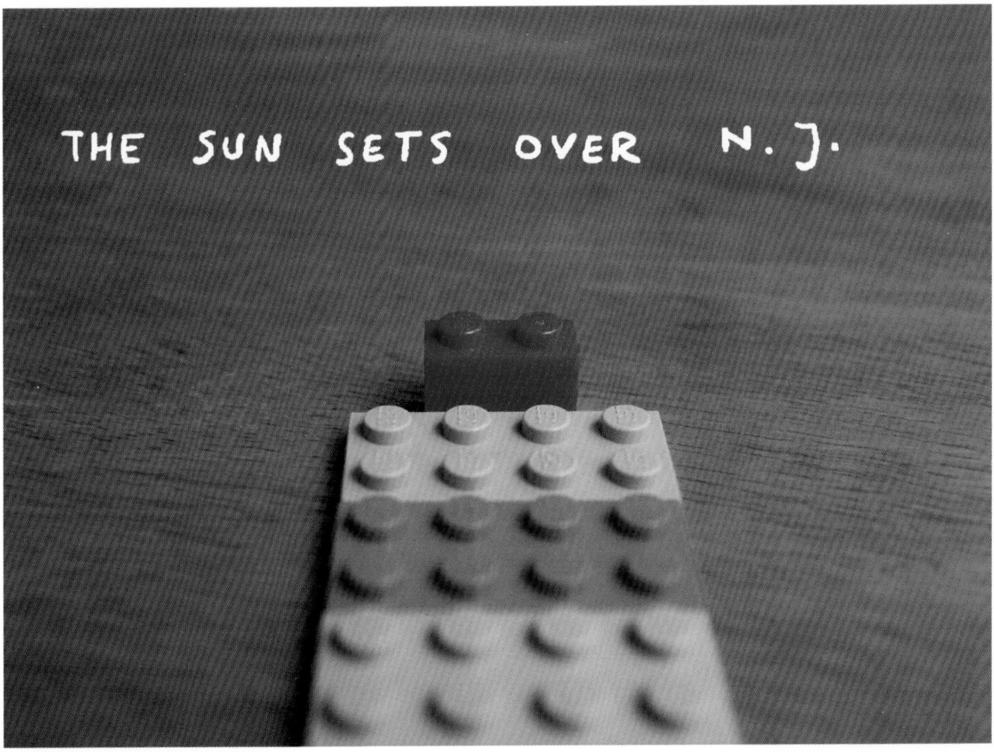
THE SUN SETS OVER N.J.

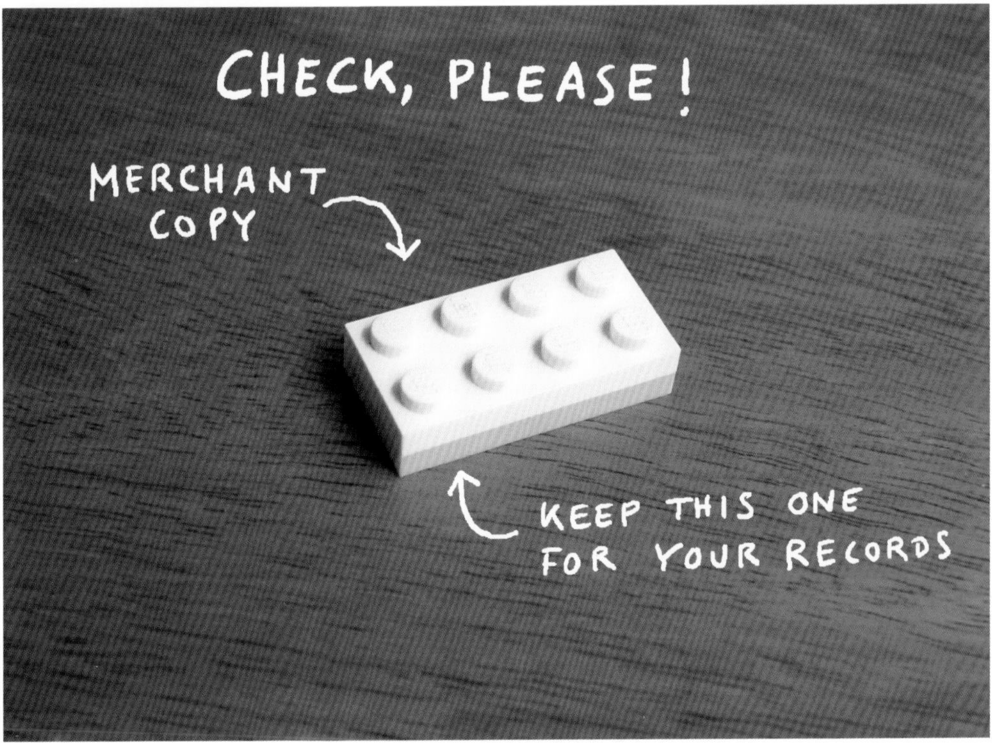
CHECK, PLEASE!
MERCHANT COPY
KEEP THIS ONE FOR YOUR RECORDS

6. My Life with Cables

Cables: Don't like 'em.

You can precipitate my problems with cables by simply calling me. There is a 50 percent chance that you will be greeted by the sound of my desk set banging against a radiator, because the spiral cord of my phone keeps tangling and assembling itself into a compact ball. Why? Am I unconsciously rotating or dancing while talking on the phone?

But my real troubles with cables occur out of sight.

My desk is far from organized, but the mess on top pales compared to the chaos lurking below. I just did a quick inventory and counted a staggering thirty-one cables running riot down there.

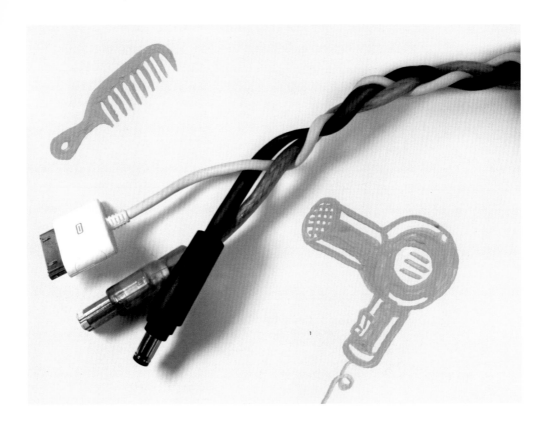

Over the years I have made multiple attempts to tame this mess. All my strategies share one fatal drawback: Replacing a single cable means I have to untie the entire arrangement.

This is how I deal with the situation these days: If I get a new device, I just stuff any new cables right into the swamp of existing ones. And if I need to remove a cable, I optimistically pull on it, like a madman.

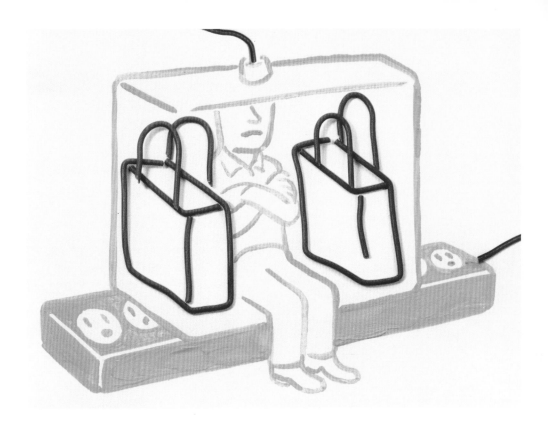

I don't even want to get started about the endless varieties of cables, chargers, and adapters out there. My biggest frustration stems from a much simpler problem: I use a lot of extension cords with multiple sockets. Although these cords are obviously designed to power six cables, I can barely squeeze in three, since most electronic equipment nowadays seems to sport absurdly large plugs. This reminds me of some very inconsiderate folks one so often encounters on the subway.

Adding to the insult: Those Franken-cables are immorally expensive. I have a habit of losing power adapters when traveling, and spend a small fortune on replacements. When I close my eyes, I can see Mr. Radio and Mrs. Shack living on an island made of solid gold.

I don't want to complain, though—I am just a designer.

A couple of years back, I tried unsuccessfully to hook up an old drum machine to an electric keyboard. This gave me a glimpse into the terrifying universe of cables that musicians and audiophiles have to deal with.

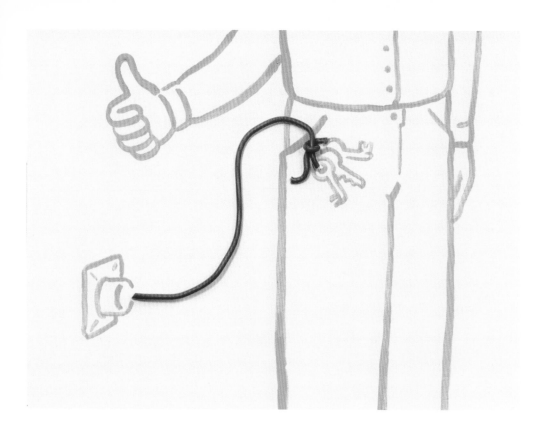

I am aware that I could reduce the number of cables in my life if I took advantage of all the advancements in wireless technology. The problem: If it's not attached to a cable, I will lose it.

If my twenty-four-inch computer screen weren't connected to the wall with a power cable, it would disappear among the sofa pillows one day.

The most venomous of all cables are headphones. The combination of thin wires and stubborn earplug hooks is an endless source of Gordian frustration (notably amplified when combined with seat belts on an airplane).

The true malice of headphones, however, is revealed when they are allowed to mingle with other cables.

Last year, as my family was packing up for our big move from New York, I was stunned at the number of cables I had amassed over the years. I had stuffed them all into a huge box, and was now confronted with one solid knot.

Upon our arrival in Berlin, I realized that there were some extremely important cables woven into miles of headphones and other junk. Untangling this mess was impossible, unless I cut some evil three-dollar headphones. Then I realized that a crucial cell phone charger had an identical thin black cable: a situation that required steady hands and a bold heart.

The storage issue has been resolved: In
a dark corner of our basement I have
attached to the wall an eight-foot plank
spiked with long nails, and all my cables
now hang untangled in neat lines.

I sometimes sneak down there and
wallow in memories of battles past.

I am sure that a generation from now, all our hassles with cables will be long forgotten. But I pledge to keep history alive, and look forward to telling my grandkids stories of SCSI cables, unpolarized NEMA 1-15 sockets, and DVI plugs.

7. Bio Diversity

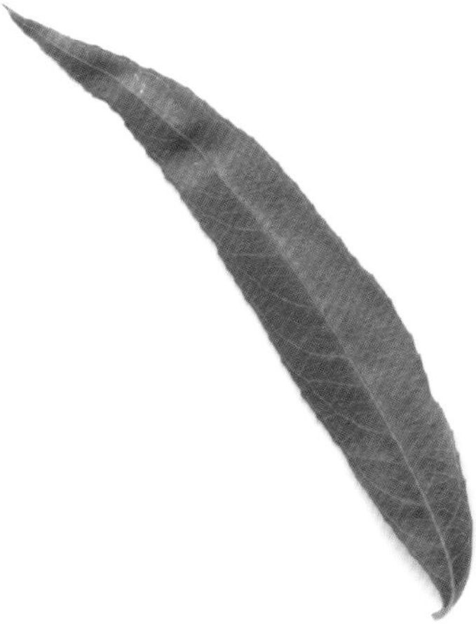

Willow

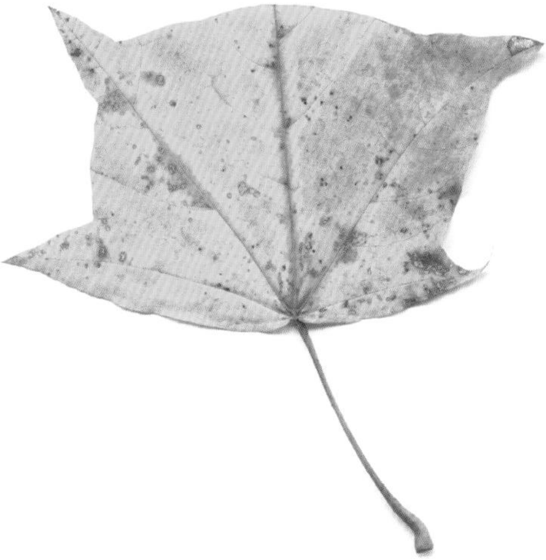

Pillow

Ernie   *and*   *Birch*

Tree-Shirt

Rod-Blagojevich's-Hair Tree

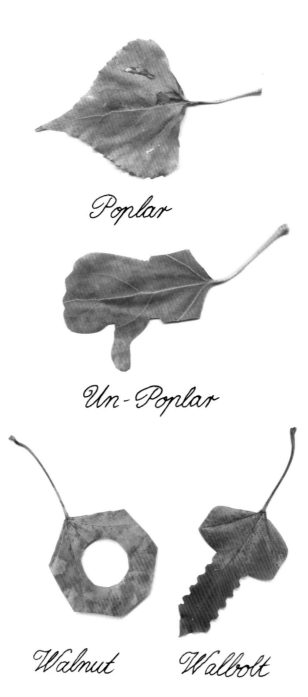

Poplar

Un-Poplar

Walnut   *Walbolt*

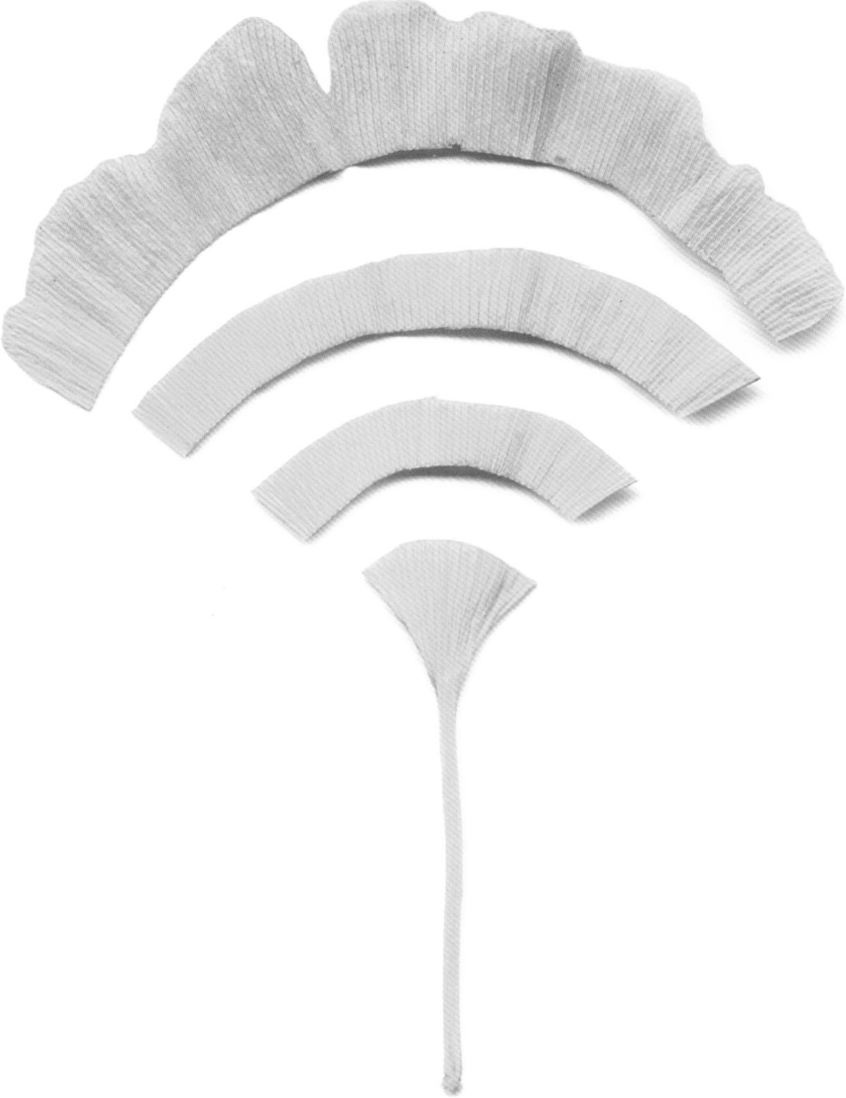

Wireless Gingko

Eighties-Jeans Tree   Eighties-Jeans Tree
(acid washed)

Tooth Bush

El-Dorado-Building-
in-Heavy-Wind Tree

Push Pine   Alder Ego

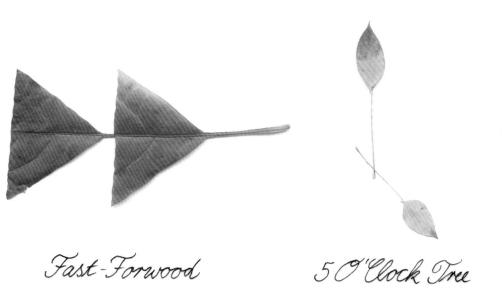

Fast-Forwood   5 O'Clock Tree

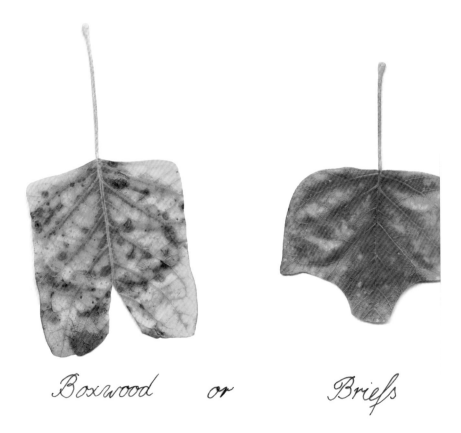

Boxwood   *or*   *Briefs*

Swiss Army
Tree

Regular Tree

Cloud Tree

Cloud-That-Actually-Resembles-a-Car Tree

1957-Ford-Thunderbird Tree

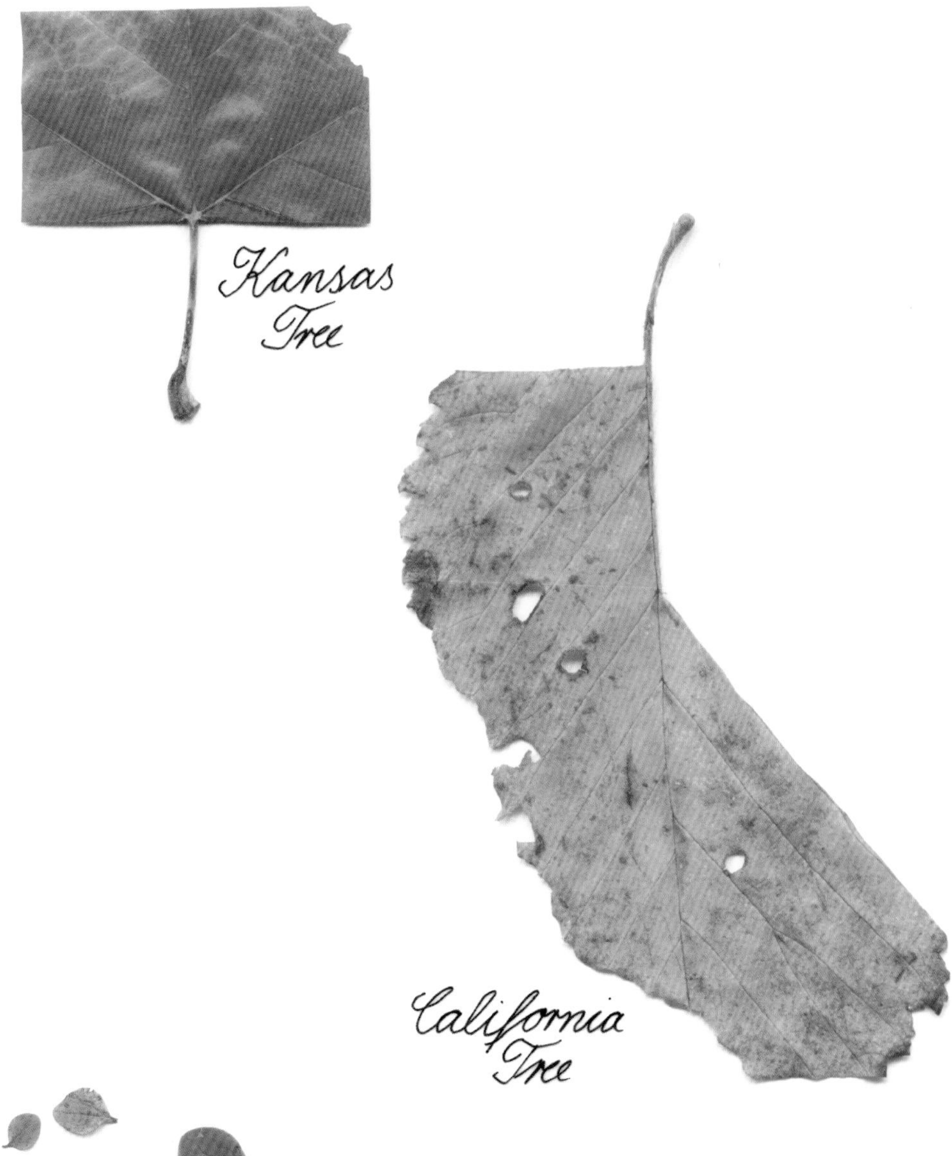
Kansas Tree
California Tree
Hawaii Tree

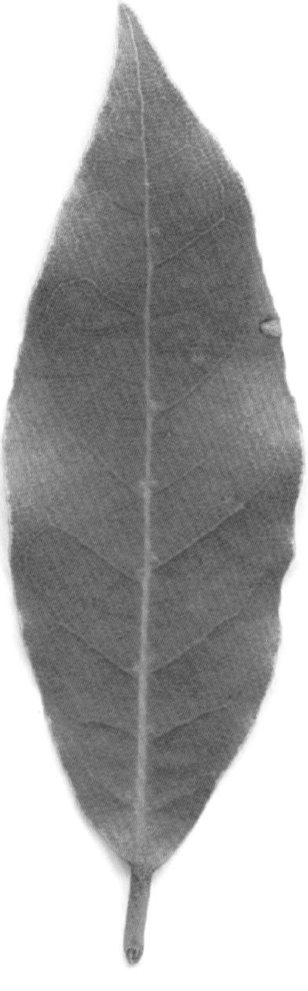

Laurel

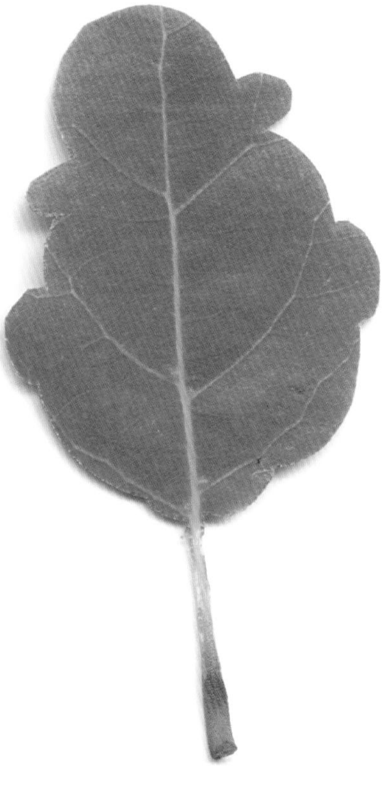

Hardy

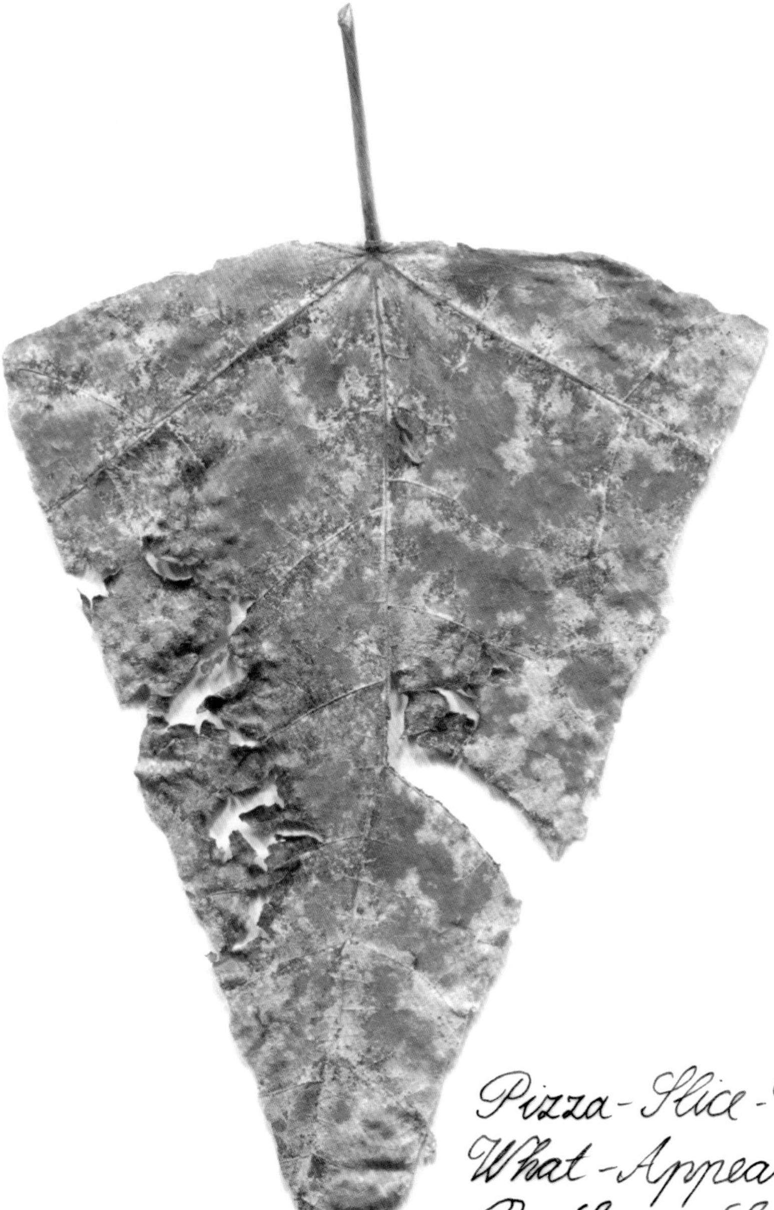

Pizza-Slice-With-What-Appears-to-Be-Some-Sort-of-Gorgonzola-Pesto-Topping Tree

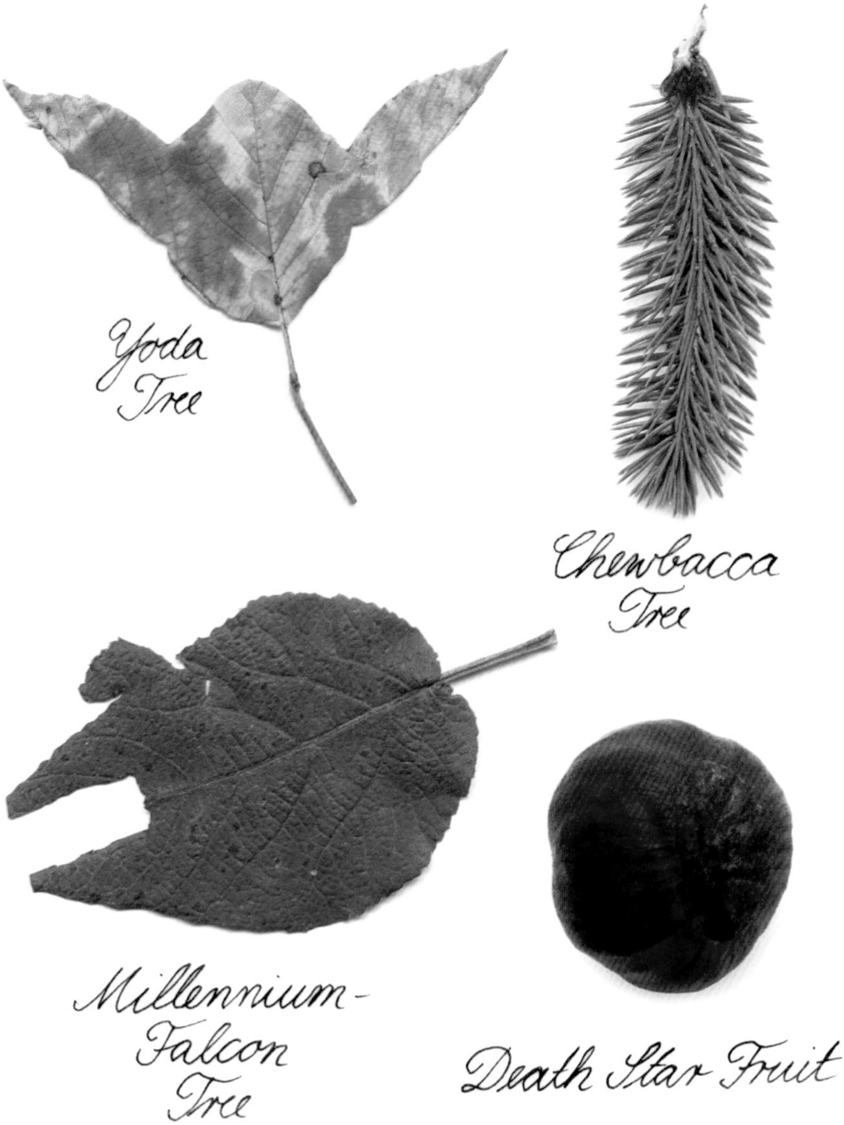
Yoda Tree
Chewbacca Tree
Millennium-Falcon Tree
Death Star Fruit

Faux Fir

8. Over the Wall

On the evening of November 9, 1989, I was watching TV. The Berlin Wall was coming down, and I was flabbergasted.

From my eighteen-year-old perspective, the wall had always been there, and I had no reason to doubt that it would remain there forever. The news of the wall coming down was like somebody telling me that the Eurasian and North American tectonic plates had reversed course overnight, and that from now on you could stroll from Hamburg to Boston.

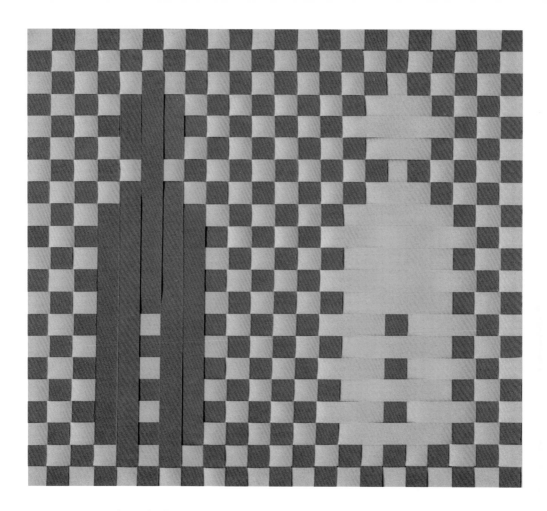

I saw pictures of people dancing on the wall in front of the Brandenburg Gate. Millions were out in the streets of Berlin, complete strangers were falling into one another's arms, smiling and weeping at the same time. The images could not have been more emotional, but since I lived in southwestern Germany and we had neither friends nor close relatives on the other side of the wall in East Germany, it remained an abstract event.

During my only visit to the divided Berlin, in 1988, I had experienced the city in all its terrifying absurdity. I vividly recall the so-called ghost stations of the subway:

Some Western subway lines passed through Eastern territory, resulting in a surreal commute. Imagine getting on the uptown 6 train at Union Square, but instead of stopping at Twenty-third, Twenty-eighth, and Thirty-third Streets, the train just slows down, and you are peeking out at dimly lit platforms patrolled by heavily armed soldiers from an enemy army. Then you get off at Grand Central to buy the paper and a bagel as if nothing had happened.

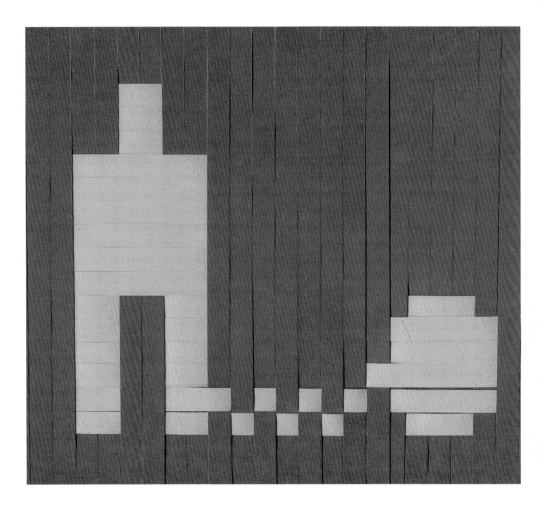

Officially, the wall existed to protect the citizens of the East from the capitalist aggressions of West Berlin. The day after the wall went up in 1961 the East German propaganda newspaper *Neues Deutschland* was filled with reports of thankful East Berliners. An article compared the orderly conduct of the socialist citizens with their counterparts in the West: "There was blood and thunder at the concert of American chief decadence apostle Bill Haley at the West Berlin Sports Palace. With our protective measures for the national border, however, everything passed off peacefully."

The real reason the wall was built was different: East Germany was simply running out of citizens. Millions had fled by crossing the open inner city border of Berlin since the end of the war.

Today my family and I live just a few hundred feet away from Bernauer Strasse, where the wall ripped most callously through the city. In the early morning of August 13, 1961, East German police brigades started to seal off the border between the Soviet and the Allied sectors, splitting the city into East and West Berlin. In other neighborhoods, the divide often ran along a natural border, or at least through open spaces. Here it followed a regular residential street. People who lived on the south side of Bernauer Strasse woke up on the very frontier—their apartments were in the East, but the sidewalk in front of their building belonged to the West.

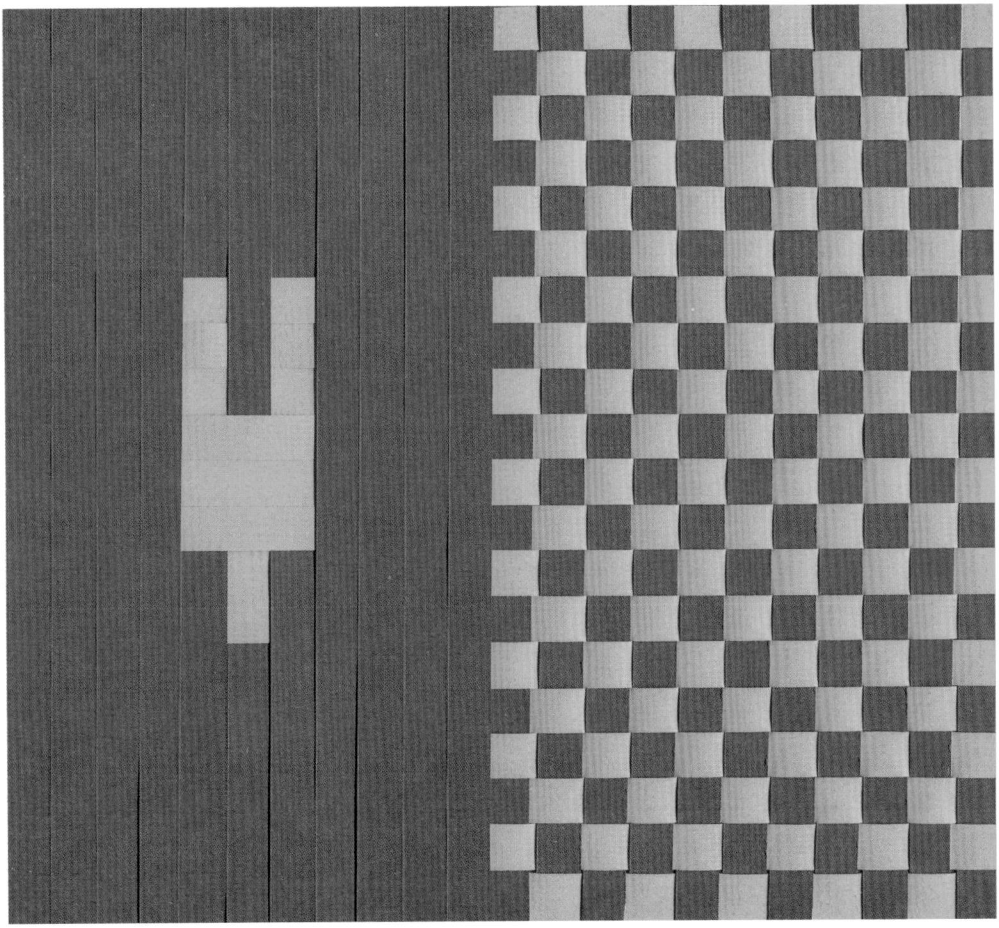

We moved from New York to Berlin last summer. Renovations at our home weren't finished yet. We were exhausted. On top of that, we had a cranky baby who was content only when I put him in the stroller and took him for long walks exploring our new neighborhood. Often we came by the Berlin Wall Memorial on the corner of Bernauer and Ackerstrasse. That's when I first saw the old photos of people jumping out of their apartment windows to escape to the West. After the lower windows had been bricked up by the police, people tried to escape from the upper floors. They left behind forever their possessions, their friends, and often their families. Ida Siekmann died right here on August 22, 1961, the day before her fifty-ninth birthday, after jumping from her third-floor apartment. She was the wall's first official victim.

And here I was, pitying myself because I had slept only a few hours and couldn't get my DSL connection up and running.

In the first days after it went up, the wall was a barbed wire barrier. Conrad Schumann, a nineteen-year-old soldier in the East German army, was standing guard on the corner of Ruppiner Strasse and Bernauer Strasse. He was taunted and insulted by passersby from the West and, on a whim, started running and hurdled the barbed wire into the West, thus becoming the subject of one of the most dramatic photographs of the time. Only recently have I realized that I often go jogging up that very sidewalk.

Today our neighborhood is filled with bustling restaurants, shops, galleries, and playgrounds, which makes it all the more jarring to find out about all the drama that unfolded here. A few feet away from where the boys and I play in a sandbox, my neighbors from forty-odd years ago had dug a tunnel through which fifty-seven people escaped before its existence was leaked to the secret police. Another photo at the memorial shows a bride and a groom waving at their parents from the other side of the barbed wire. They had probably lived just a few blocks from each other, and now found themselves in two separate, hostile nations. I think of our parents, who can just hop a train to come to Berlin to see their grandchildren perform a song in kindergarten.

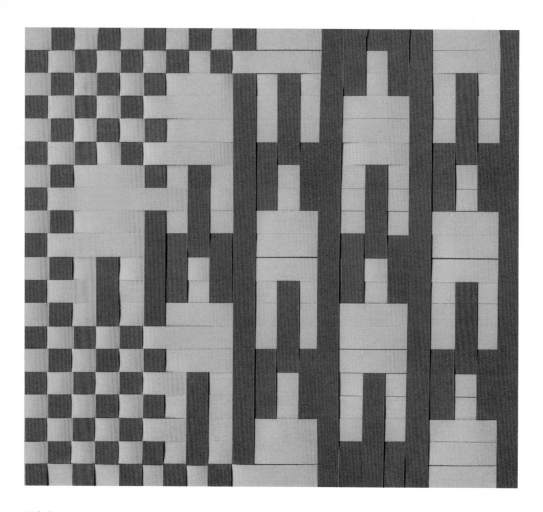

While I try to get in touch with history through museums, books, and TV, twenty years ago history was actually being made, just a few blocks east in the church communities of the Prenzlauer Berg district. People risked losing their jobs, ruining their children's prospects, and even being taken to one of the notorious Stasi prisons, yet they still worked in opposition groups for years. Like similar groups in Leipzig, they began organizing open demonstrations in the fall of 1989. Within weeks, these grew from a few dozen brave men and women to hundreds of thousands across the country, ultimately leading to the collapse of the socialist regime.

Germany, with a history so full of iron-fisted terror, war, and wanton violence, had finally experienced a revolution without a single bullet being fired.

For twenty-eight years the wall in Berlin was one of the world's most frightening and impermeable borders. Few made it to the other side; most who tried were captured and thrown into prison, and many were killed in the attempt. Today, there are only very few places where the wall still exists. Instead, a twin row of cobblestones is laid into the streets of Berlin, indicating where the wall once stood.

Every time I ride my bike across this artificial scar, I quickly close my eyes and appreciate the small, humbling bump.

9. Master of the Universe

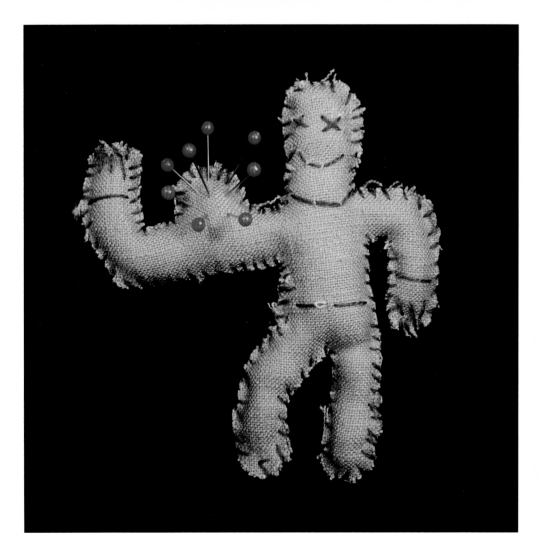

Remember the Knicks making it to the
finals in 1999? That was me.

The blizzard of 2006? I just felt like it.

Barack Obama being elected president?
You're welcome.

I first became of my super natural powers
when I was eleven.

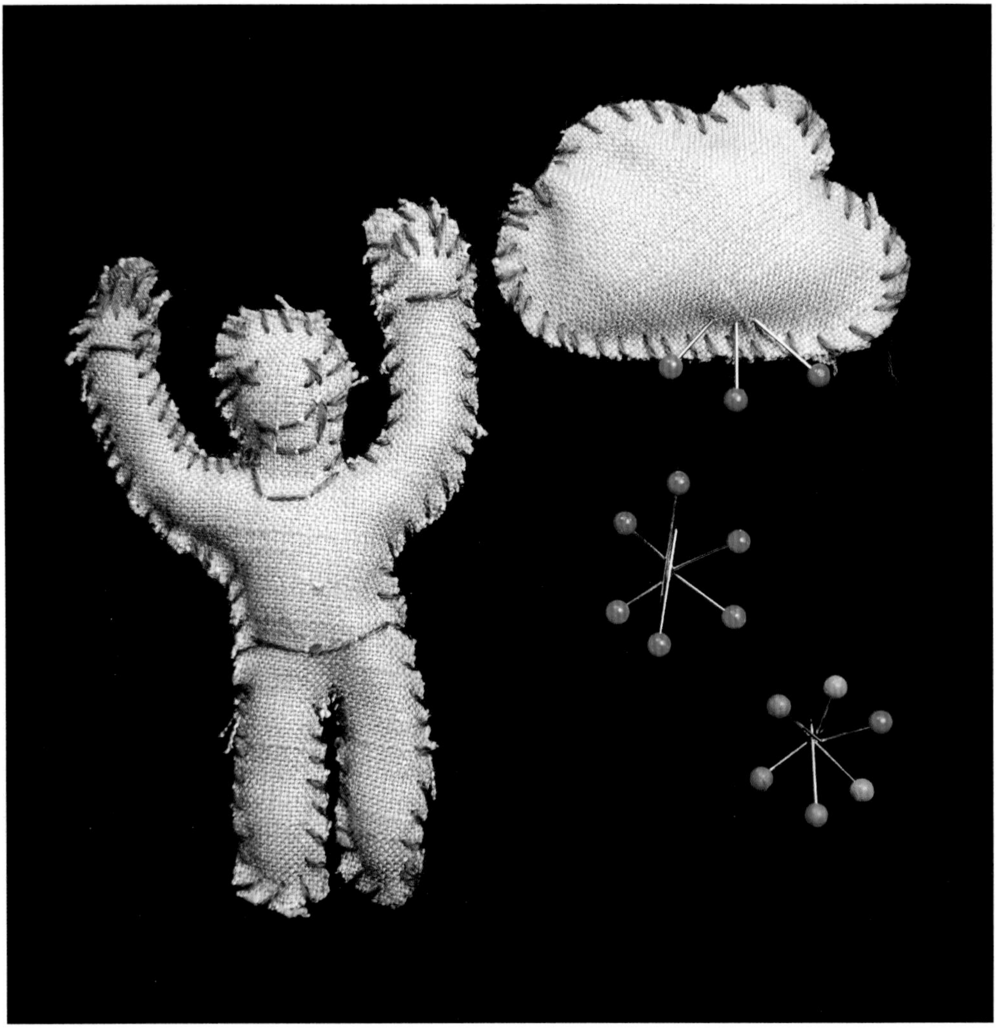

It was the winter of 1982, and I loved nothing more than snow. By February there still hadn't been a proper snowfall, and I had an epiphany: If I managed to walk the whole way home from school without stepping on a single line on the pavement, my wish would be granted.

The next morning I woke up to a whopping eight inches.

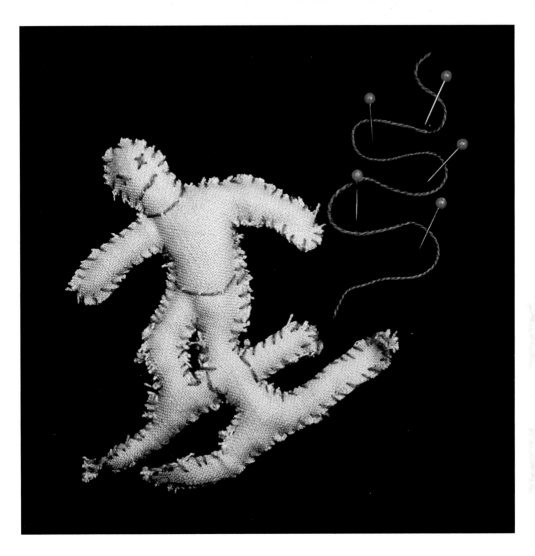

Most miracles I perform require that I accomplish a challenging task.

For example: Removing the peel in one piece from at least three consecutive tangerines will greatly increase the chances that an overdue check will arrive in the mail the following day.

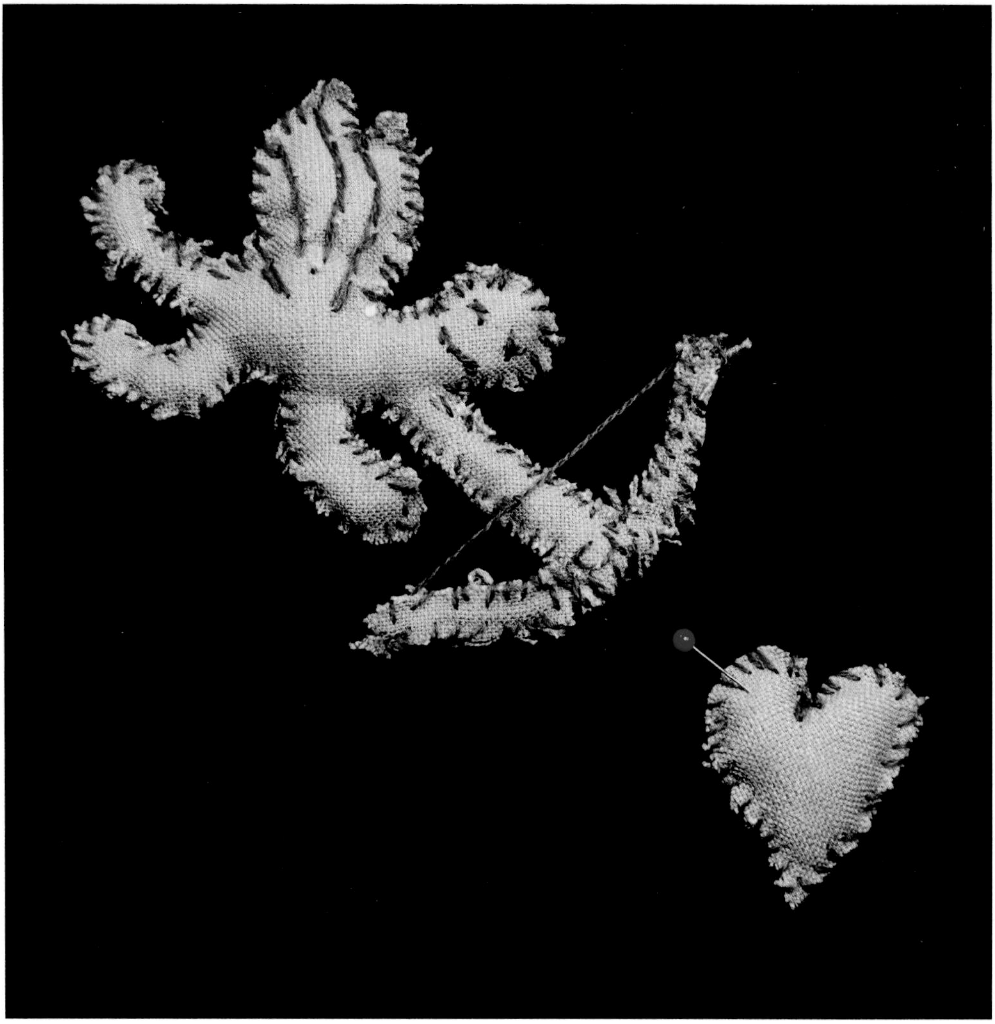

As a kid, I spent a lot of time on the neighborhood basketball court. To a passerby, it may have looked like I was a lonely guy, mindlessly shooting hoops for half the afternoon. But I was actually developing elaborate systems, in which a certain sequence of continuous made shots would generate a decent grade in a math test or (more importantly) a lucky encounter with a girl I had a crush on.

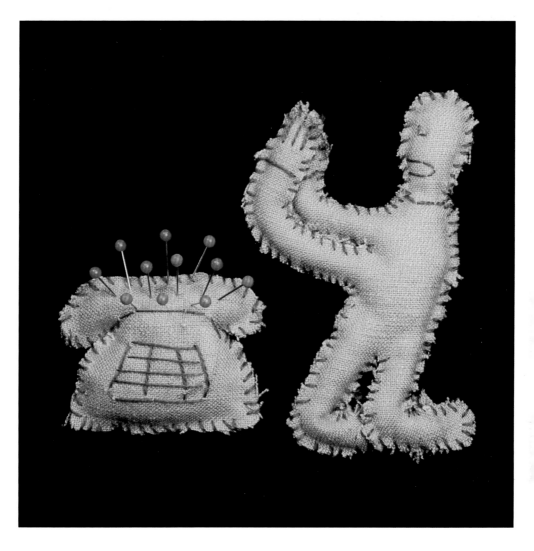

Teenagers spend hours staring at their phones, desperately waiting for the person of their dreams to call. Not me—I would grab life by the horns: Pacing through our living room I would scan the spines of all the books for the letter J. I knew that as soon as I had found 99 of them, she would call.

Or 150.

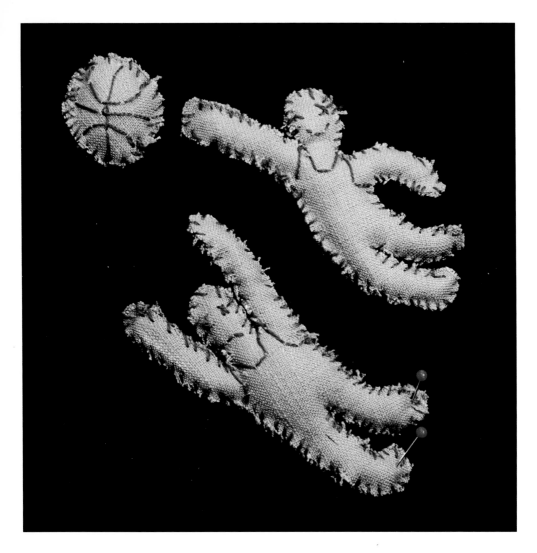

At times I have needed support from those around me. A few years back I was watching a Knicks game with a friend. By strategically switching salsas late in the third quarter we had managed to engineer a turnaround. The Knicks were up by two as regulation time was winding down. Meanwhile, my pal's girlfriend had fallen asleep on the sofa in an awkward position. Obviously there was a direct correlation between her posture and Marcus Camby's remarkable free throw percentage.

When she suddenly awoke, we had to beg her not to remove her left hand and right knee from under that pillow.

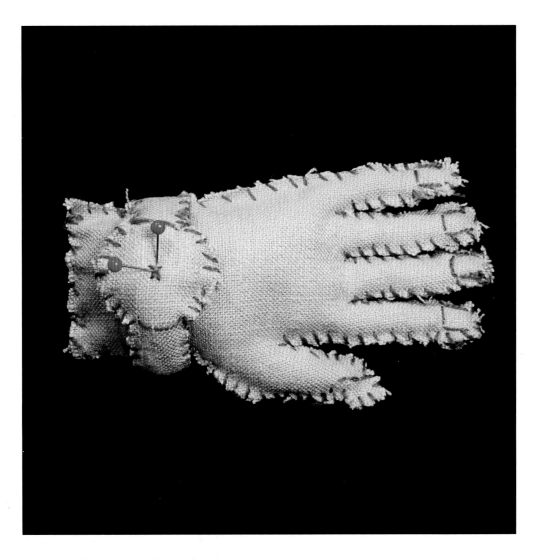

To save a close game, I have often had
to sit through an entire quarter with my
tongue stuck in a beer bottle. However,
with all those commercial breaks, a quarter can easily last forty-five minutes.
When you are almighty, you have a very
tight schedule. Consequently I had to end
my NBA career in 2001, to focus on other
responsibilities. Look at what has happened to the Knicks since.

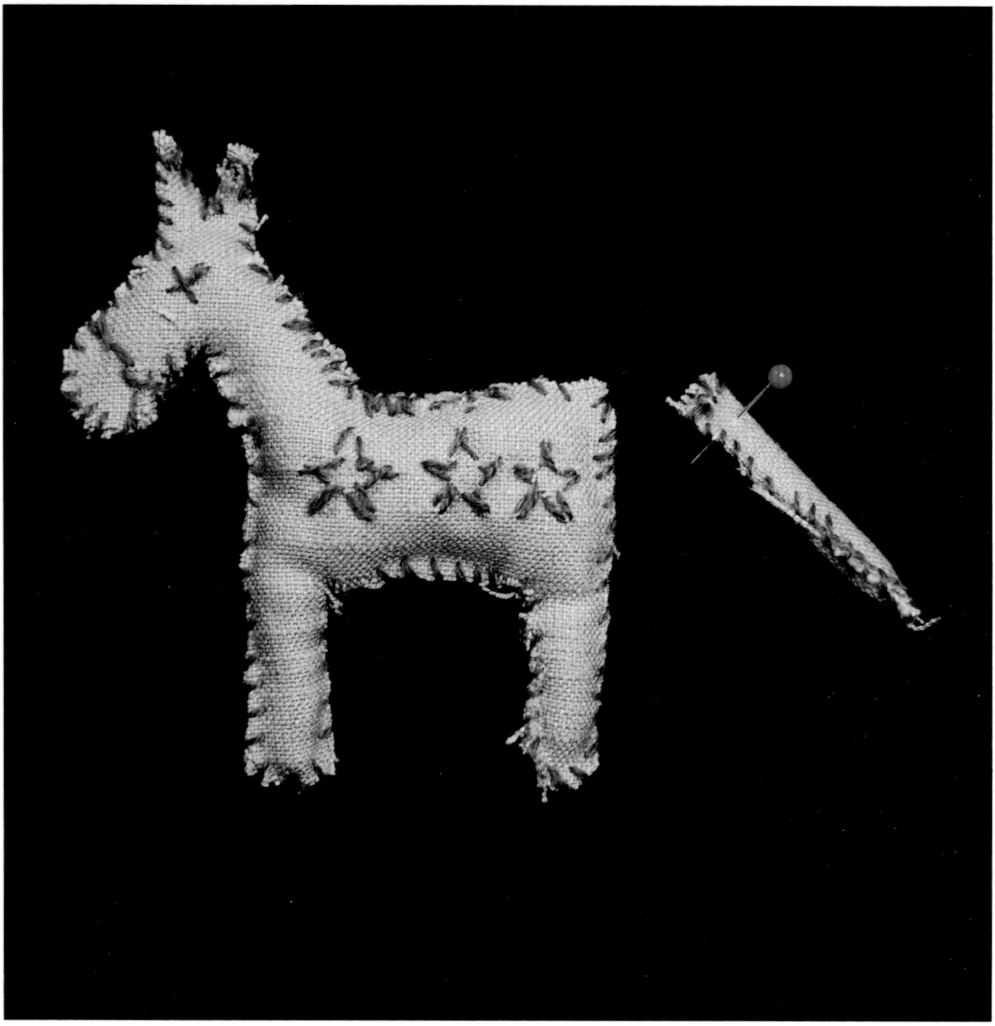

Despite his flawed campaign, John Kerry had a good shot to win the presidency in 2004. All it would have taken was me spotting five Kerry-Edwards campaign stickers on cars on my way to work on November 2, 2004. There were only three.

I gave the ticket a second chance on my way home, but when I failed to find a car with either an Ohio or Florida license plate on Hicks Street in Brooklyn, I knew that George Bush had it won.

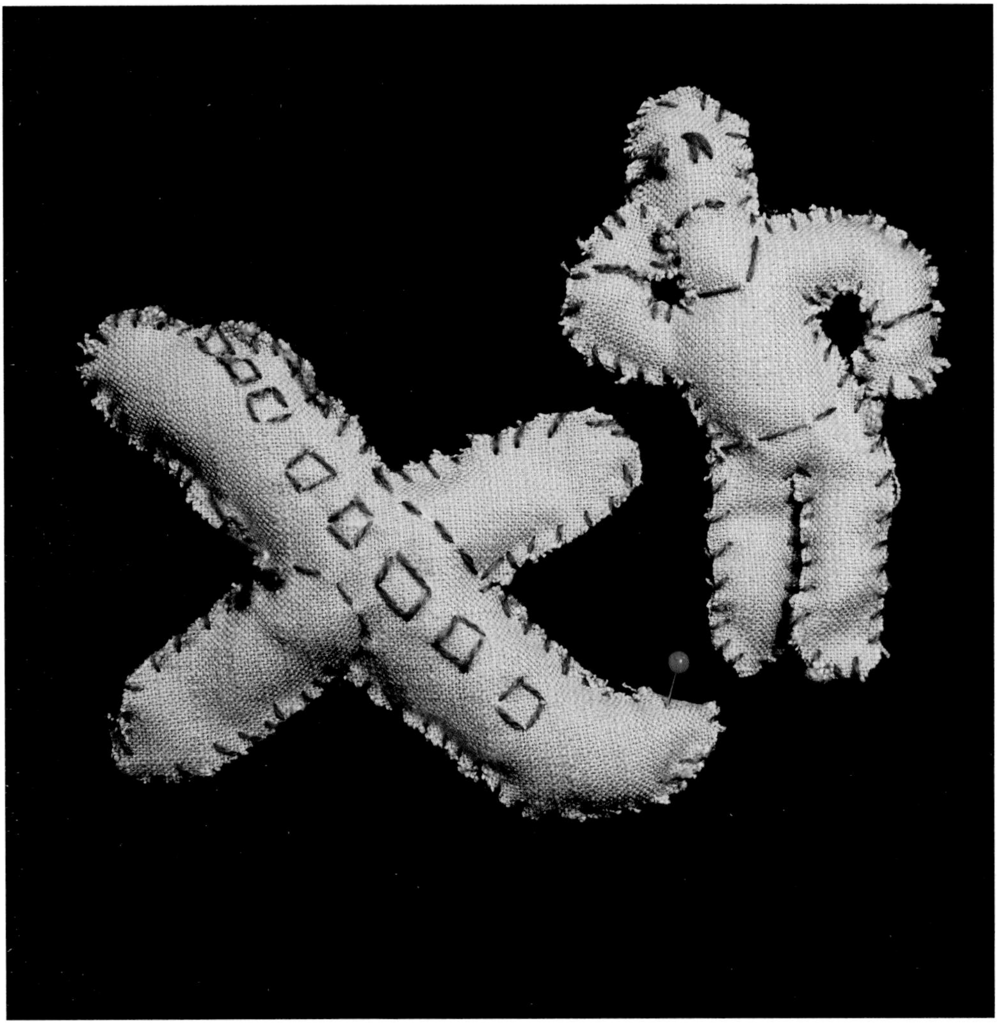

Fate is one sneaky chap. I often have to try out several maneuvers to find the one that clicks. Recently I was stuck on the tarmac at LaGuardia Airport in New York, waiting to fly to Chicago. The burden of getting us going was on me. At first I thought it would suffice to slowly rotate my index finger around my thumb three dozen times (counterclockwise). Unfortunately, this was not the formula of the day, and it took me more than an hour of trial and error until I came up with the proper remedy (filling each square of the in-flight magazine's Sudoku with cross-hatching—duh). Only then were we ready for takeoff.

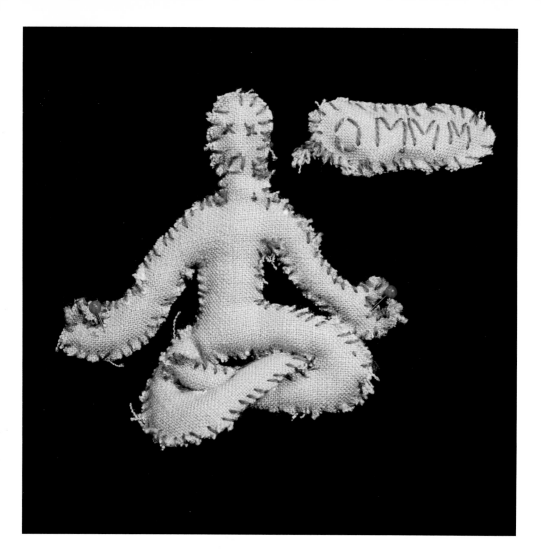

My powers seem limitless when I am not emotionally invested in the outcome of an event: I didn't grow up with football, so I watched the 2008 Super Bowl with blissful detachment. While my friends were nervously following the game, I quietly sat back. Using a gummy bear and a screw cap, I initiated the Giants' stunning last-minute comeback.

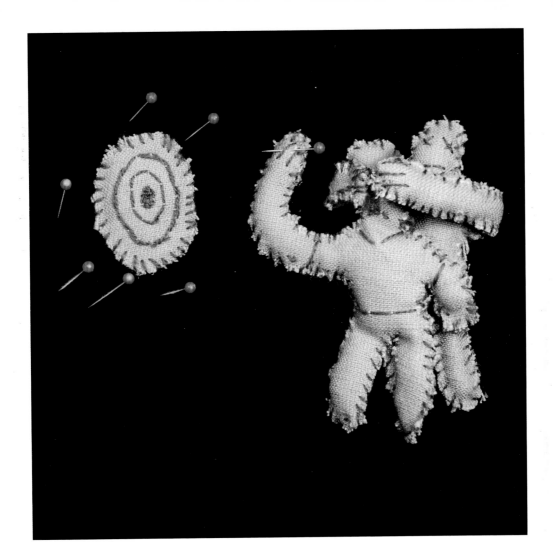

A few times, my powers have failed me. Usually this happens when others distract me. Creating a late goal in a soccer stadium thousands of miles away is no small feat and requires utter concentration.

Germany would certainly have beaten Italy in the last World Cup semifinal had it not been for the disturbing chatter in the New Jersey living room where I was watching the game.

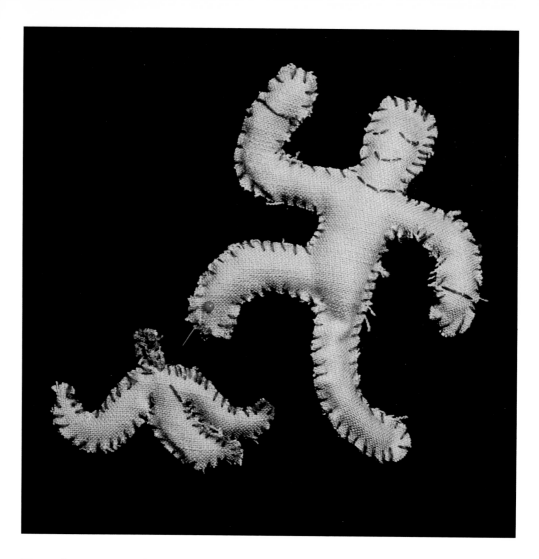

These days I am so exhausted from running after my kids (who seem to be immune to my powers) that I haven't been quite as active as in the past. I am afraid, however, that every time I hit a daisy with a cherry pit or find that the number of salt grains on a pretzel stick is divisible by three, I unwittingly topple governments, award undeserved grades to students, and cause random people across the world to fall madly in love with each other.

10. Good Night and Tough Luck

Getting a good night's sleep is actually a lot more complicated than one would think.

LIFE
BEING AWAKE
SLEEPING
COMPLICATED
SIMPLE
= ONE WOULD THINK
= ACTUALLY

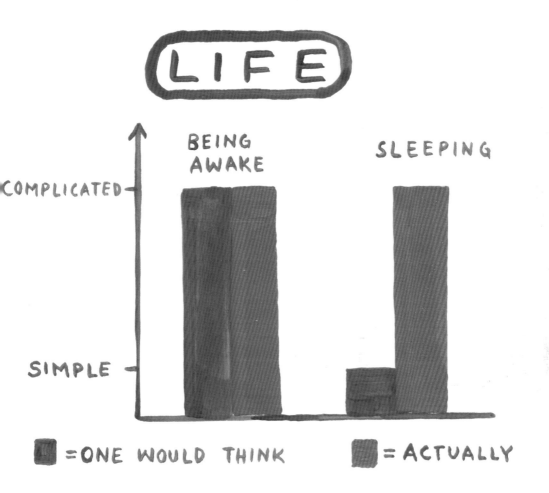

Usually the trouble starts with my having to use the bathroom. Even though I am thirty-eight years old, I still find myself hoping the urge will just pass. Which it doesn't.

Another terrible nuisance: midnight hypochondria. In the light of darkness, I have diagnosed many a sore throat as some dreadful disease that will soon turn my wife into a widow.

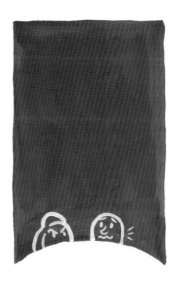

Next up: a visitor from the kids' room.
They start all sweet and cuddly, but
their little bodies become more brazen
by the minute.

To make things worse, our kids always
insist on sleeping ON TOP of our blanket,
creating a whole new set of problems.

fig. a:
sans child

fig. b:
child under
blanket

fig. c:
child on top
of blanket

After weeks of sweet-talking, serenading, and heartbreaking Ferberizing, we think we have reclaimed our bed.

Until a short trip or a quick flu undoes everything again.

I hate mosquitoes.

What with all that buzzing and itching, the hubbub they cause is disproportionate to the micro-drop of blood they make away with. Besides, I am the world's most formidable mosquito hunter.

I have brought to justice every single mosquito that has ever attacked me (except when I spend nights in rooms with patterned wallpaper, which makes mosquito hunting impossible).

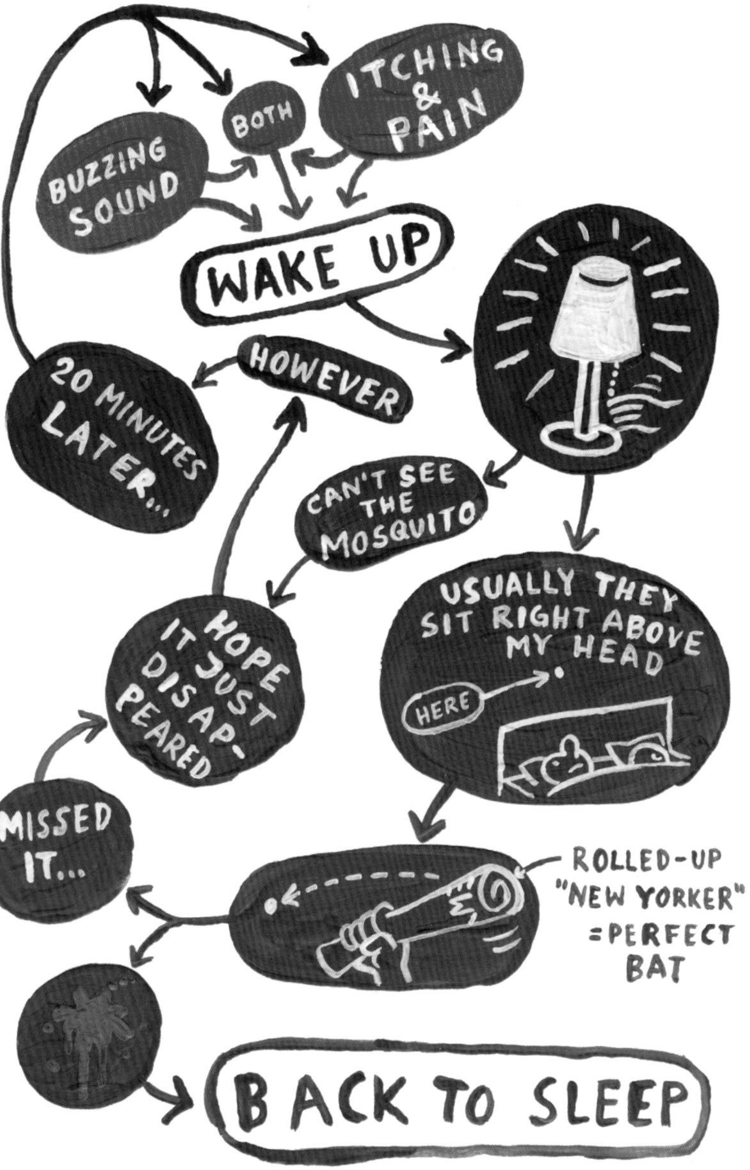

BUZZING SOUND
BOTH
ITCHING & PAIN
WAKE UP
HOWEVER
20 MINUTES LATER...
CAN'T SEE THE MOSQUITO
USUALLY THEY SIT RIGHT ABOVE MY HEAD
HERE
HOPE IT JUST DISAP-PEARED
MISSED IT...
ROLLED-UP "NEW YORKER" =PERFECT BAT
BACK TO SLEEP

If there are any mosquitoes reading this, I would like to offer you a deal: I'll volunteer an ounce or two of my blood each Memorial Day. This should be enough to get you and some of your pals comfortably through the season, and you can spare all of us a lot of suffering.

The opposite of a mosquito is spooning:
Mosquitoes are awful, whereas spooning
is super. The one thing I haven't really
figured out is where the person in the
back is supposed to put that bottom arm.

The second-most wonderful thing about sleeping is the sensation of your cheek meeting the cool half of the pillow after you've turned from one side to the other. I found that it takes about forty-five minutes for the other end to completely cool down again so the procedure can be repeated.

Winter is coming, and slipping into a cold bed is tough. But believe it or not, sometimes when I go to bed before my wife does, I will offer her the half that I have just warmed up.

I obviously love her very, very much.

To summarize what we've learned so far:

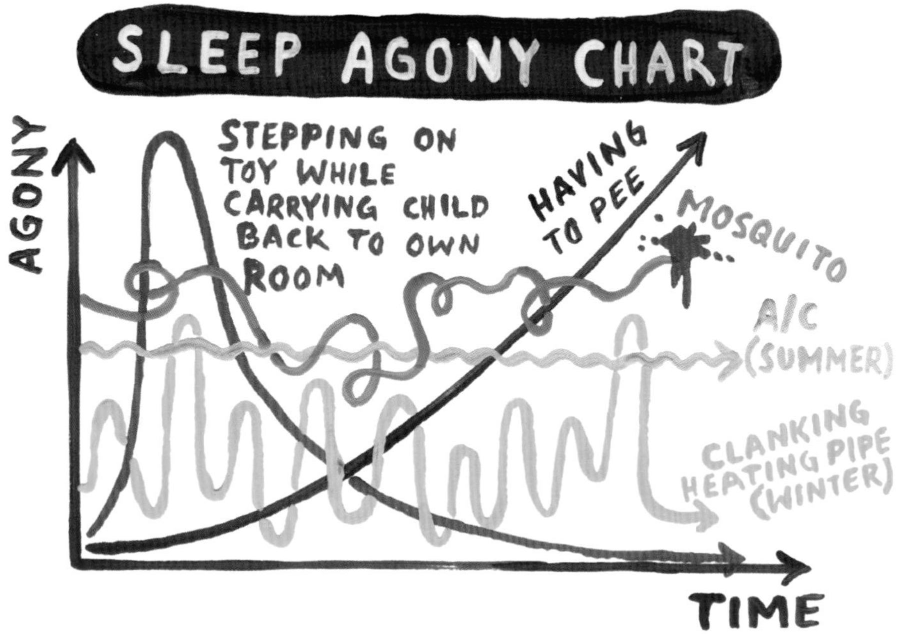
SLEEP AGONY CHART
AGONY
STEPPING ON TOY WHILE CARRYING CHILD BACK TO OWN ROOM
HAVING TO PEE
MOSQUITO
A/C (SUMMER)
CLANKING HEATING PIPE (WINTER)
TIME

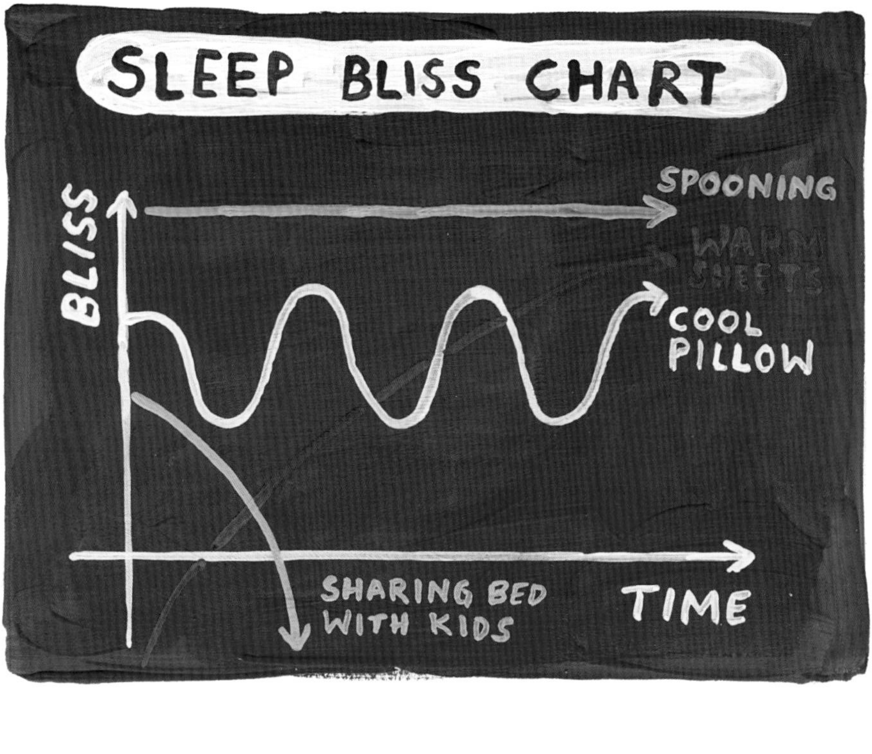
SLEEP BLISS CHART
BLISS
SPOONING
WARM SHEETS
COOL PILLOW
SHARING BED WITH KIDS
TIME

Finally, the kids are back in their own room, the mosquitoes are on the cover of the *New Yorker*, the bed is well tempered, and I can finally go back to sleep, which brings me to the most annoying aspect of sleeping: dreams.

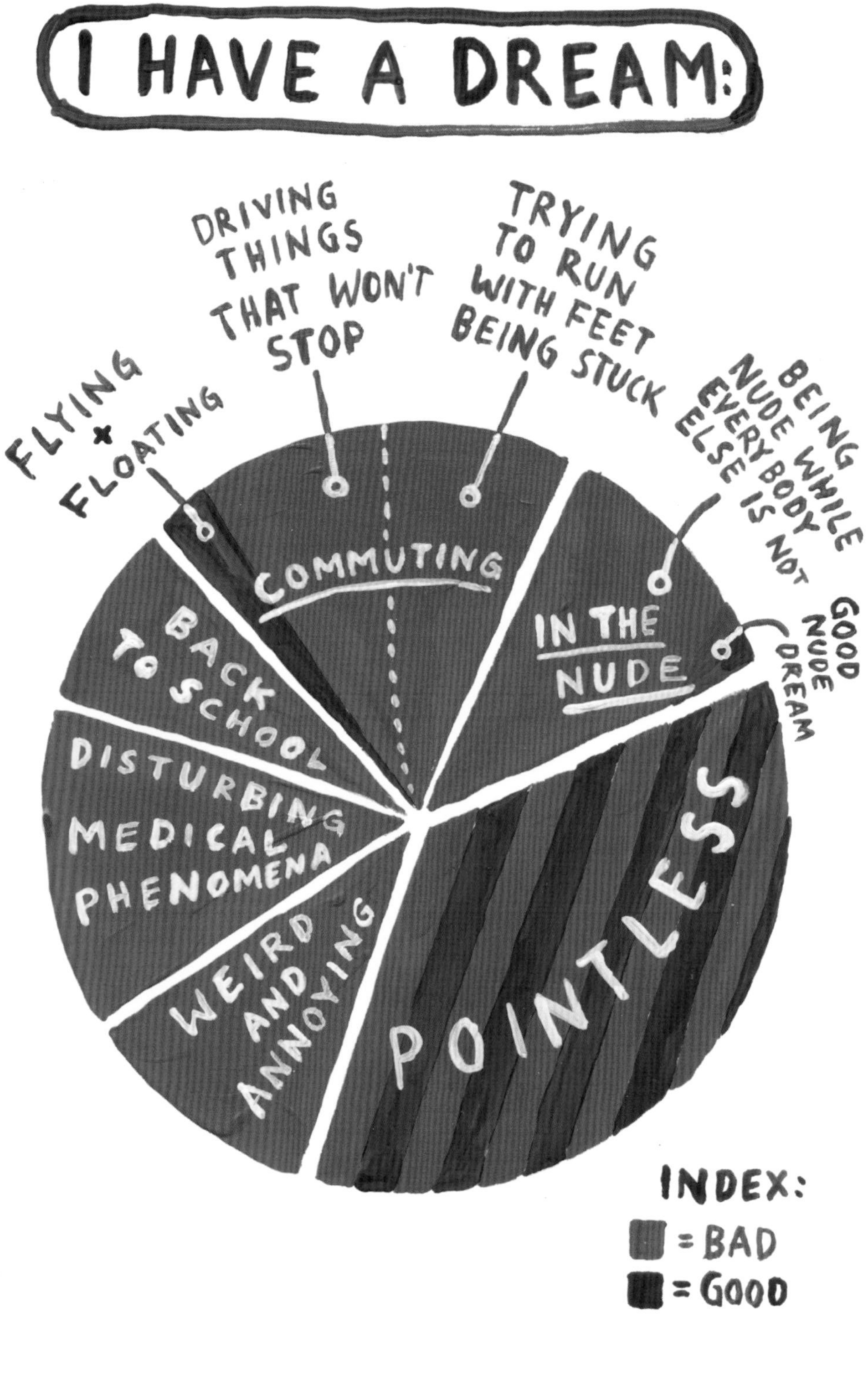

I HAVE A DREAM:
DRIVING THINGS THAT WON'T STOP
TRYING TO RUN WITH FEET BEING STUCK
FLYING + FLOATING
BEING NUDE WHILE EVERYBODY ELSE IS NOT
COMMUTING
IN THE NUDE
GOOD NUDE DREAM
BACK TO SCHOOL
DISTURBING MEDICAL PHENOMENA
WEIRD AND ANNOYING
POINTLESS
INDEX:
= BAD
= GOOD

Just one recent example: Last Tuesday, I had at one point studied a map of Queens with my sons. Later that day I spilled some yogurt. Sure enough, I ended up having a feature-length dream the following night about getting a yogurt stain in the shape of Queens on my pants. Worse, my dreaming self found this very upsetting, and I woke up all exhausted.

But even if a night doesn't work out, I can always rely on sleep's wonderful little sibling: the daytime nap!

11. Come Rain or Come Shine

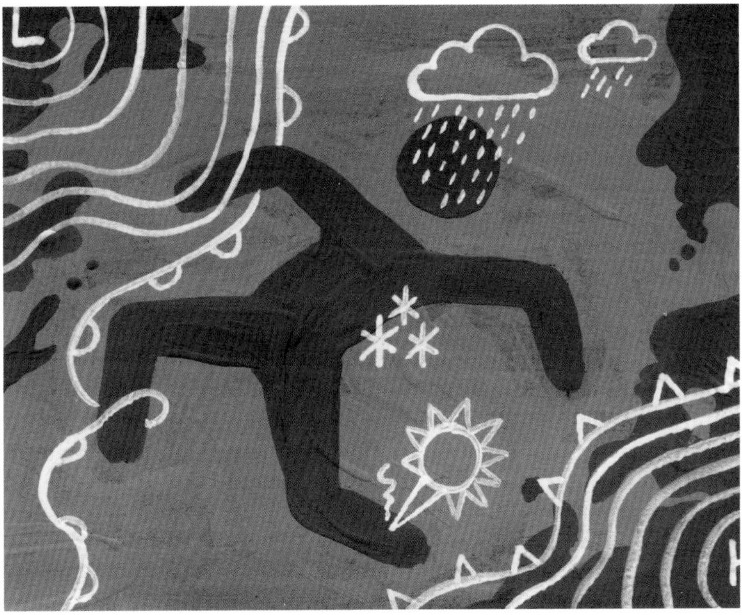
L
H

And now for
my personal
weather forecast
for the year.

January 21:

A 50 percent chance of slush puddles.

January 21:

A 90 percent chance of me over-estimating my ability to jump across slush puddles.

February 28:

Local fog for bespectacled people entering warm room.

March 10:

Spontaneous showers and umbrella purchases.

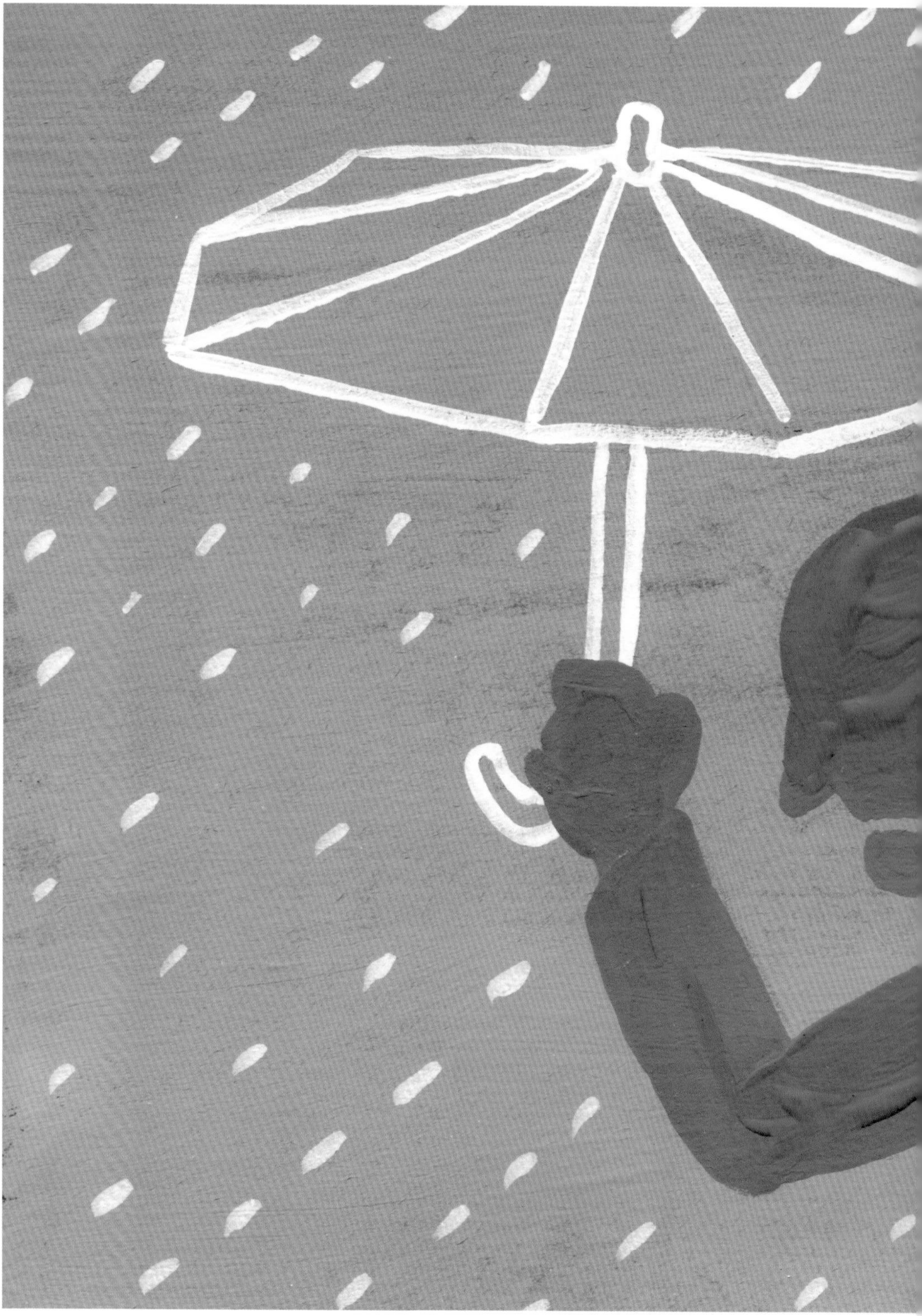

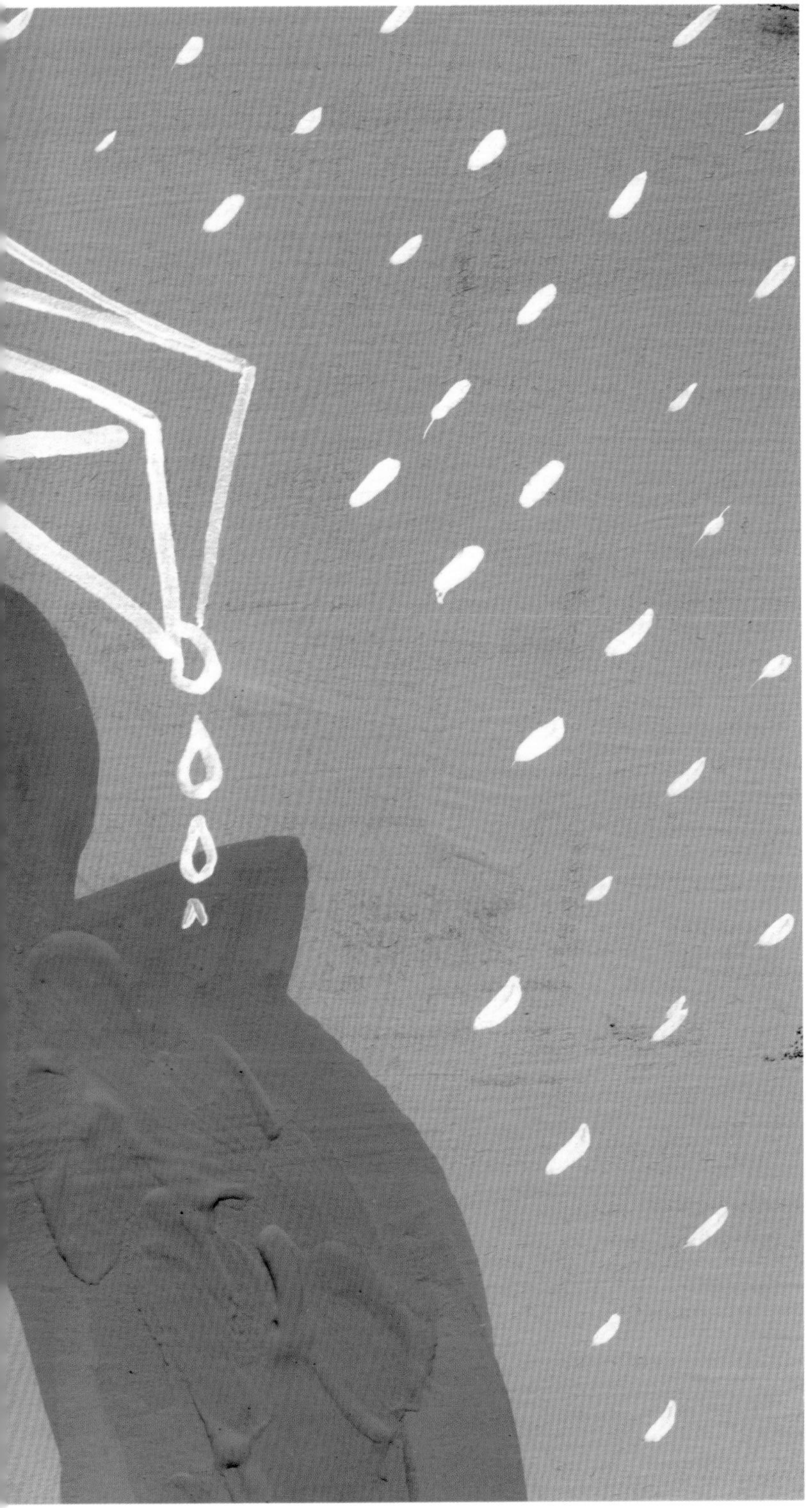

March 12:

Isolated precipitation.

March 13:

Umbrella dissipating.

March 14:

Developing weather pattern.

April 23:

Sudden climate change from nagging about the cold to whining about the heat.

May 5:

The whole world looks absolutely gorgeous. Strong advisory: Do not go on real-estate hunt.

June 15:

Increased chance of grown men wearing shorts.

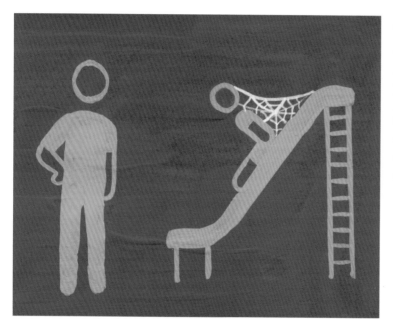

July 3:

Young children, on the other hand, look perfectly adorable in shorts. The only downside: their bare legs stick to playground slides.

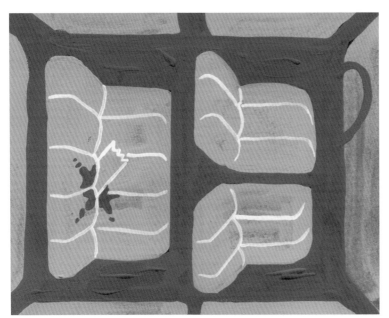

August 12:

Hot car mixed with high probability of regret about those chocolate bars on family trip to the beach last week.

September 9:

Most people back to wearing long pants, with lingering socks and sandals.

October 16:

A 10 percent chance of strong fall winds making my hair look wild and audacious.

Or, 90 percent chance of strong fall winds making my hair look really stupid.

November 25:

Half-frozen gummy bears from that beach trip dis-covered in glove compartment. Surprisingly tasty.

December 29:

Freezing, 75 percent chance of young parents going nuts while spending a whole weekend indoors. Playground visit exposes remarkable velocity of synthetic winter outfits.

All year:

Severe threat of conversational drought, if it weren't for weather-related small talk.

12. My Way

Friday
Thursday
Saturday
Wednesday
Sunday
Tuesday
Monday
Birth
Death

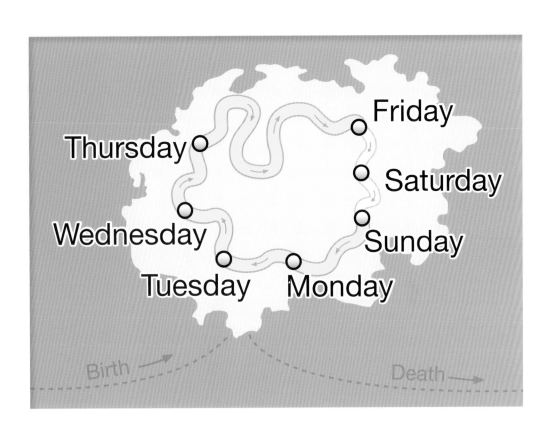

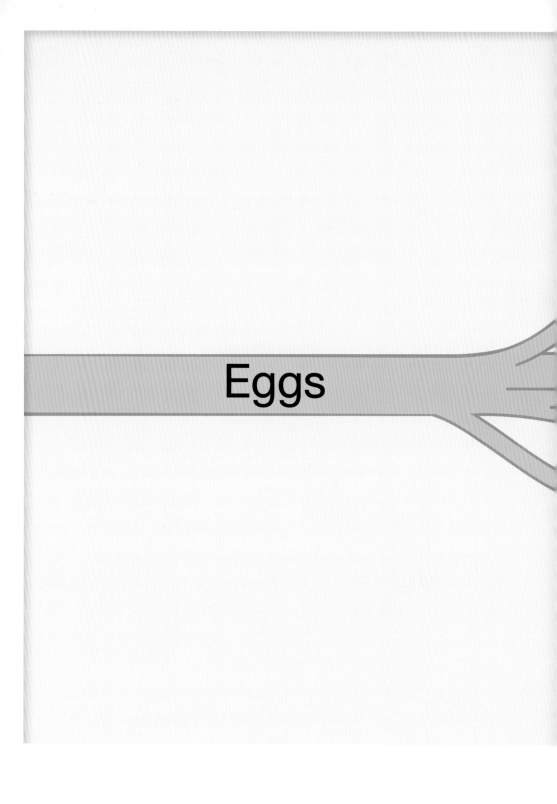

Eggs

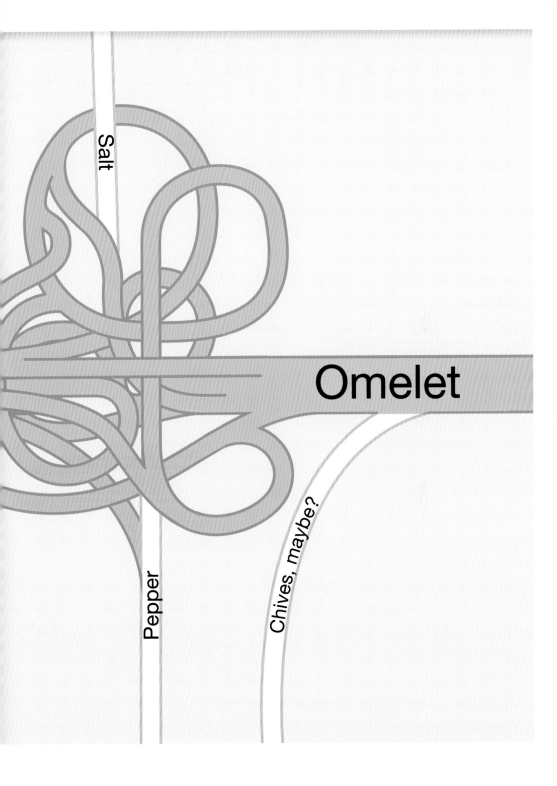

Salt

Omelet

Pepper

Chives, maybe?

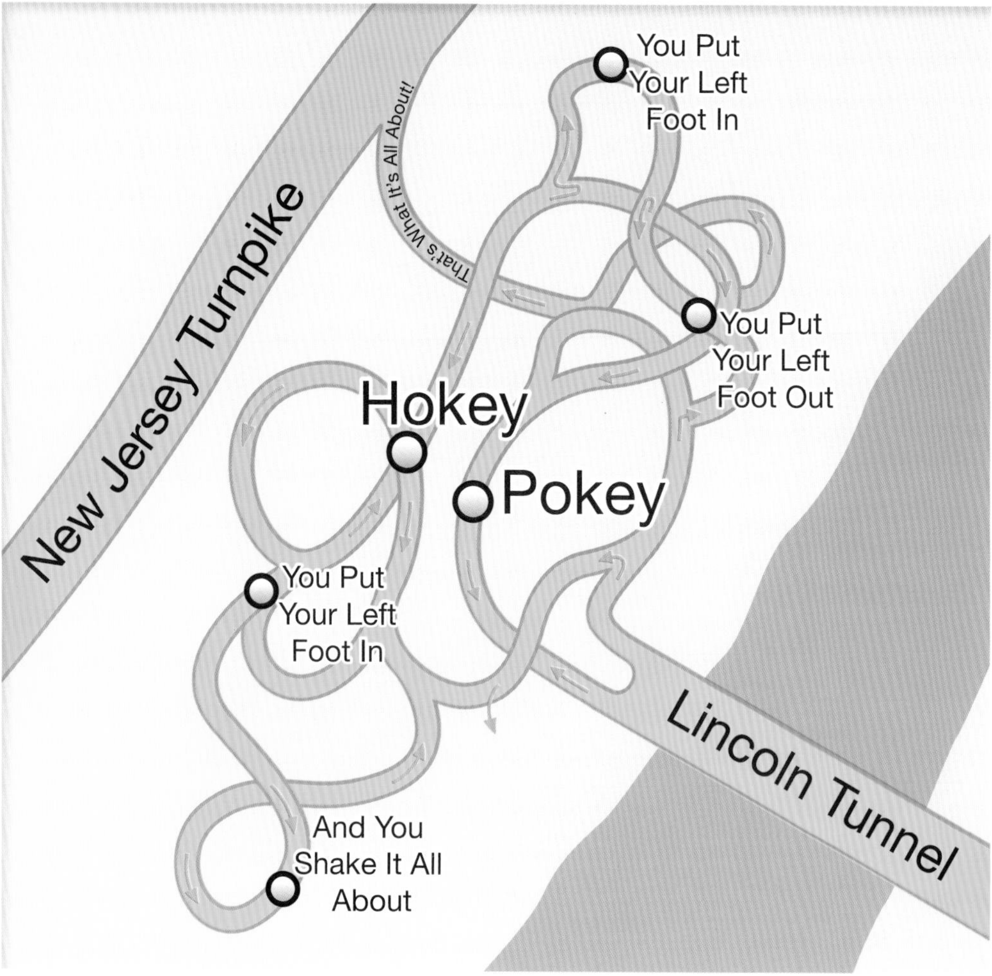
You Put
Your Left
Foot In
That's What It's All About!
New Jersey Turnpike
You Put
Your Left
Foot Out
Hokey
Pokey
You Put
Your Left
Foot In
Lincoln Tunnel
And You
Shake It All
About

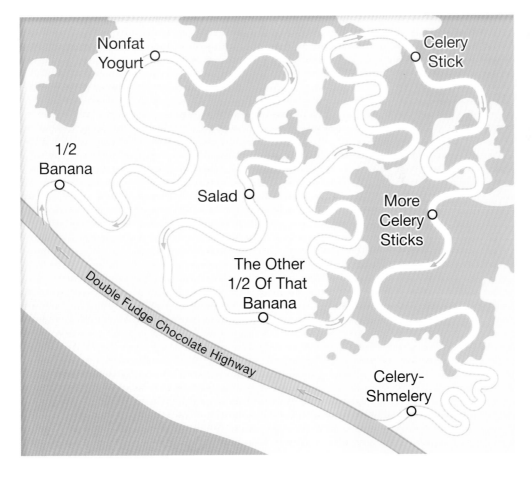

Nonfat Yogurt

Celery Stick

1/2 Banana

Salad

More Celery Sticks

Double Fudge Chocolate Highway

The Other 1/2 Of That Banana

Celery-Shmelery

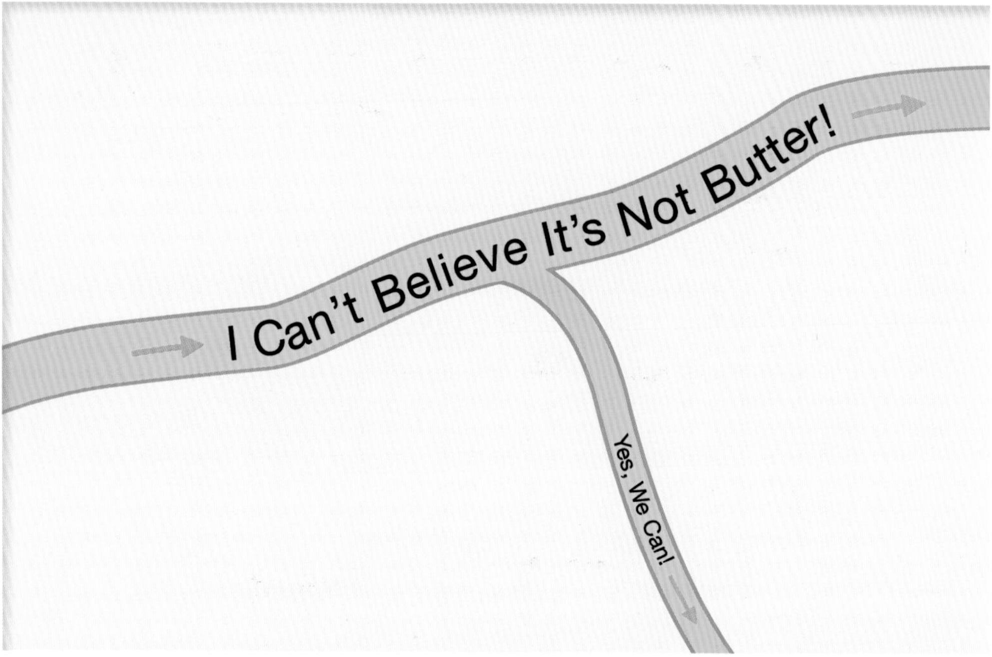
I Can't Believe It's Not Butter!
Yes, We Can!

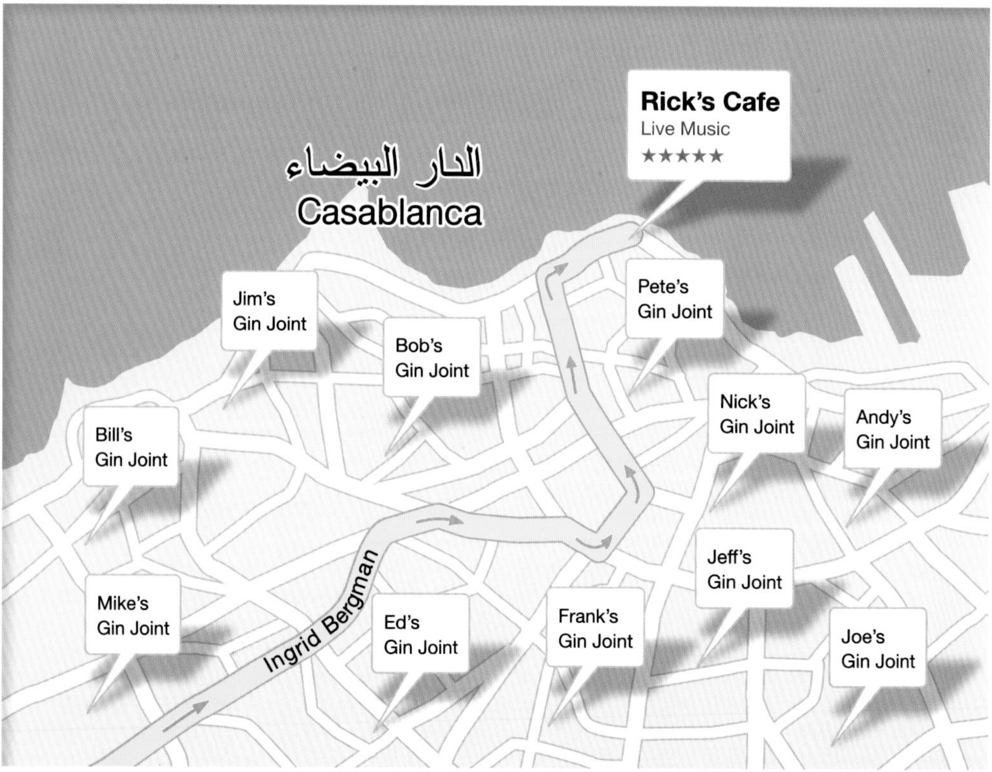
Rick's Cafe
Live Music
★★★★★
الـار البيضاء
Casablanca
Jim's Gin Joint
Pete's Gin Joint
Bob's Gin Joint
Nick's Gin Joint
Andy's Gin Joint
Bill's Gin Joint
Jeff's Gin Joint
Mike's Gin Joint
Ingrid Bergman
Ed's Gin Joint
Frank's Gin Joint
Joe's Gin Joint

Reserve
Battery
Park

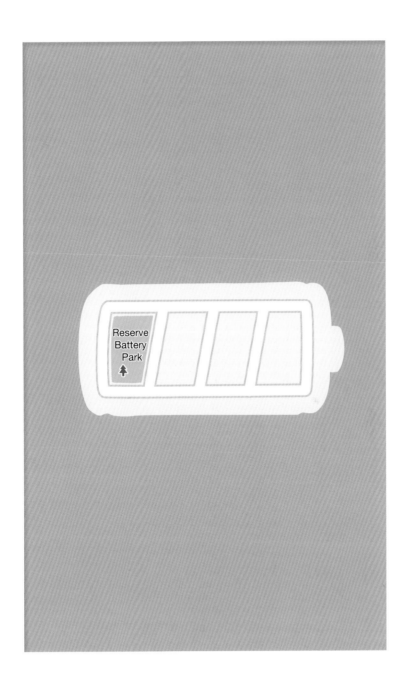

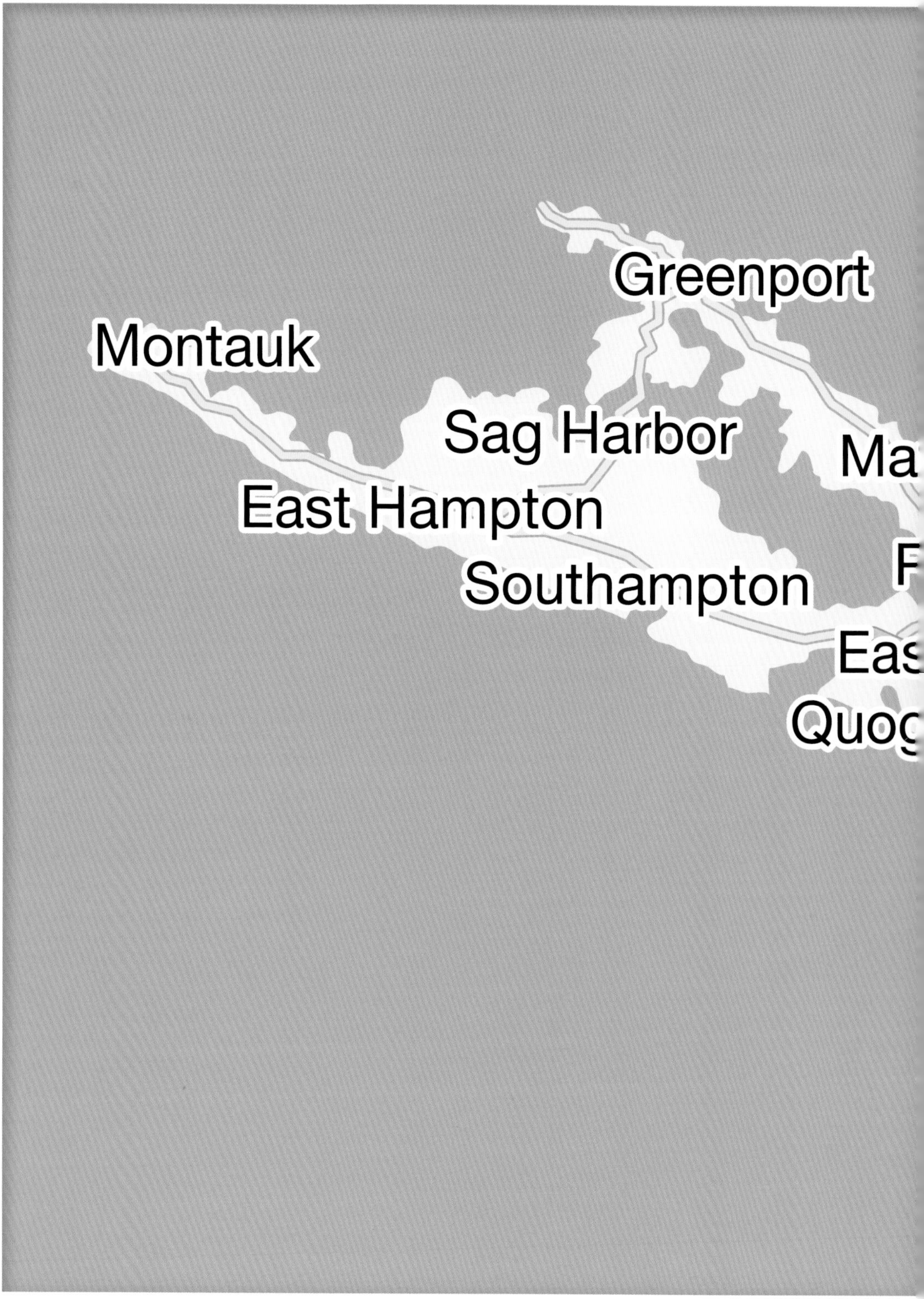
Greenport
Montauk
Sag Harbor
Ma
East Hampton
Southampton
Eas
Quog

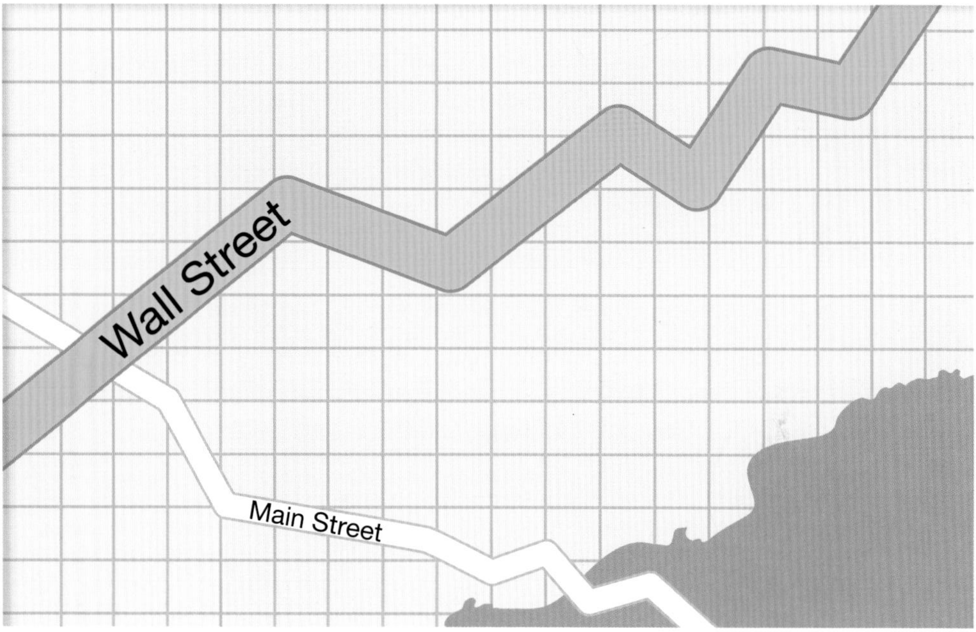
Wall Street
Main Street

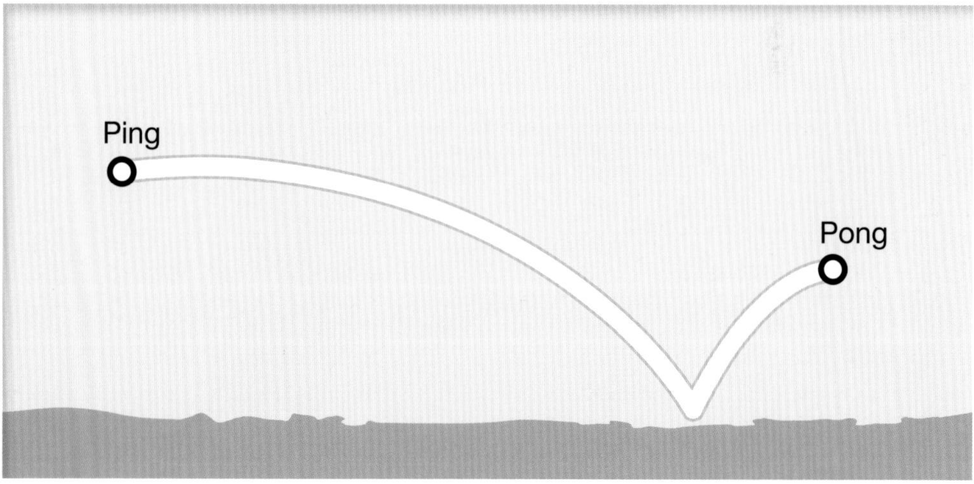
Ping
Pong

land

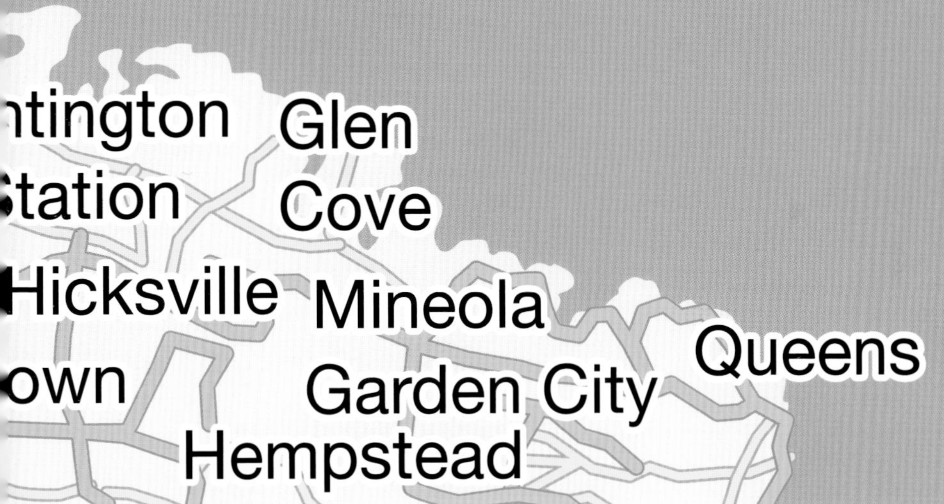
ntington
Station
Glen
Cove
Hicksville
Mineola
Queens
own
Garden City
Hempstead
Freeport
Brooklyn
Long Beach

Wrong Is

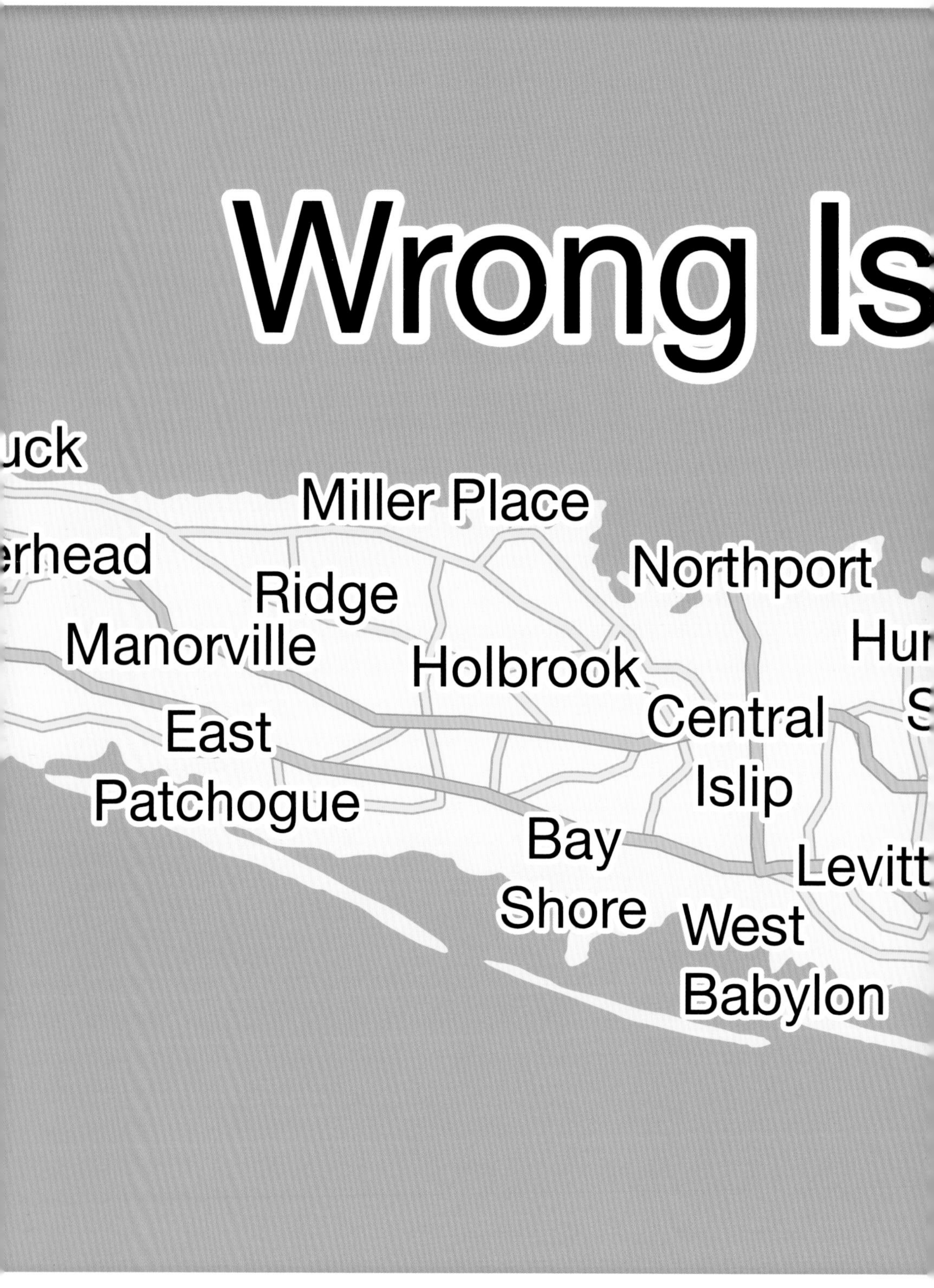
Miller Place
Northport
Ridge
Manorville
Holbrook
Central
Islip
East
Patchogue
Bay
Shore
West
Babylon

Fiction
Nonfiction
CDs

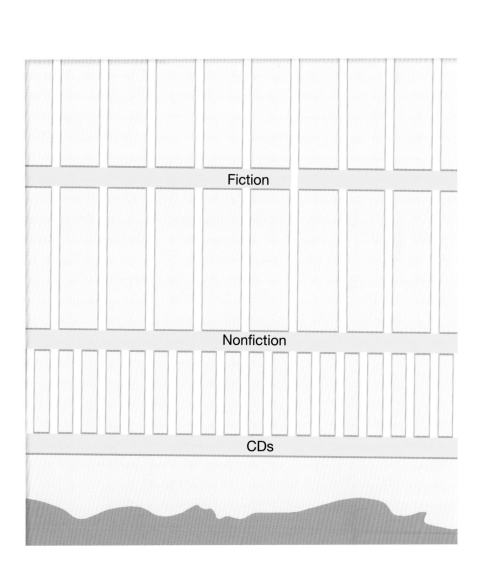

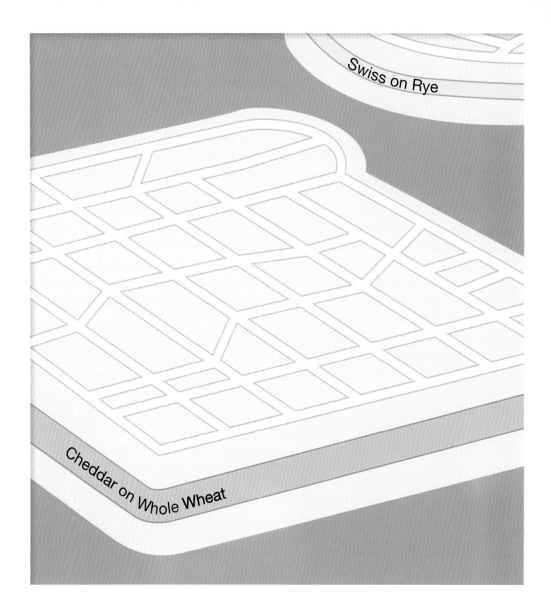

Swiss on Rye

Cheddar on Whole Wheat

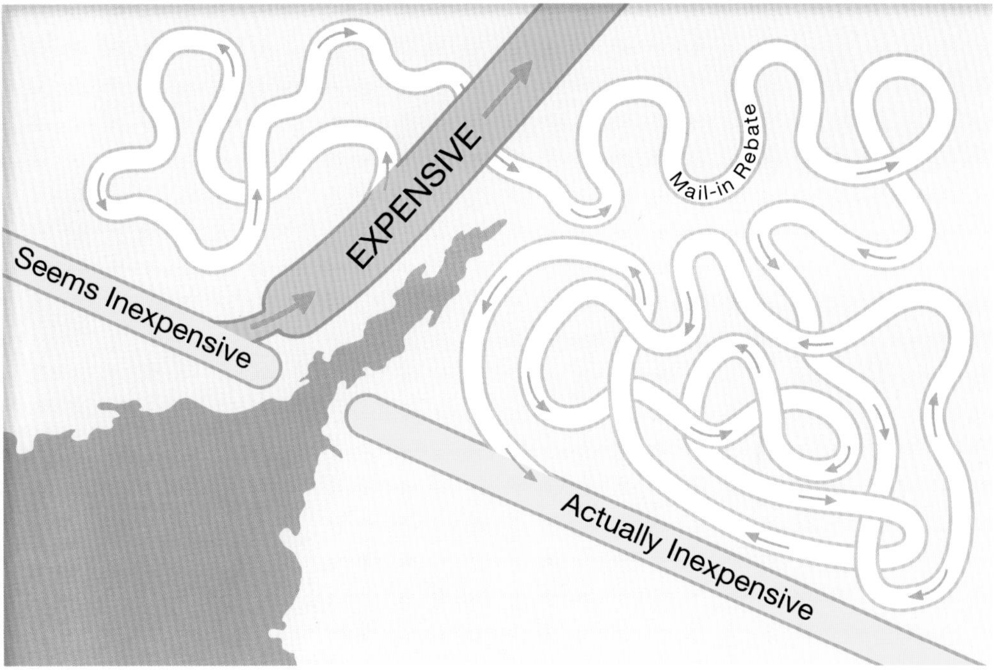
EXPENSIVE
Mail-in Rebate
Seems Inexpensive
Actually Inexpensive

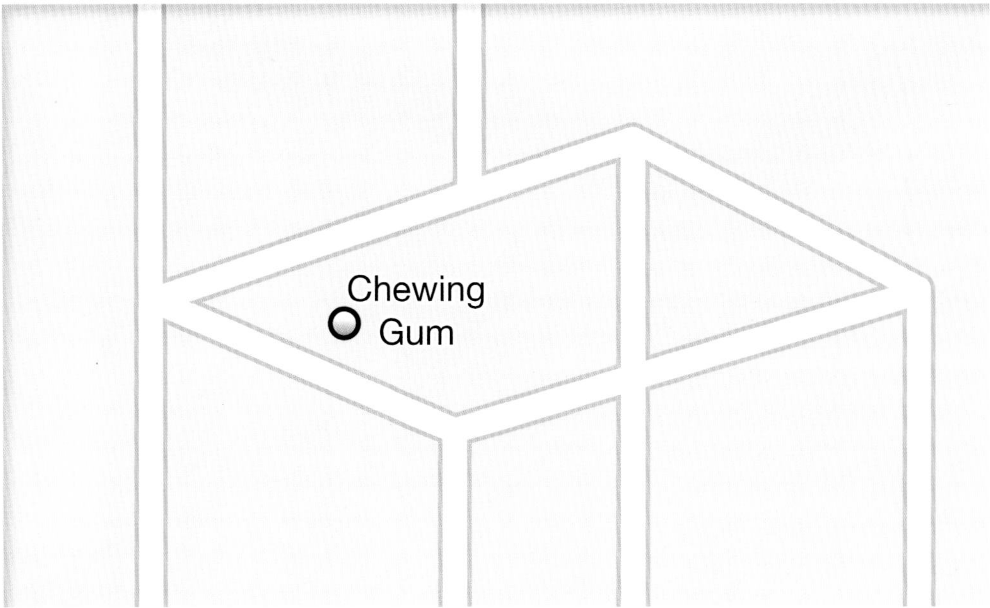
Chewing Gum

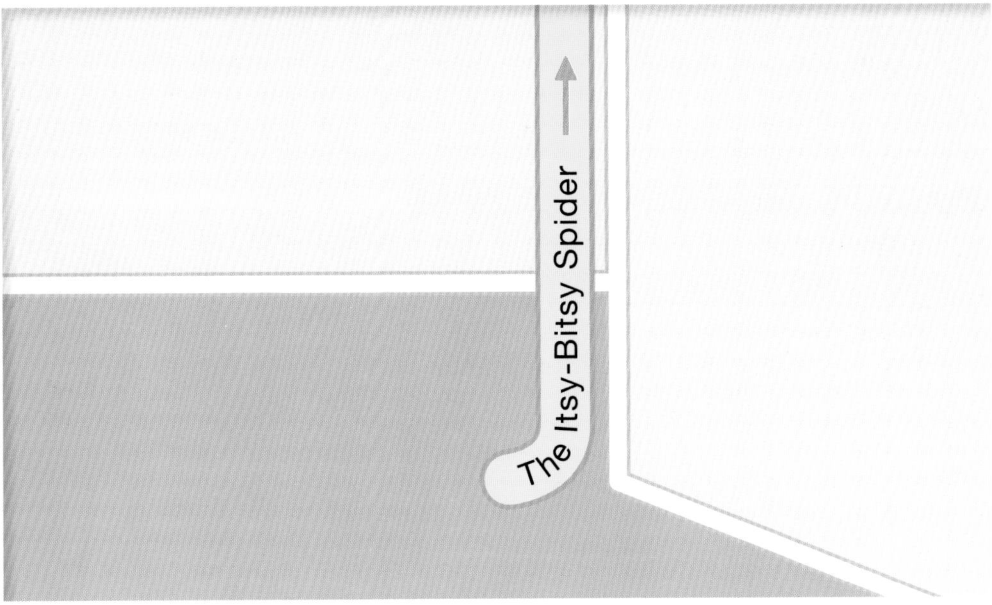
The Itsy-Bitsy Spider

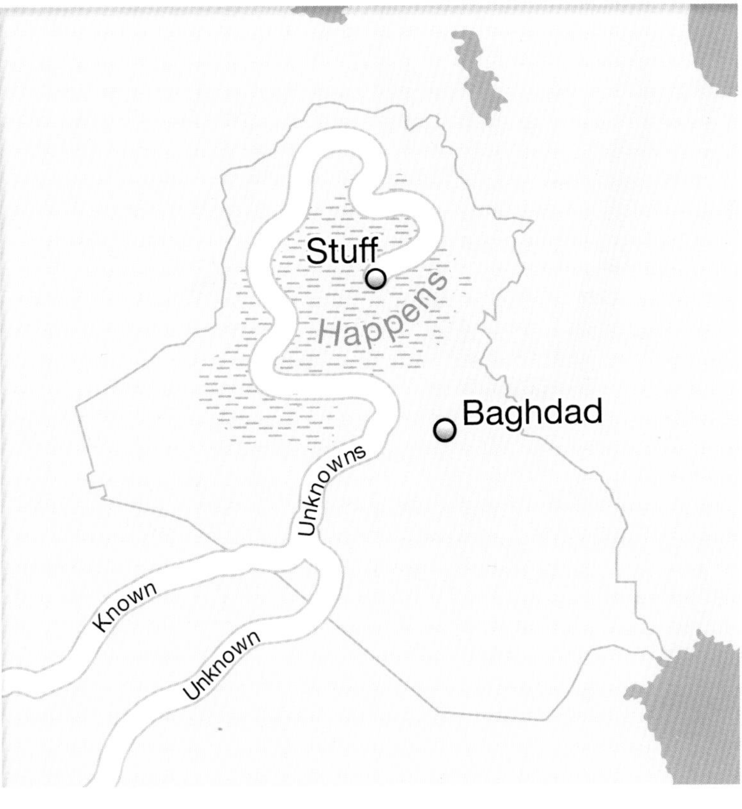
Stuff
Happens
Baghdad
Unknowns
Known
Unknown

The Beltway
K Street

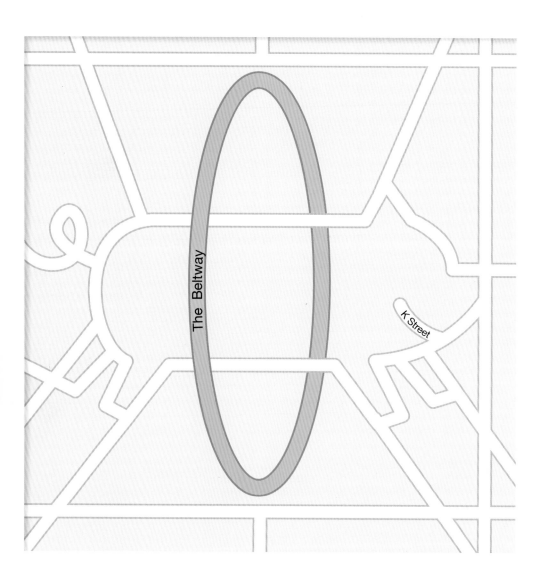

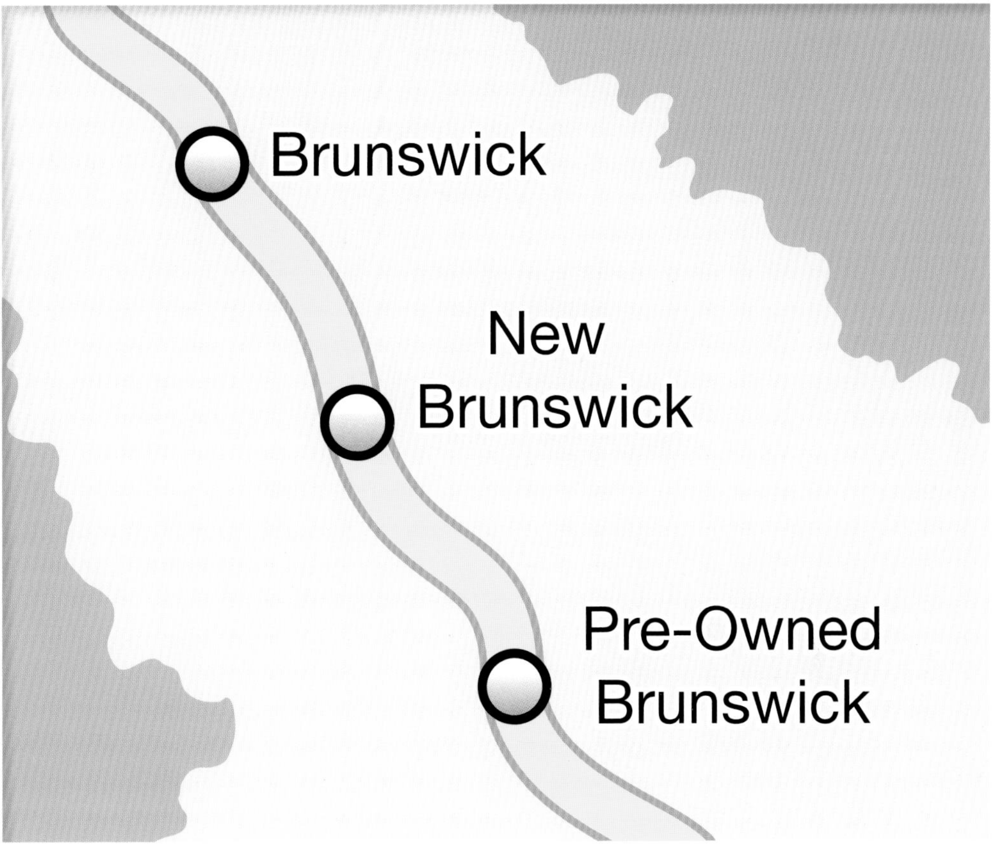
Brunswick
New Brunswick
Pre-Owned Brunswick

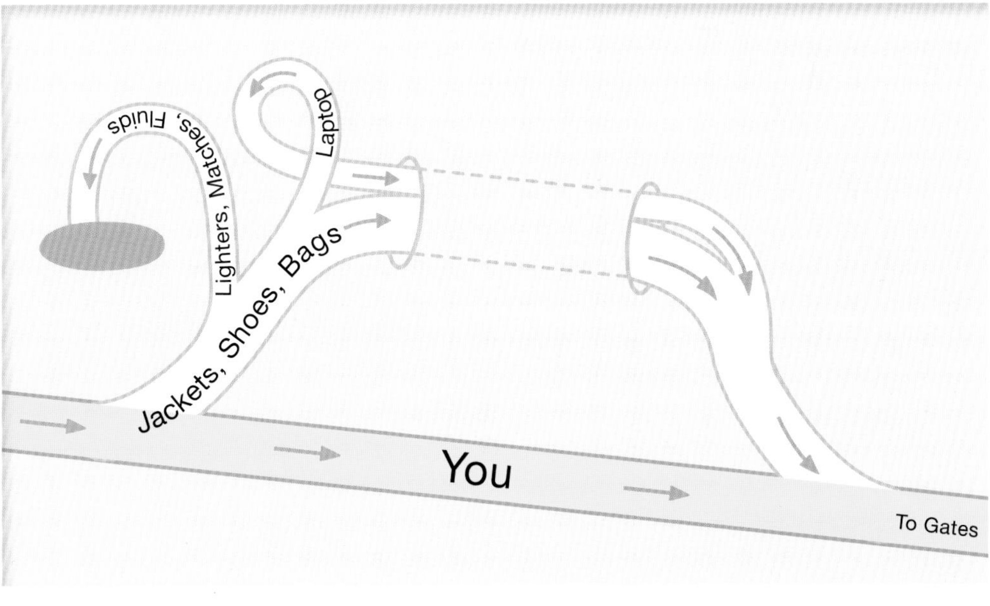
Fluids, Matches, Lighters
Laptop
Jackets, Shoes, Bags
You
To Gates

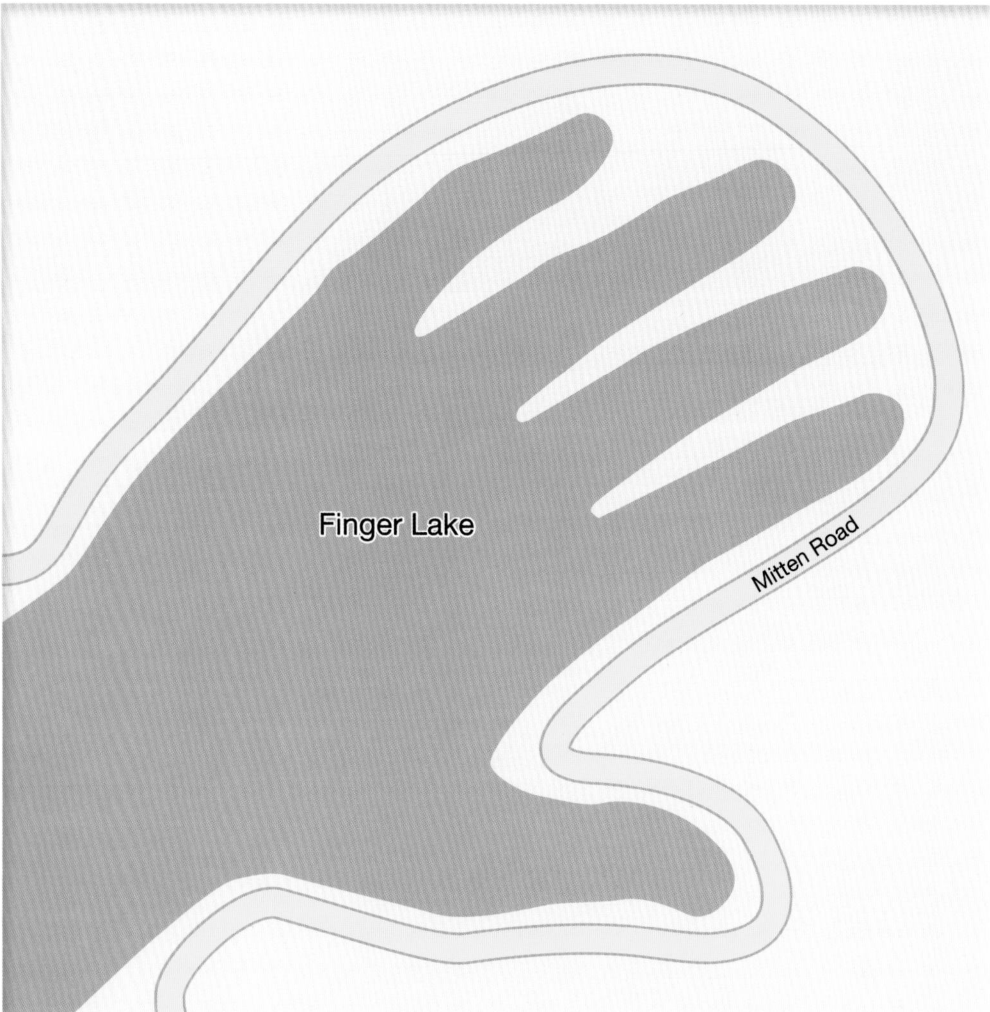
Finger Lake
Mitten Road

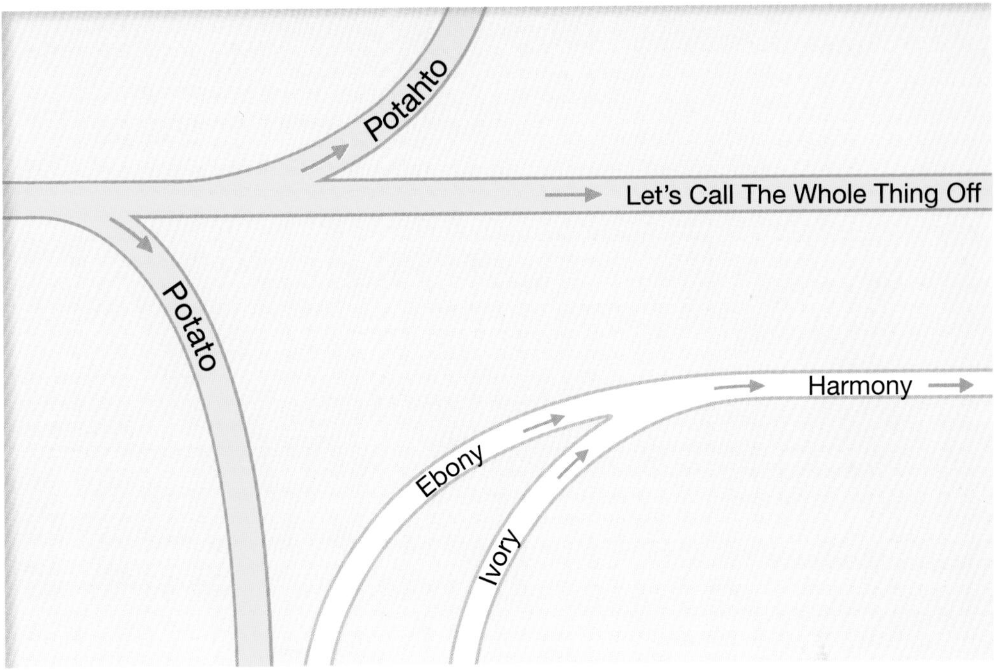
Potahto
Let's Call The Whole Thing Off
Potato
Harmony
Ebony
Ivory

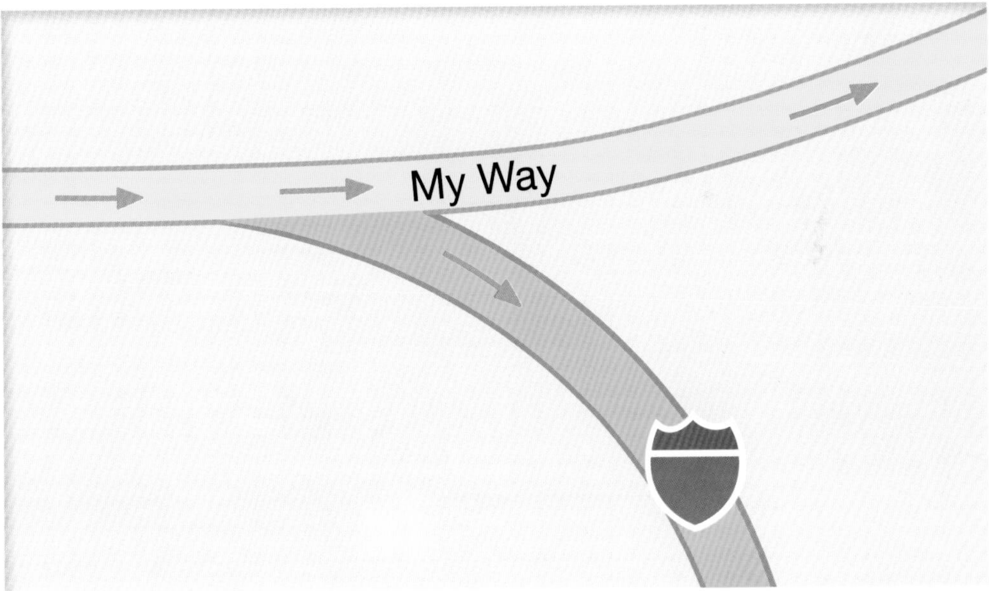
My Way

13. The Haunted Household

Maintaining a home is an uphill battle. For quite some time I've suspected that little goblins are sabotaging my efforts.

We try to keep our place tidy. I sweep the floor, I sit back, relax, and ponder my good work, yet ...

. . . a few seconds
later . . .

. . . ta-da! One of
those little beasts
jumps out to
mock me.

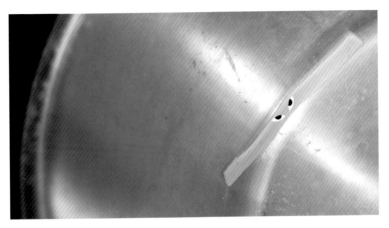

These creatures make life difficult in myriad ways.

I love pasta. But there's always one straggler that stays in the pot and, once dry, will never leave again.

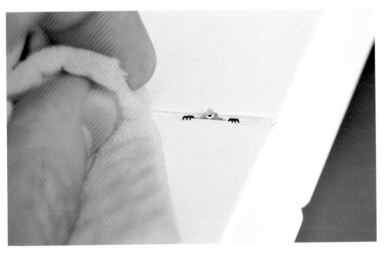

Another formidable opponent is the little crumb of whatever, which gets stuck between the two parts of our tabletop.

They ridicule my
handiwork.

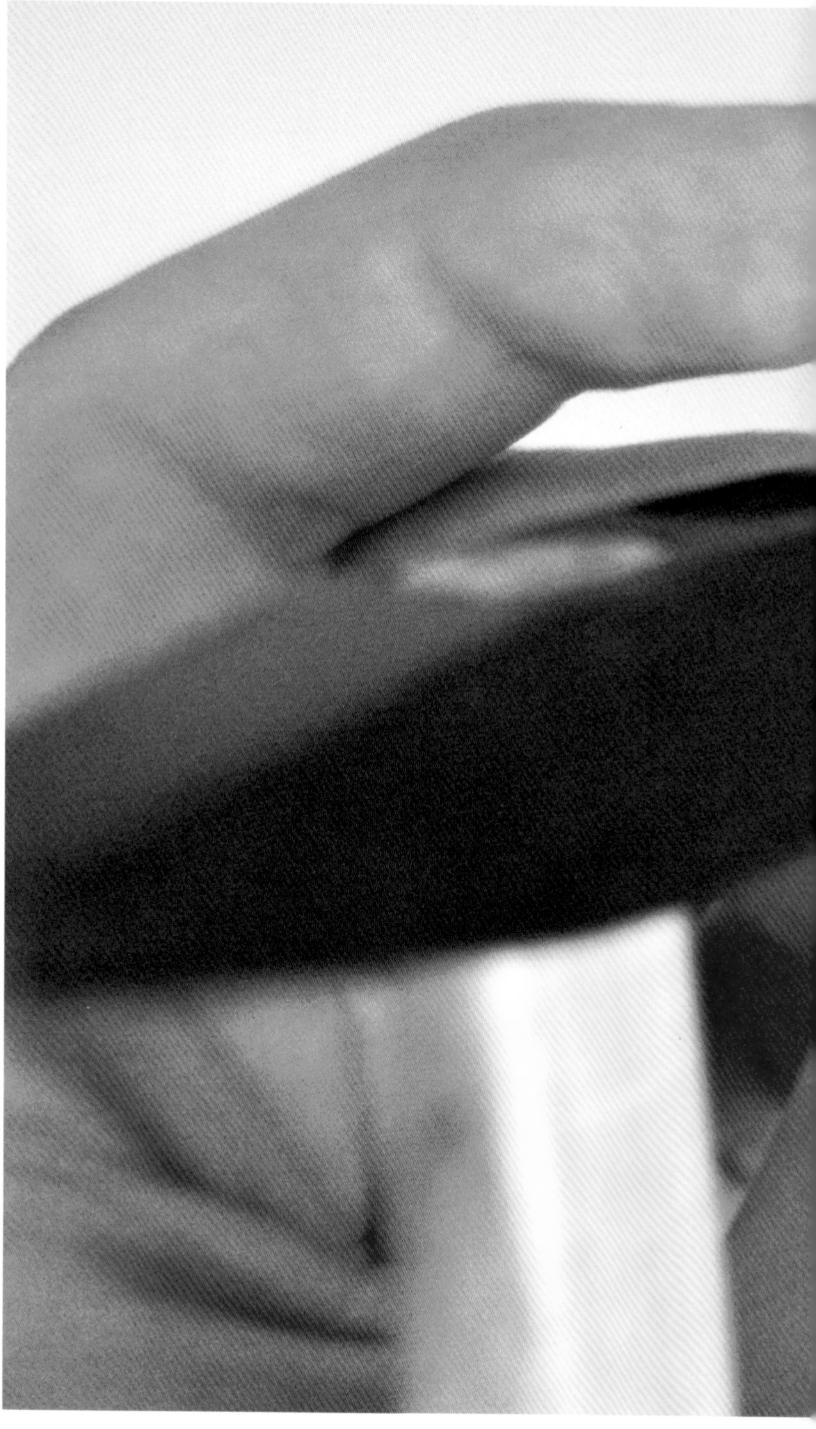

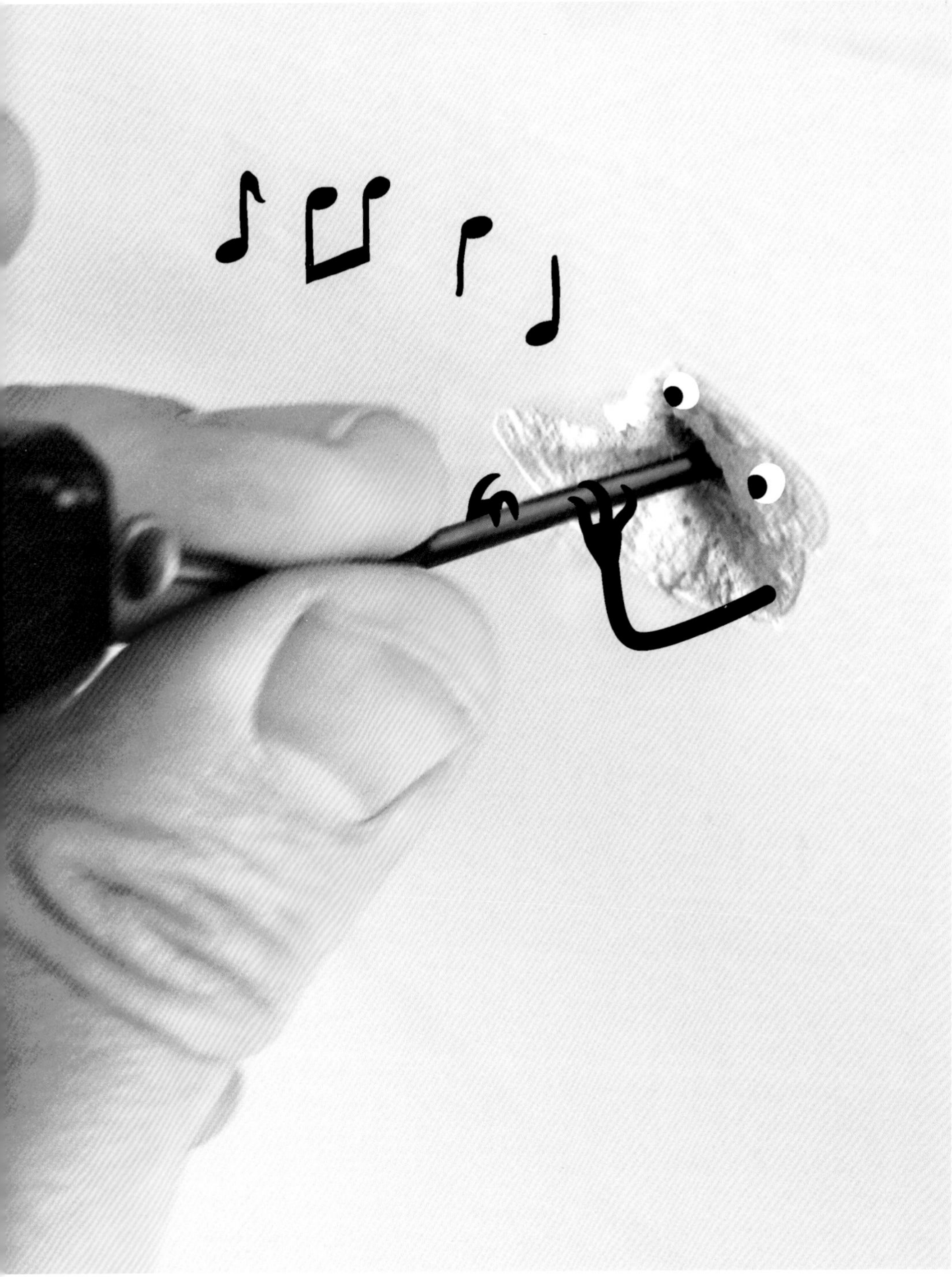

This guy gets upset when I take off my jacket.

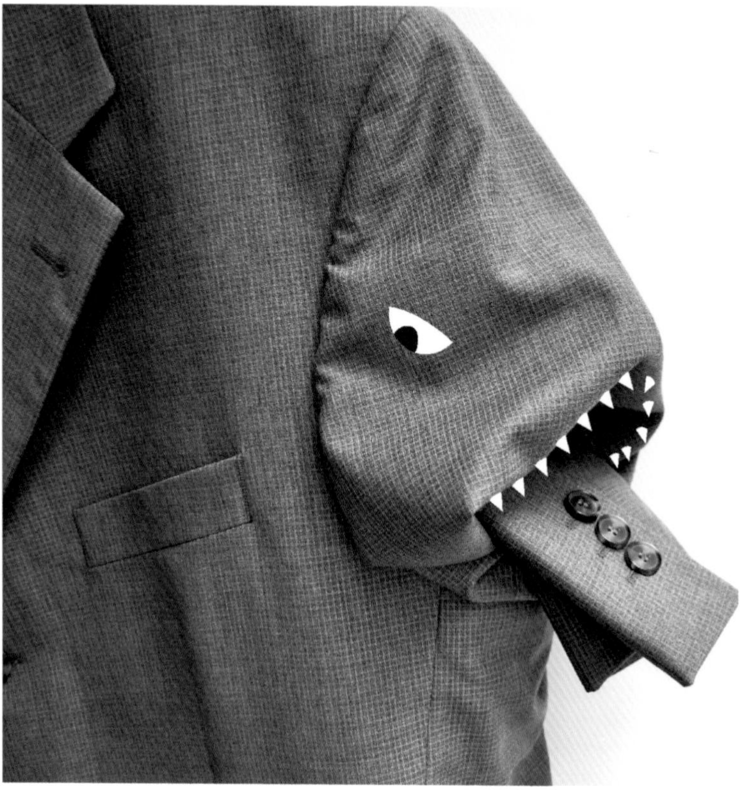

I am deeply embarrassed by my laptop's scruffy smile.

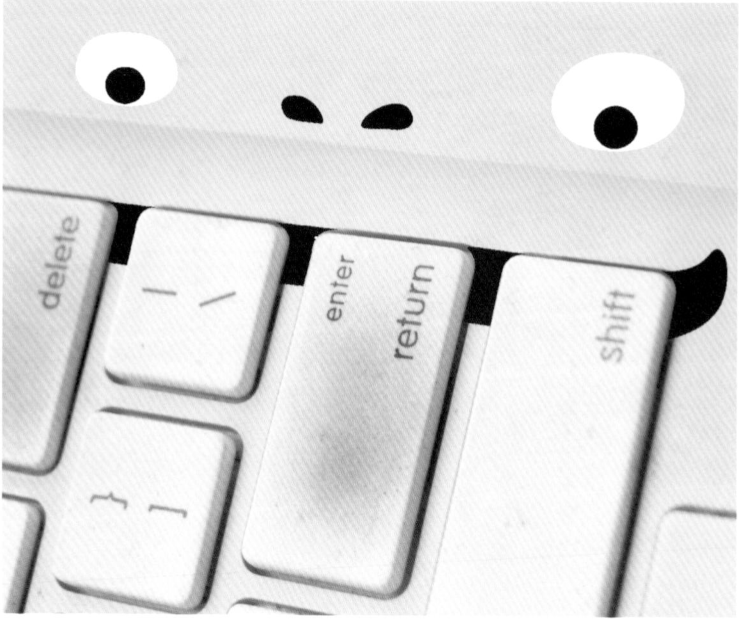
delete
enter
return
shift

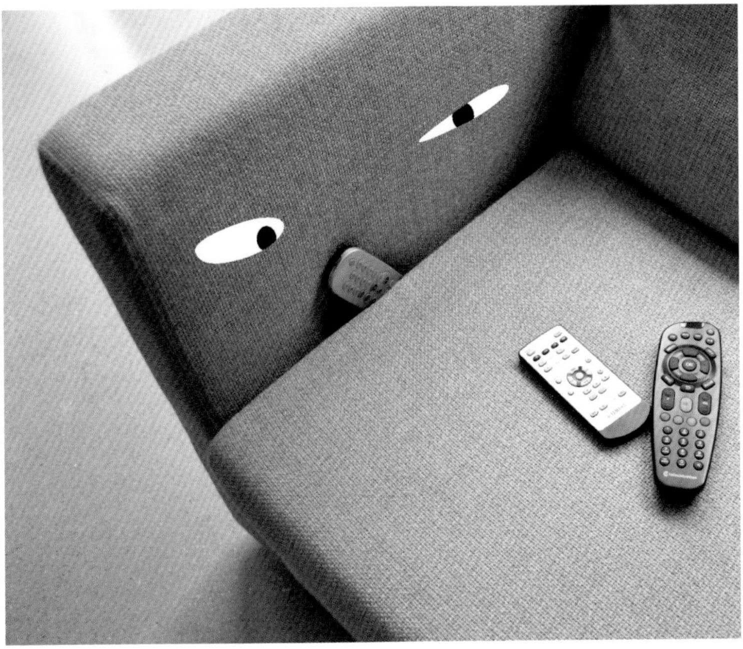

There goes another remote.

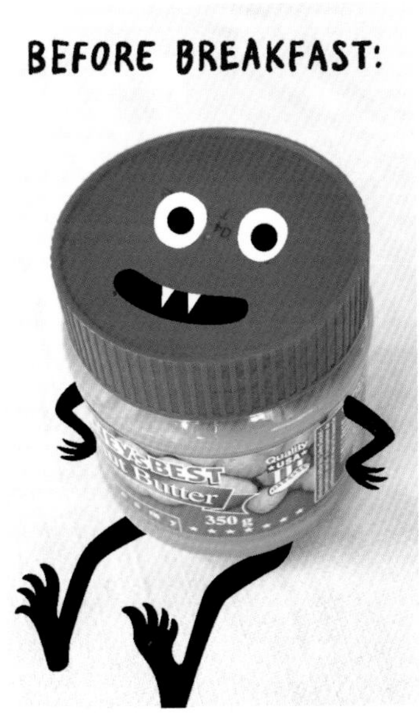

BEFORE BREAKFAST:

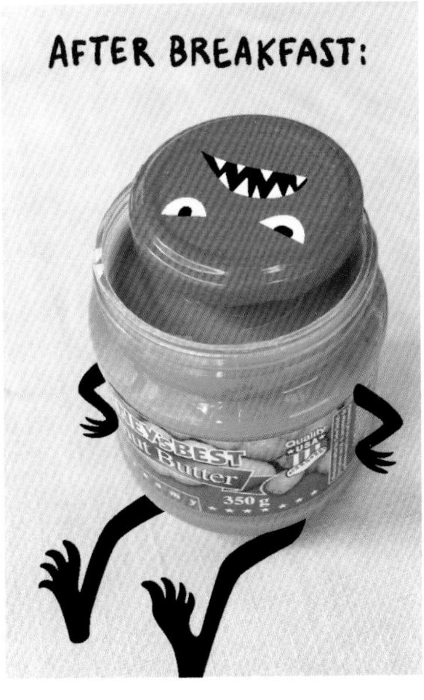

AFTER BREAKFAST:

When I set the table in the morning, all the jars are A-OK. When I clean up, none of the lids seem to fit anymore.

Speaking of break-
fast, why does
this guy begrudge
me that last bit of
marmalade?

Even more
annoying is that
our dishwasher is
always—always!—
already full or not
yet emptied.

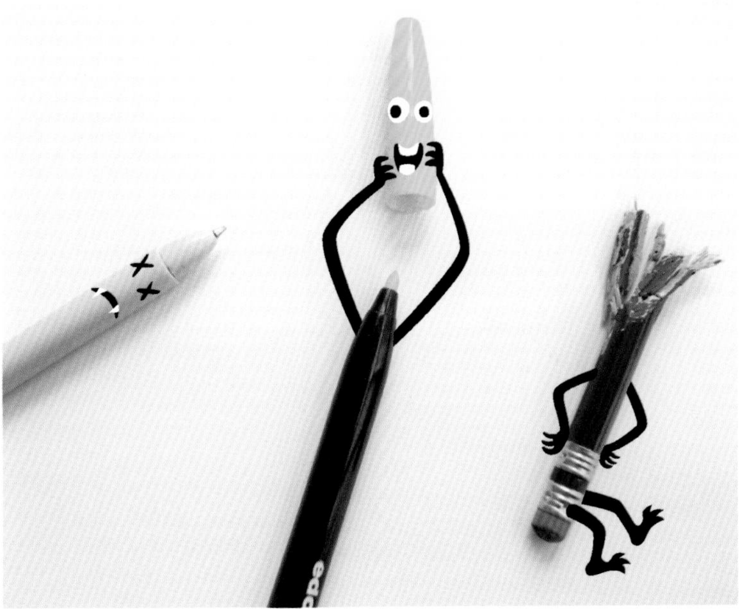

Whenever I have to jot down a phone number, the writing tool I find on my desk will be:

a) dried up.
b) a useless color.
c) utterly disfigured, because the other day I used it to open a shrink-wrapped package, which I know was not a good idea, but I couldn't find those darned scissors.

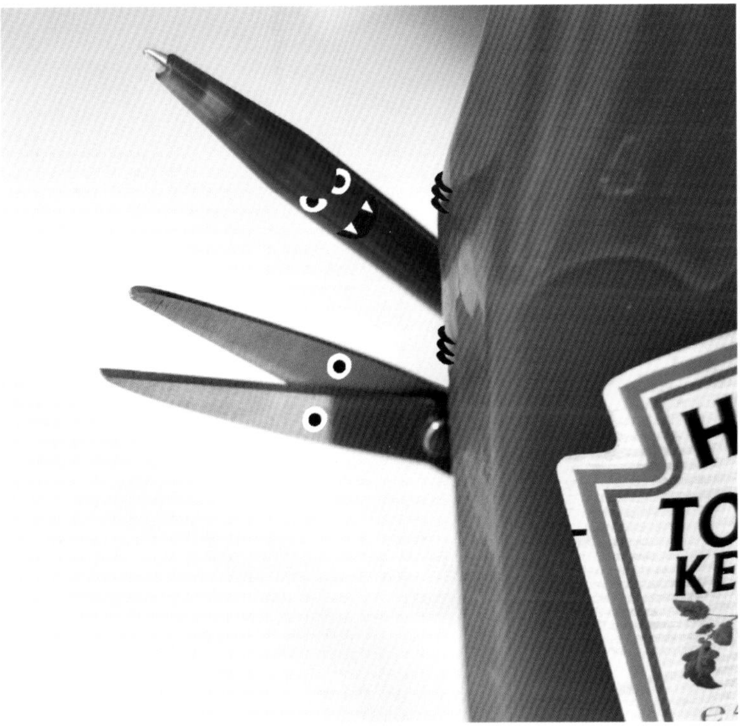

All the while, the one operational pen is hiding in some ridiculous spot. Joined by the scissors, for all I know.

Things have not improved since we had children.

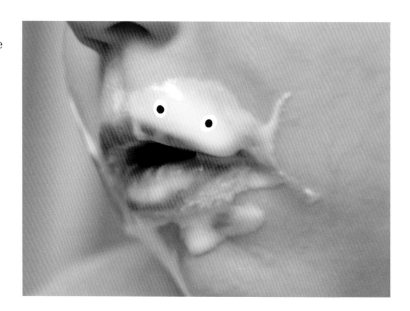

I am always amazed at the diverse lot underneath the high chair of our toddler.

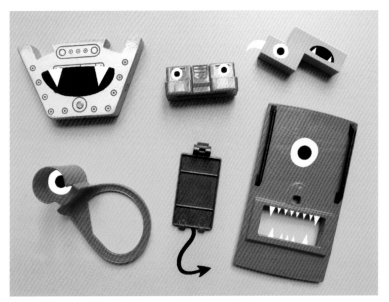

The kids' room is populated by a wildly procreating tribe of orphaned bits and pieces, who all claim to be descendants of some fancy toy.

By now, I have learned to live with their trickery. Even when they bewitch my wallet and my cell phone.

I actually value their reliability. The lonely playing card, the battery (that may or may not be charged), the mysterious key, and the piece of string have been fixtures in the top drawer of the kitchen cabinet since I was a child.

My little household friends may be wicked, but they are dependable companions. And they are welcome to stay.

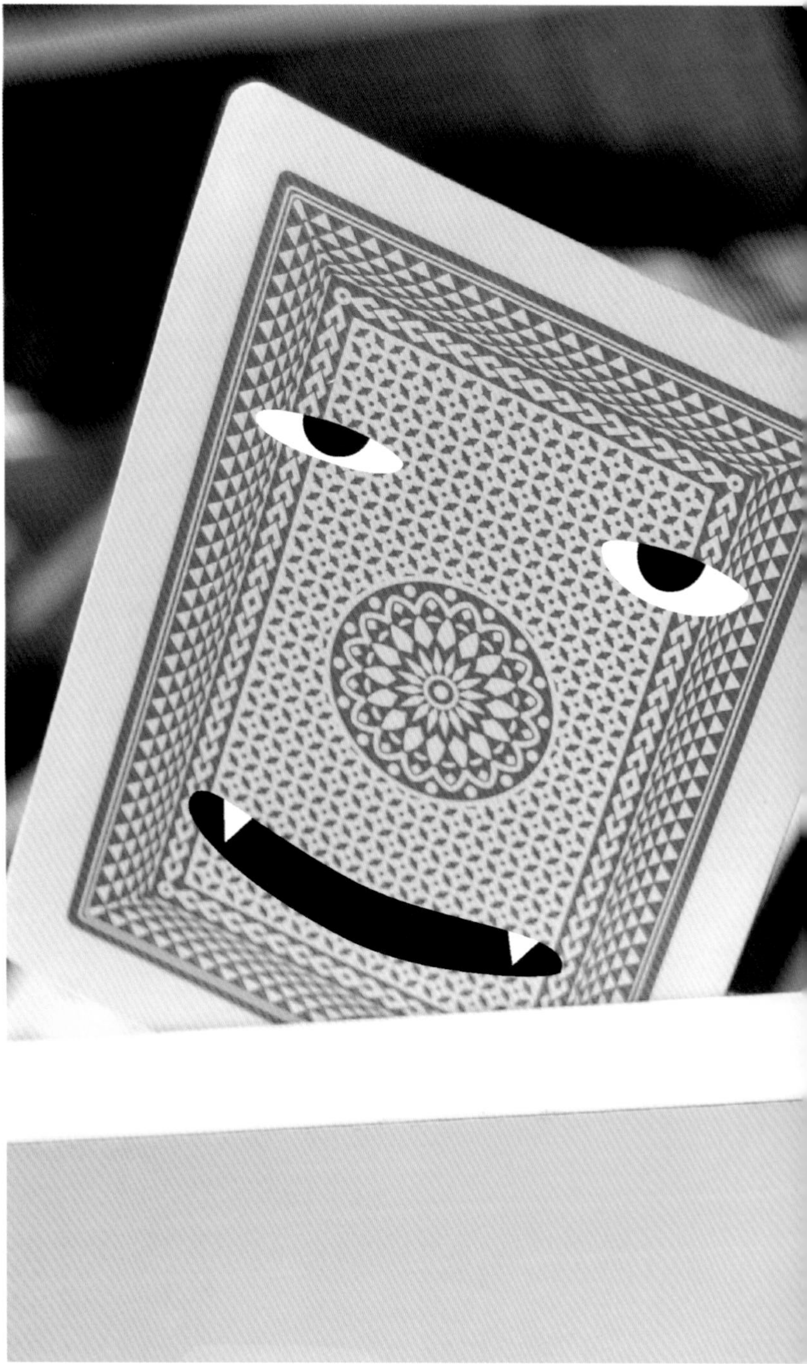

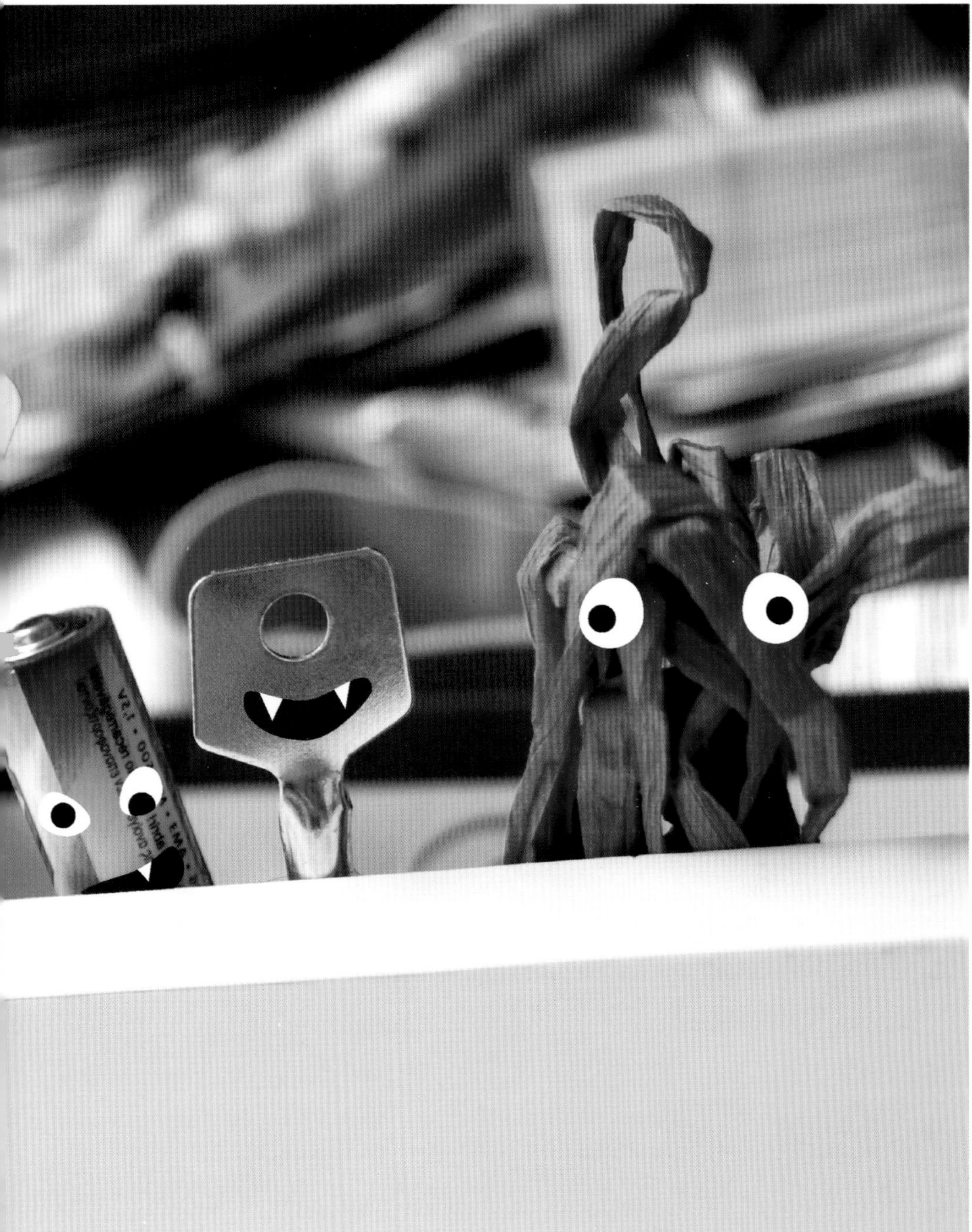

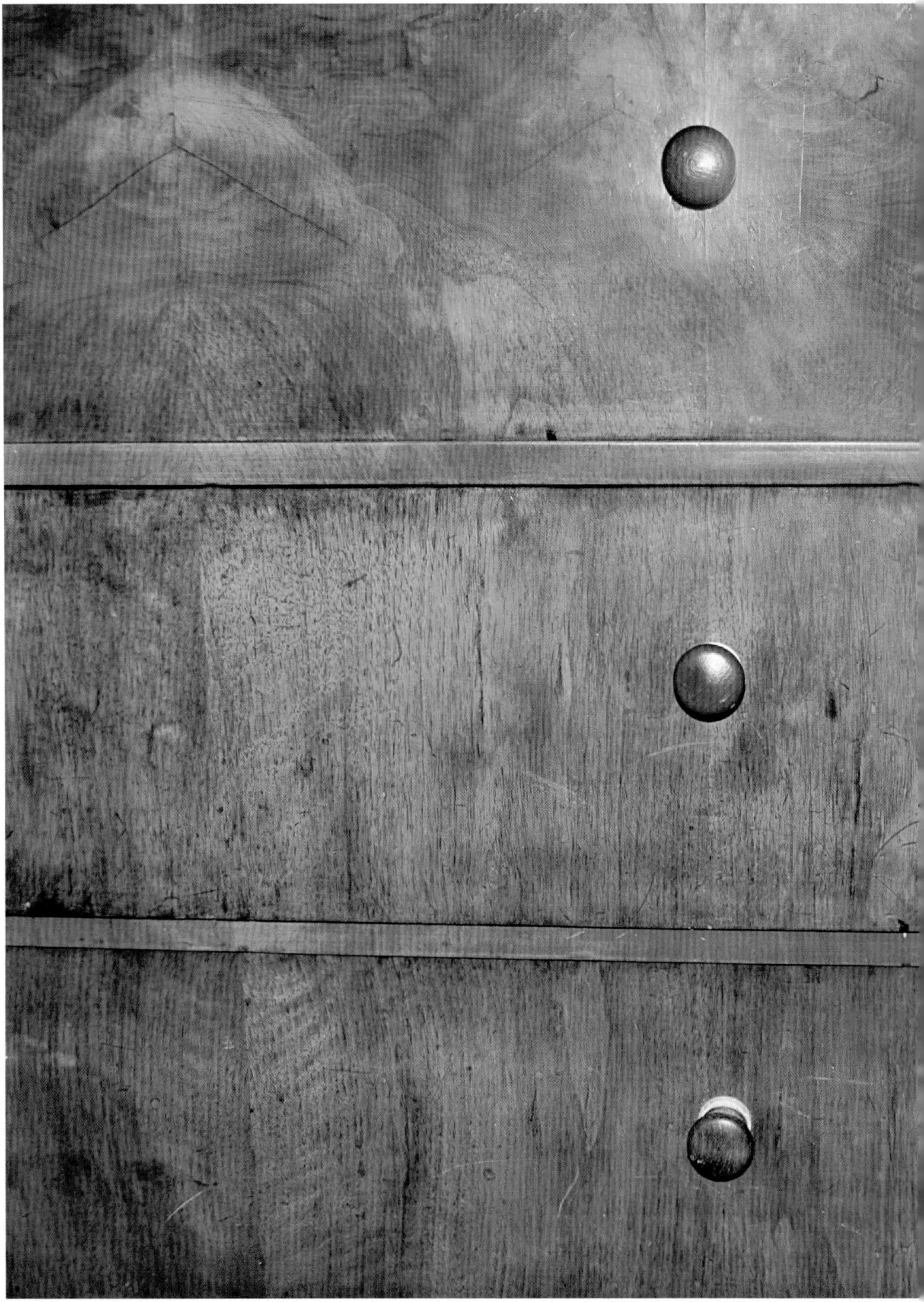

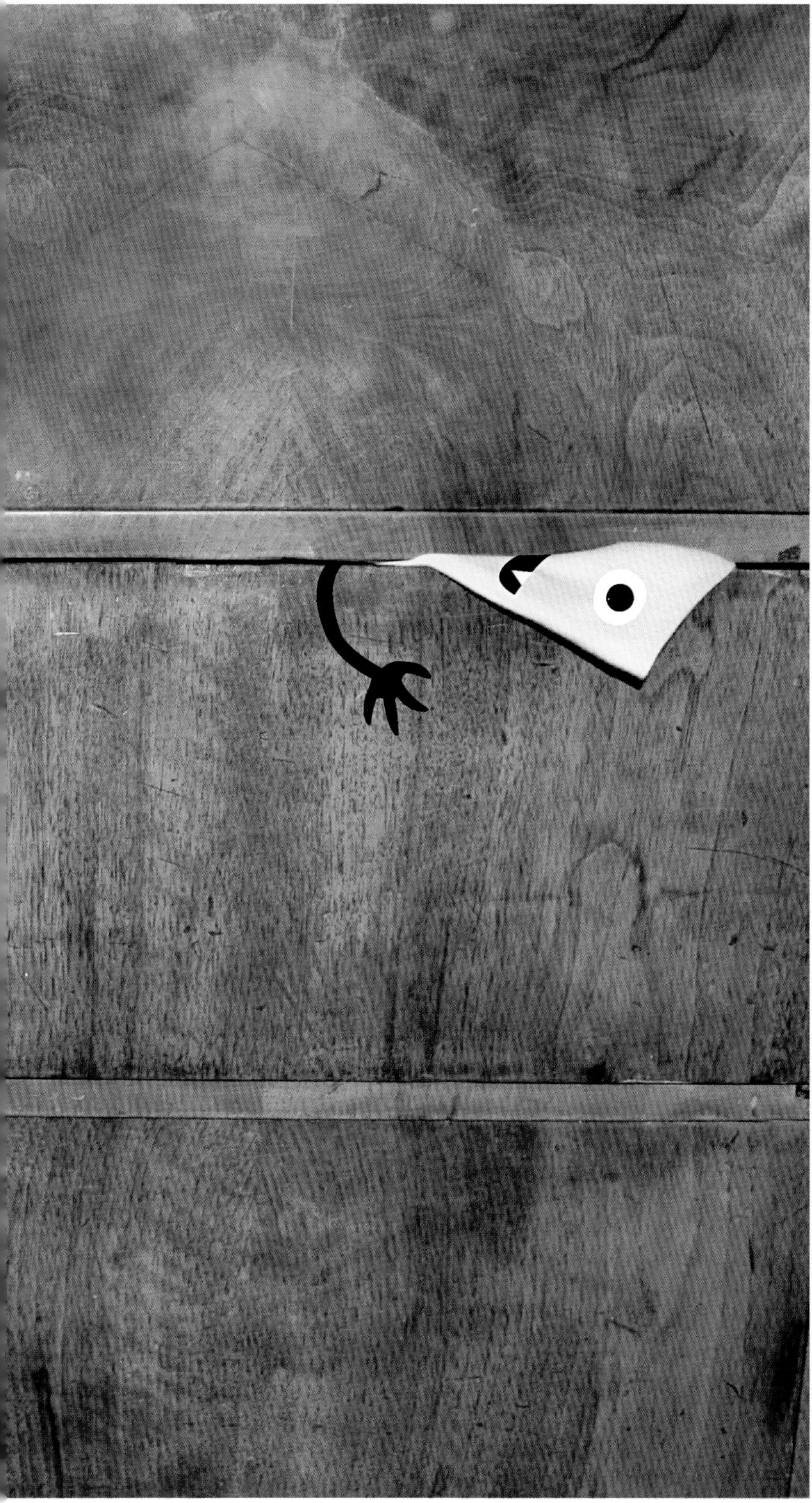

Except for you,
T-shirt Houdini!

Red Eye

New York, JFK
to Berlin, TXL
via London, LHR

6:53 p.m.
Takeoff!
The fight for armrest supremacy begins!

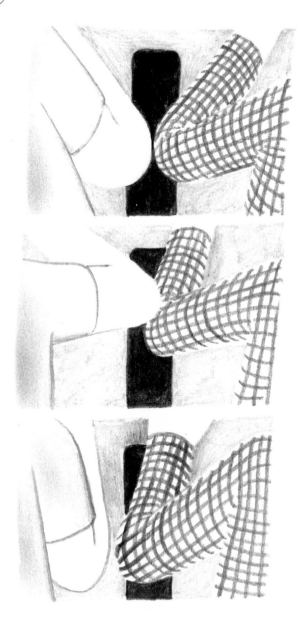

8:15 p.m.   Maine

Peanuts.

8:16 p.m.
Trying not to devour them right away.
What if I stack them to pass more time?

8:17 p.m.

Could have sworn there was one left.

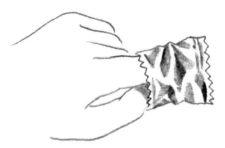

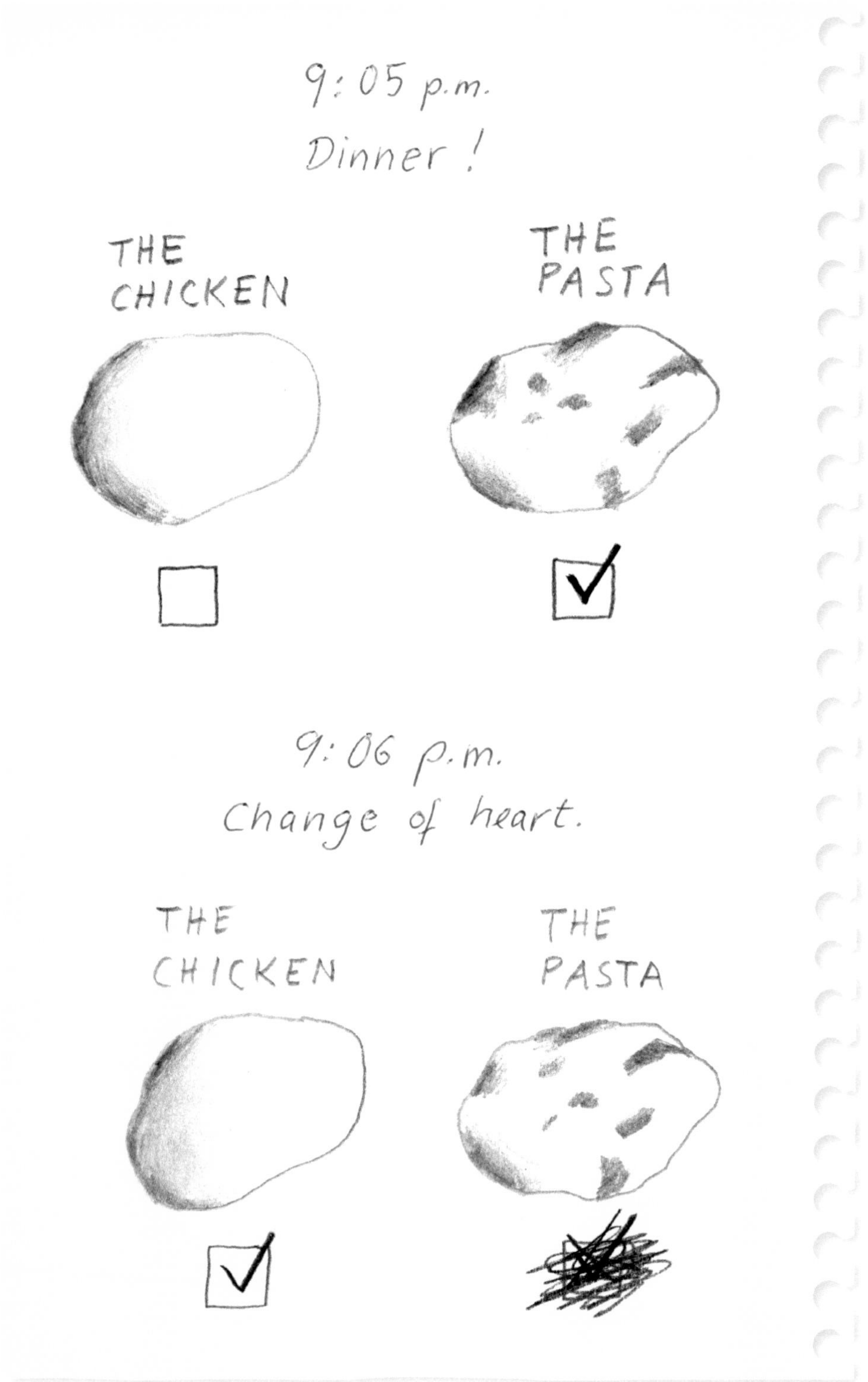
9:05 p.m.
Dinner!
THE CHICKEN
THE PASTA
9:06 p.m.
Change of heart.
THE CHICKEN
THE PASTA

10:00 p.m.
Wish my seat would recline farther.

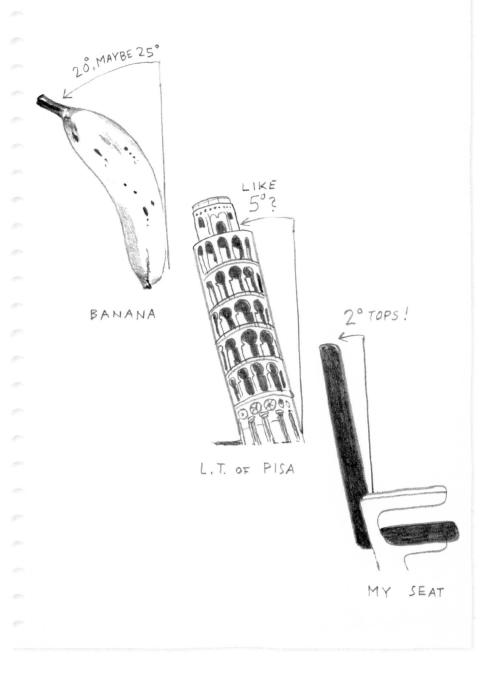

20°, MAYBE 25°

BANANA

LIKE 5°?

L.T. OF PISA

2° TOPS!

MY SEAT

10:43 p.m., 10:47 p.m., 10:50 p.m. Halifax

I ♥ my seat-back monitor.

HALIFAX
HALIFAX
HALIFAX

10.08 p.m. St. John, New Brunswick

Cool! Seems that my remote has a button to delete neighbor.

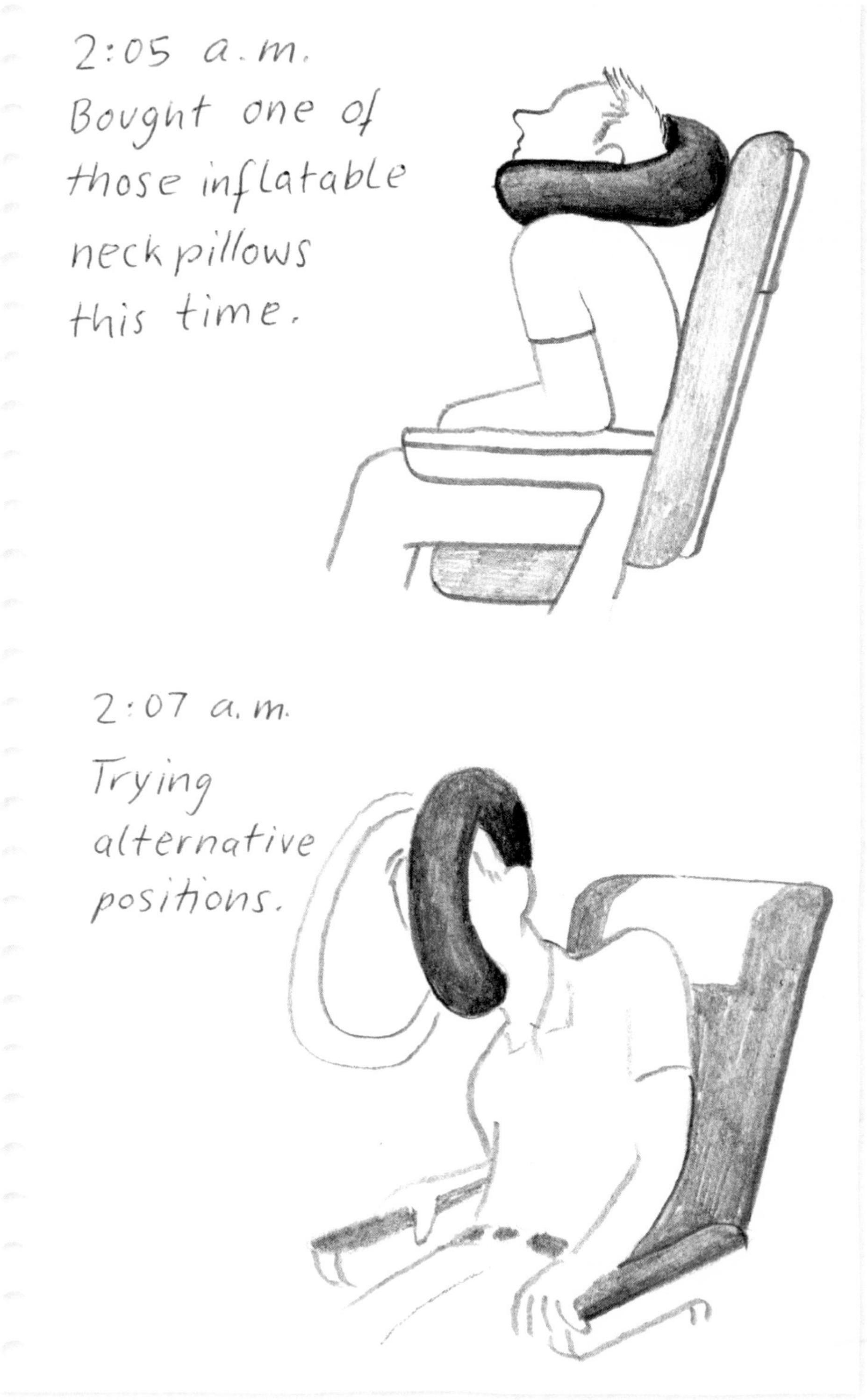
2:05 a.m.
Bought one of those inflatable neck pillows this time.
2:07 a.m.
Trying alternative positions.

2:15 a.m.

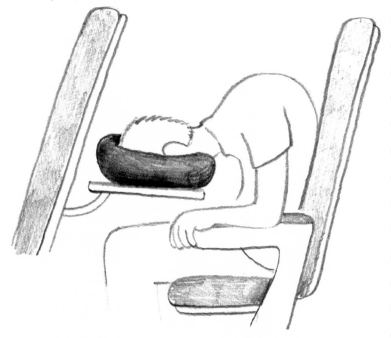

4:12 a.m.   North Atlantic

Not sure if I slept or just entered brief coma.
Not sure how to describe taste in my mouth either.

5:10 a.m.

Giving baby girl in front row the evil eye.

I don't mind that the poor thing is crying
I'm just envious of her bassinet.

7:50 a.m. Cork, Ireland

"Put your seat in the upright position!"
You mean, as opposed to where it is now?

8:05 a.m.
Cleanup.

CRUMPLED NEWSPAPER

NOVEL

ALL SORTS OF GARBAGE AND GLASSES.

BROKEN PLASTIC CUP

8:07 a.m.
By the way:

NOVEL
I HAD
PLANNED
TO READ
ON FLIGHT

PORTION
OF NOVEL
I ACTUALLY
READ

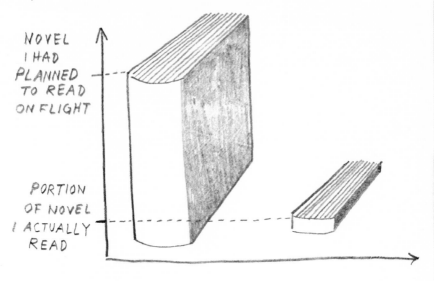

8:35 a.m.
Putting shoes back on.

9:30 a.m. London Heathrow
Layover.
Heathrow bathrooms equipped with
nuclear-powered hand dryers.

9:50 a.m. Heathrow food court
They have awesome poppy seed pretzels here!

9:57 a.m.
Desperately trying to find equally awesome spot
to discreetly remove the single poppy seed
stuck between front teeth.

11:30 a.m. Groningen, Netherlands
Back in the air.
Wow! Cloud outside looks just like
Henry Moore's "Reclining Figure" (1939).

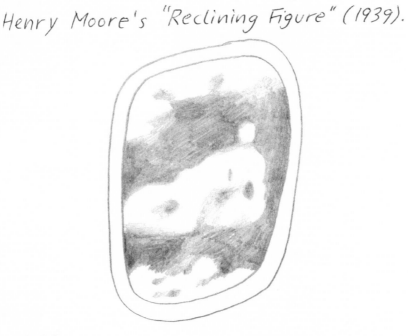

11:35 a.m.
So does the "croissant."

11:52 a.m.

Unable to sleep, read, or even think.
Spending the remaining 45 minutes contemplating
the little hole in airplane window.

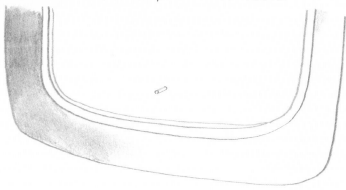

12:46 p.m. Berlin, Tegel airport (baggage claim)

A glimpse of happiness at last.
Looks like it wasn't _my_ suitcase that
broke open during the flight.

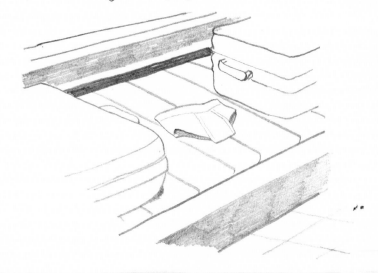

15. Unpopular Science

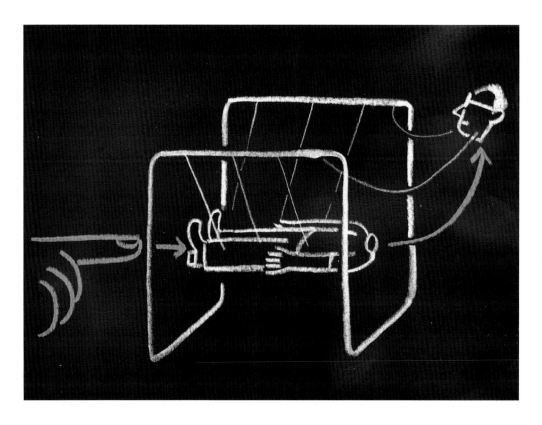

Whether we like it or not, human life is
subject to the universal laws of physics.

My day, for example, starts with a demonstration of Newton's First Law of Motion. It states, "Every body continues in its state of rest, or of uniform motion in a straight line . . .

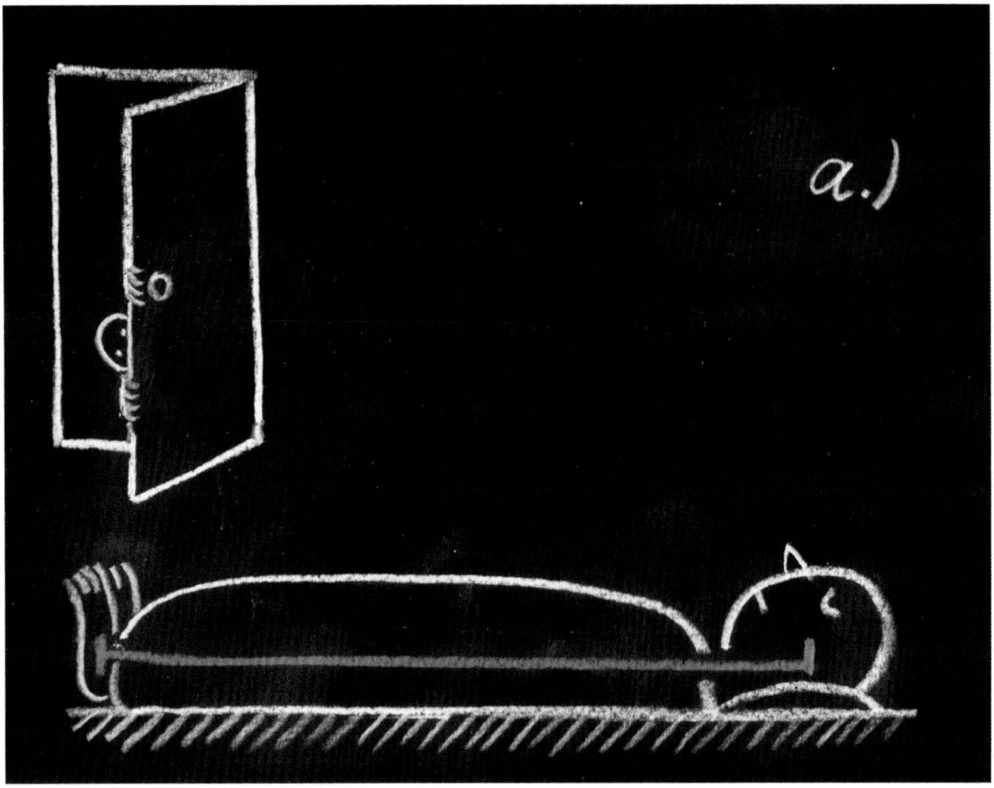
a.)

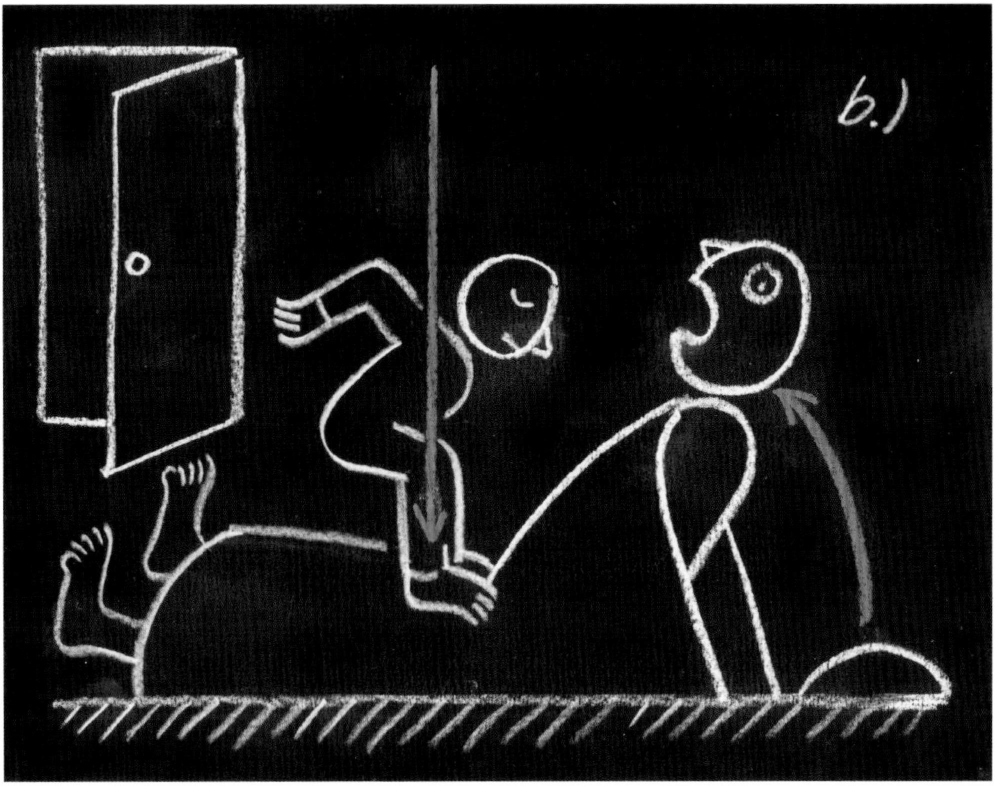
b.)

". . . unless it is compelled to change that state by forces impressed upon it."

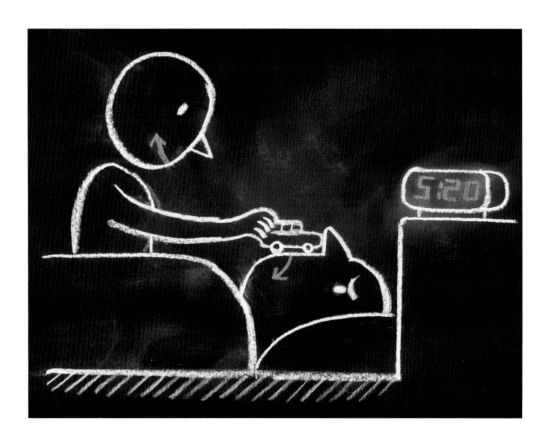

Based on super-complicated physical observations, Einstein concluded that two objects may perceive time differently. Based on simple life experience, I have concluded that this is true.

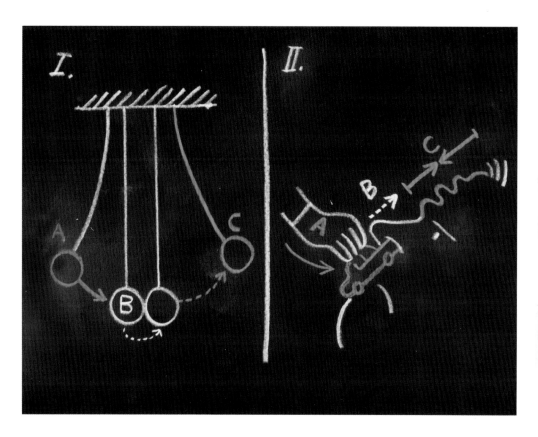

Newton's Cradle shows how energy
travels through a series of objects. In our
particular arrangement, kinetic energy is
ultimately converted into a compression
of the forehead.

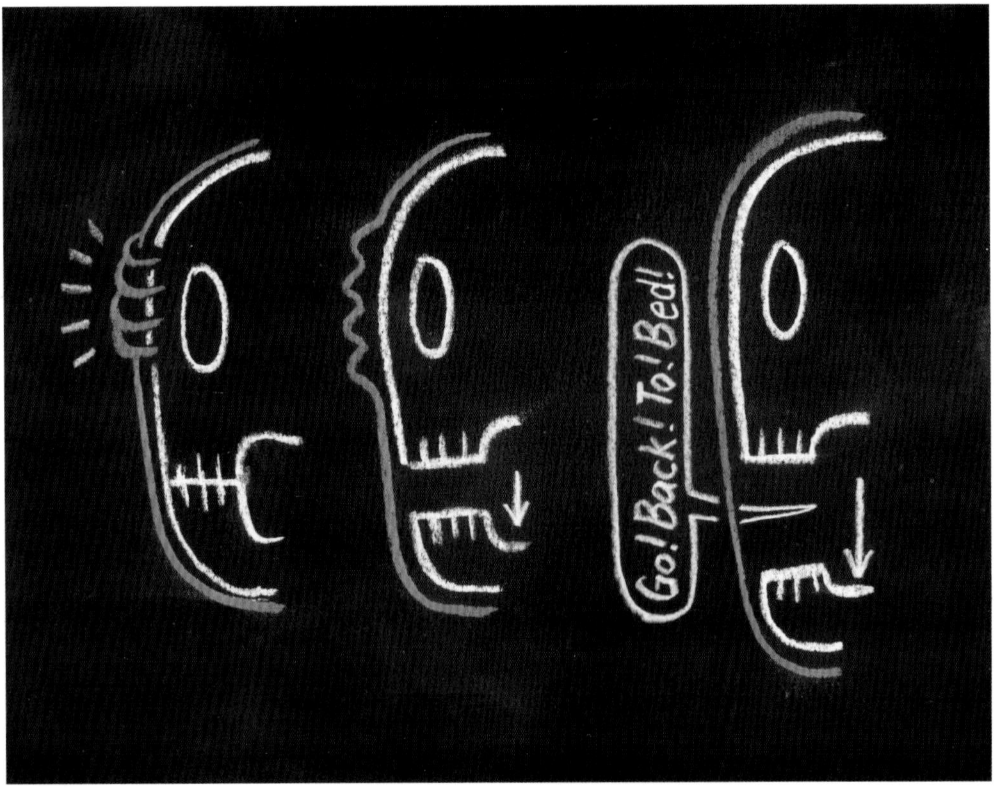
Go! Back! To! Bed!

The forehead can be uncrumpled by a downward movement of the jaw.

Excessive mechanical strain will compromise the elasticity of most materials, though.

The human body functions like a combustion engine. To produce energy, we need two things:

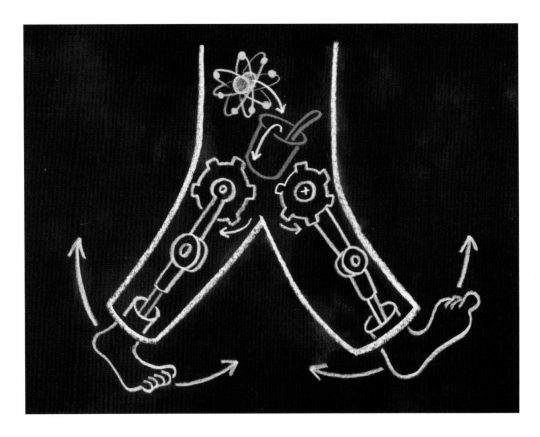

– Oxygen, supplied through the nostrils (once the toy car is removed, that is).

– Carbohydrates, which come in various forms (vanilla, chocolate, dulce de leche).

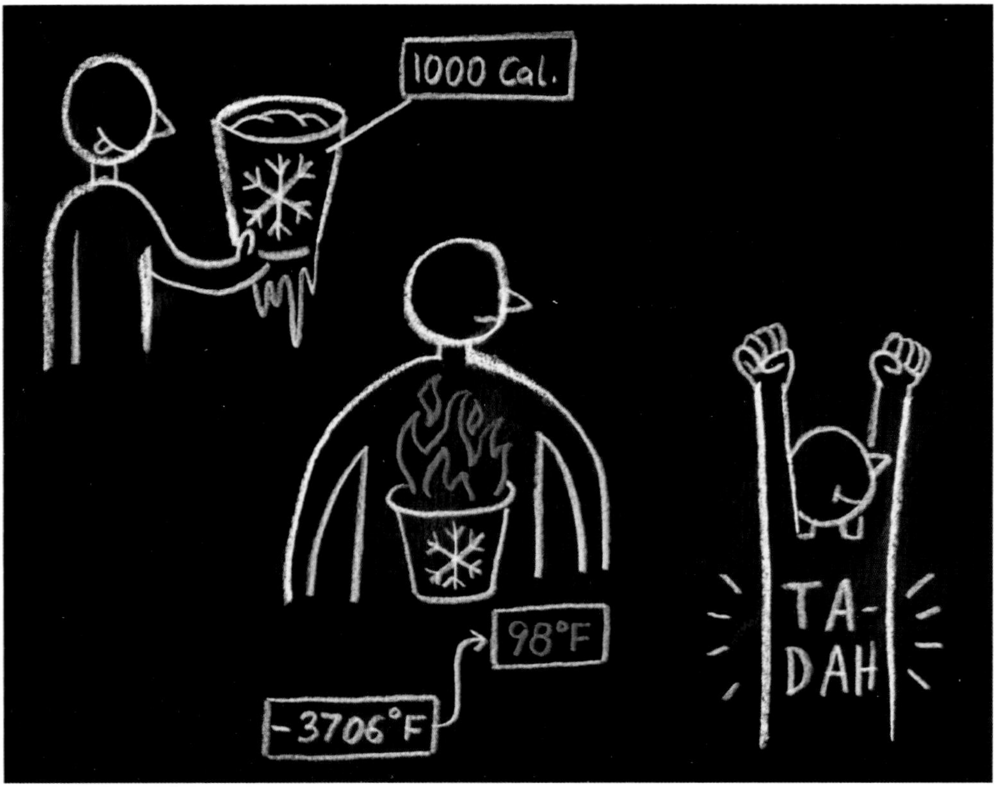
1000 Cal.
98°F
-3706°F
TA-
DAH

By the by: I had an idea for a carb-neutral ice cream. All you need is to freeze a pint of ice cream to -3706 degrees Fahrenheit. The energy it will take your system to bring the ice cream up to a digestible temperature is roughly 1,000 calories, neatly burning away all those carbohydrates from the fat and sugar. The only snag is the Third Law of Thermodynamics, which says it's impossible to go below -459 degrees Fahrenheit. Bummer.

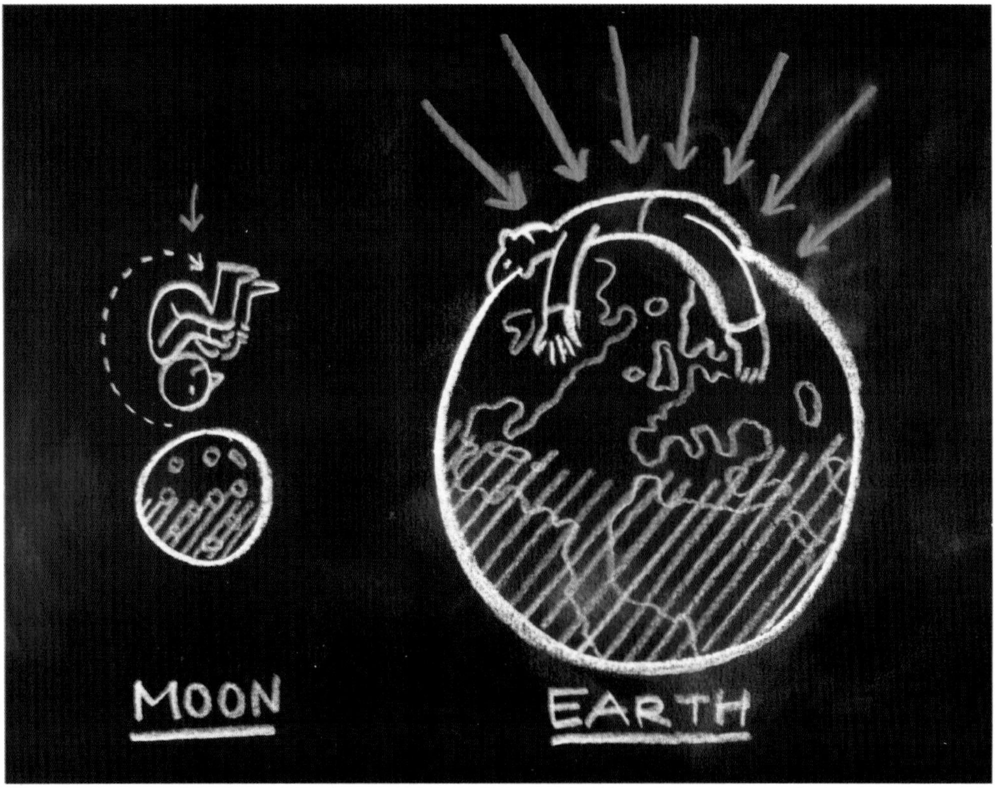
MOON
EARTH

But back to Newton: He discovered that any two objects in the universe attract each other, and that this force is proportional to their mass. The Earth is heavier than the moon, and therefore attracts our bodies with a much greater force.

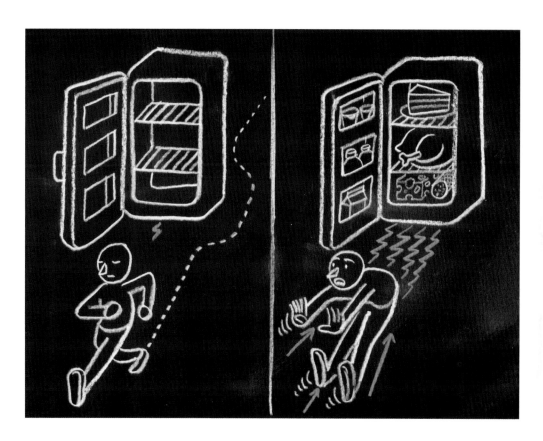

This explains why an empty refrigerator administrates a much smaller gravitational pull than, say, one that's stacked with fifty pounds of delicious leftovers. Great: That means we can blame the leftovers.

(Fig. A): Let's examine the behavior of particles in a closed container.

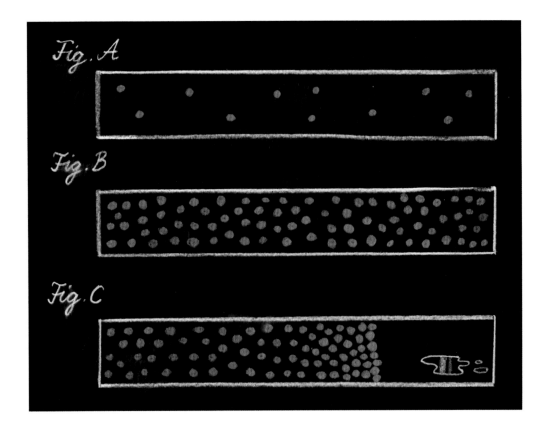

Fig. A

Fig. B

Fig. C

(Fig. B): The more particles we squeeze into the container, the testier they will become, especially if the container happens to be a rush-hour downtown local at Eighty-sixth and Lex.

(Fig. C): Usually the particles will distribute evenly, unless there is a weird-looking puddle on the floor.

The probability of finding a seat on the subway is inversely proportional to the number of people on the platform.

Even worse, the utter absence of people is 100 percent proportional to just having missed the train.

To describe different phenomena, physicists use various units.

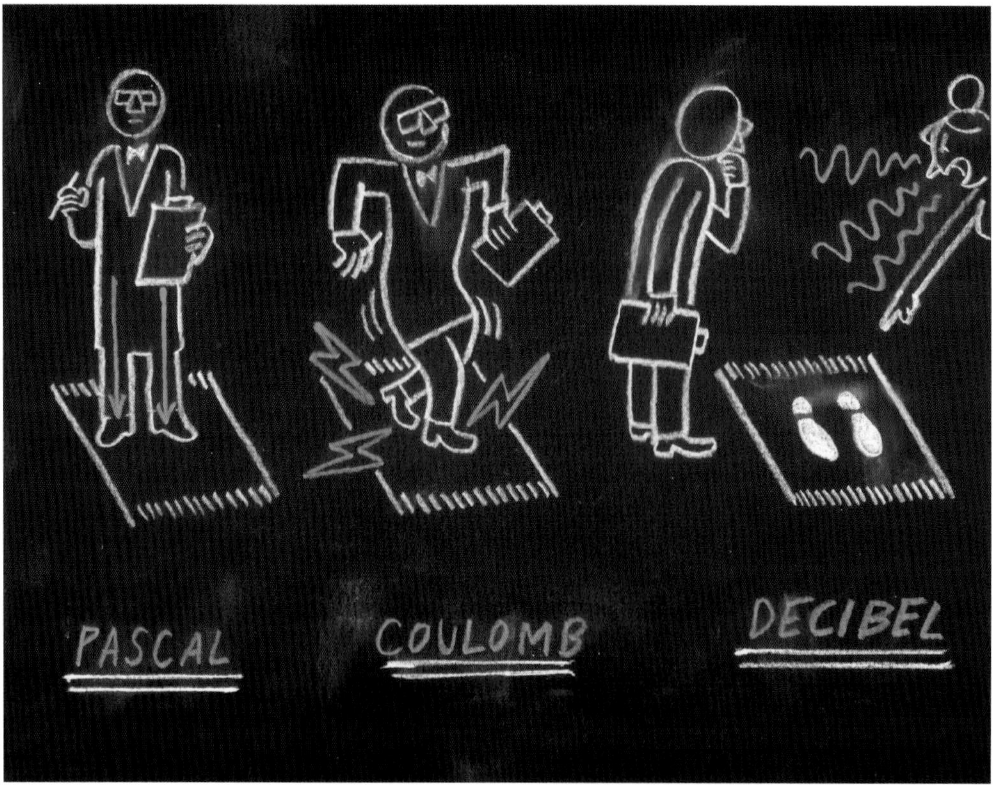
PASCAL
COULOMB
DECIBEL

PASCALS, for example, measure the pressure applied to a certain area.

COULOMBS measure electric charge (that can occur if said area is a synthetic carpet).

DECIBELS measure the intensity of the trouble the physicist gets into because he didn't take off his shoes first.

$$1\ Newton = 1\ \frac{kg * m}{s^2}$$

$$1\ Niemann = \frac{3y * (2s + J)}{LfK}$$

Often those units are named after people to recognize historic contributions to their field of expertise.

One NEWTON, for example, describes the force that is necessary to accelerate one kilogram of mass by one meter per second squared.

This is not to be confused with one NIEMANN, which describes the force necessary to make a three-year-old put on his shoes and jacket when we're already late for kindergarten.

Once the child is ready to go, I search for my keys. I start spinning around to scan my surroundings. This rotation exposes my head and all its contents to centrifugal forces, resulting in loss of hair and elongated eyeballs. That's why I need to wear prescription glasses, which are yet another thing I constantly misplace.

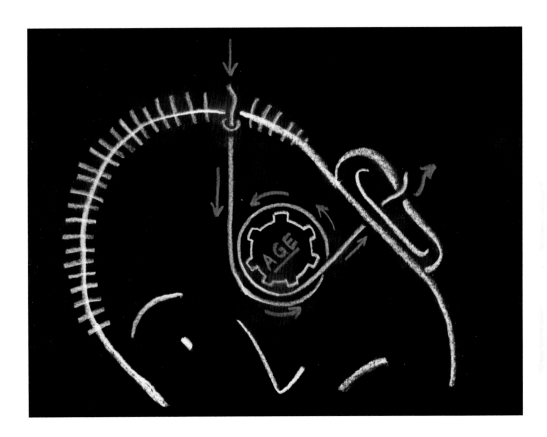

Obviously, the hair loss theory I just presented is bogus. Hair can't be "lost." Since Antoine Lavoisier, we all know that "matter can be neither created nor destroyed, though it can be rearranged," which, sadly, it eventually will.

Not everything can be explained through physics, though. I've spent years searching for a rational explanation for the weight of my wife's luggage. There is none. It is just a cruel joke of nature.

16. Let It Dough!

IN THE BEGINNING, I CREATED
THE HEAVENS AND THE EARTH.

AND THE EARTH WAS
WITHOUT FORM AND VOID.

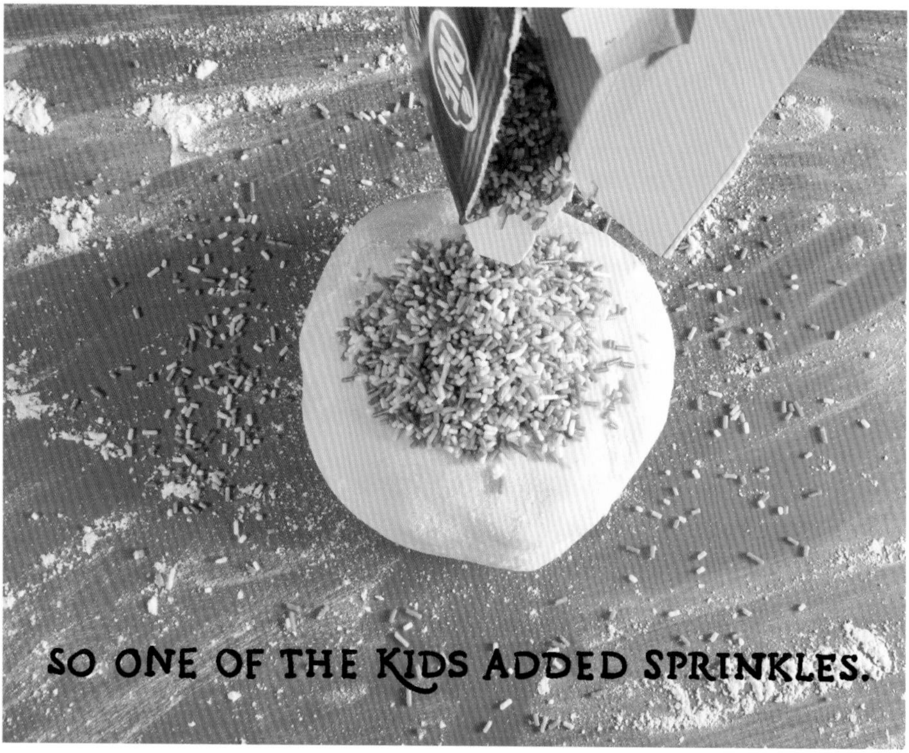
SO ONE OF THE KIDS ADDED SPRINKLES.

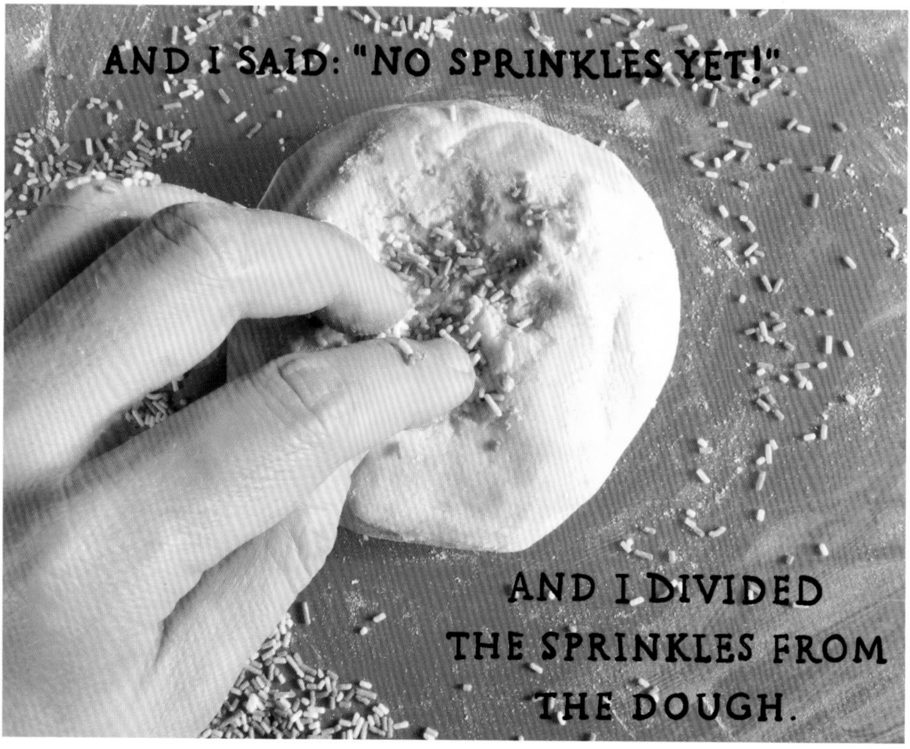
AND I SAID: "NO SPRINKLES YET!"
AND I DIVIDED THE SPRINKLES FROM THE DOUGH.

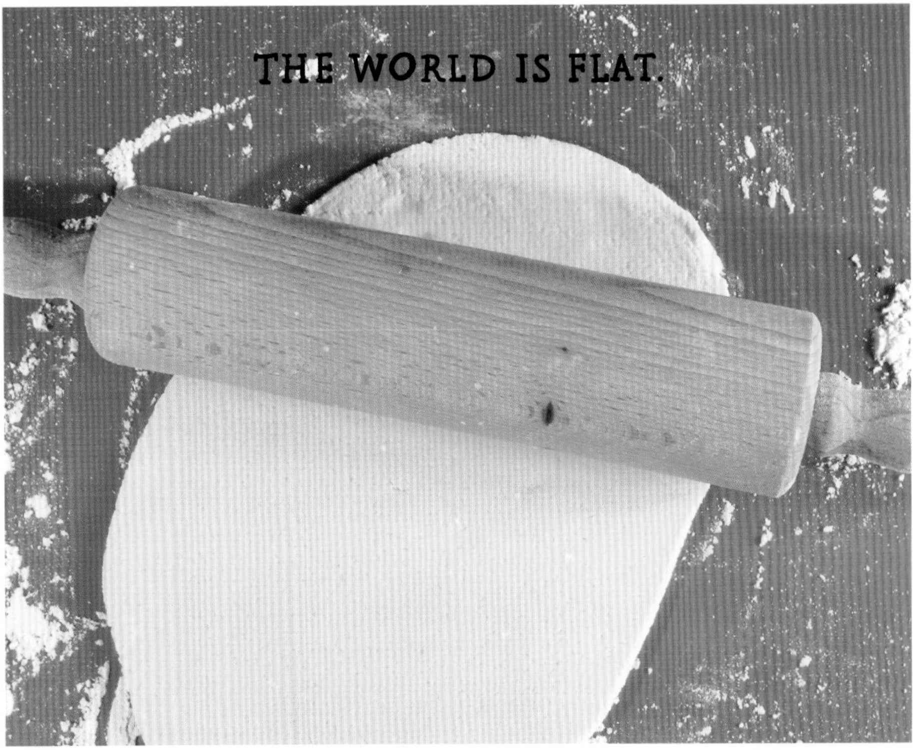
THE WORLD IS FLAT.

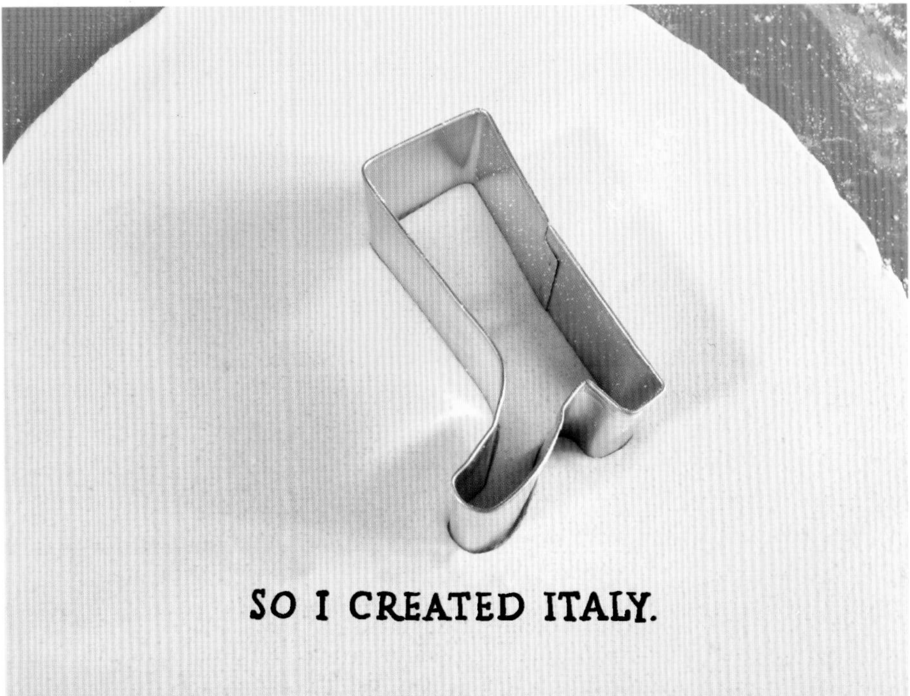
SO I CREATED ITALY.

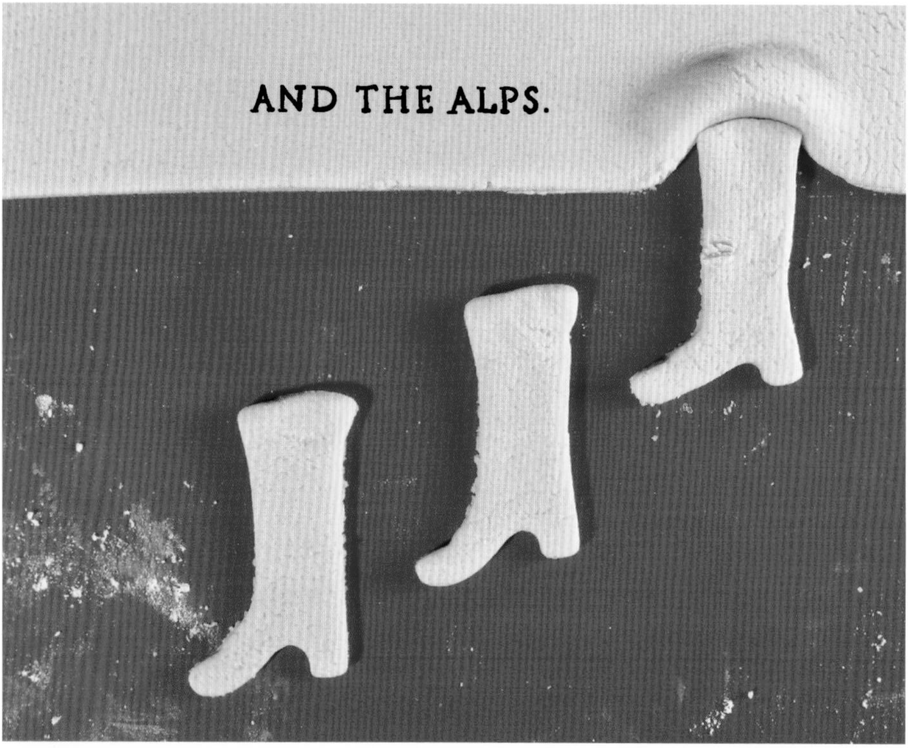
AND THE ALPS.

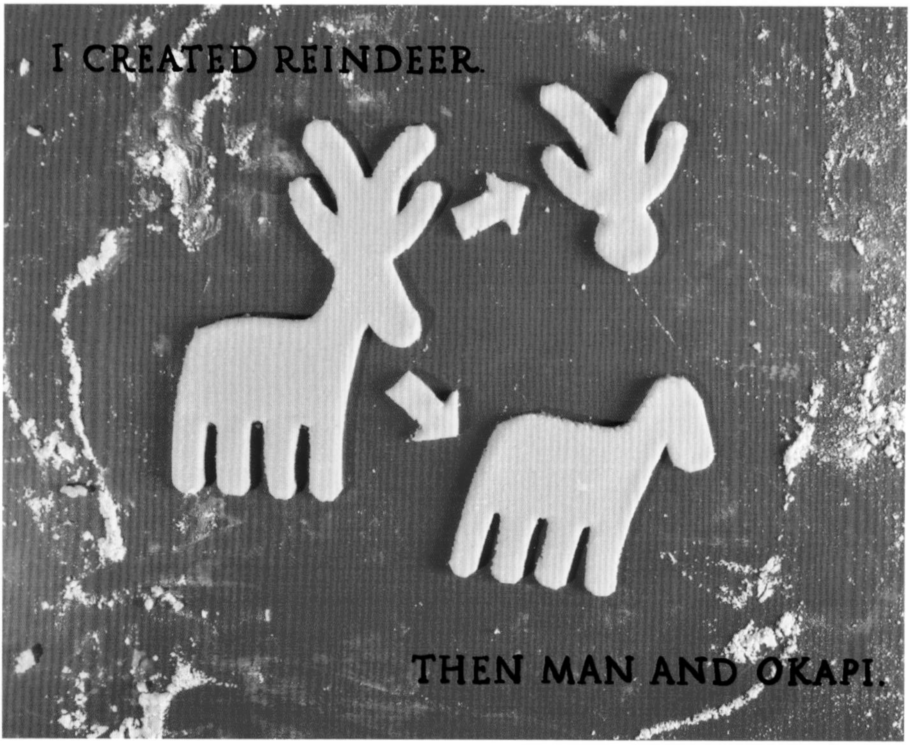
I CREATED REINDEER.
THEN MAN AND OKAPI.

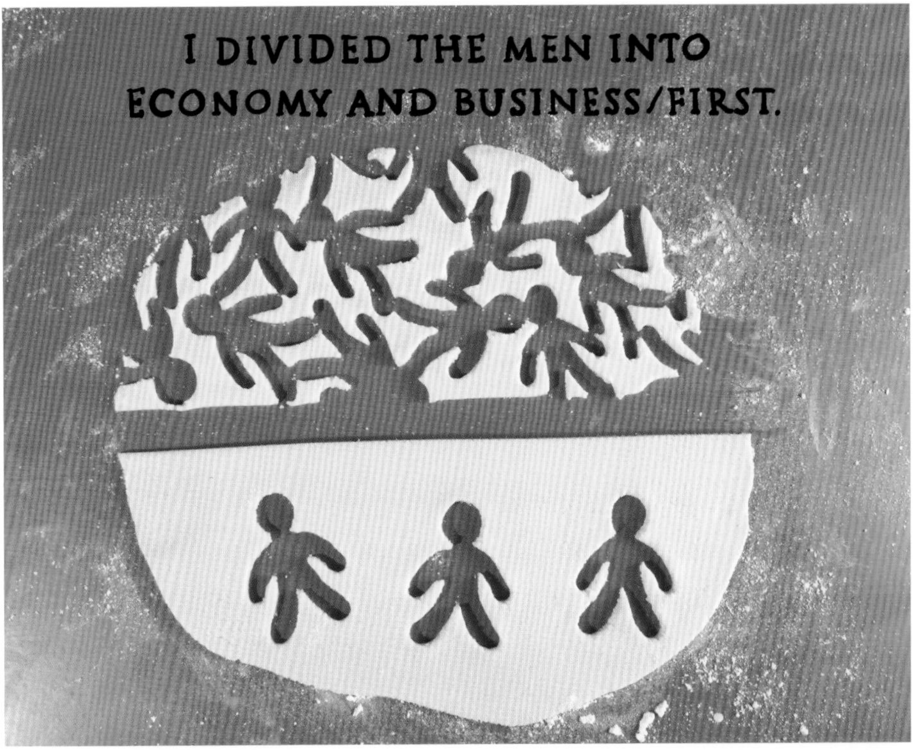
I DIVIDED THE MEN INTO
ECONOMY AND BUSINESS/FIRST.

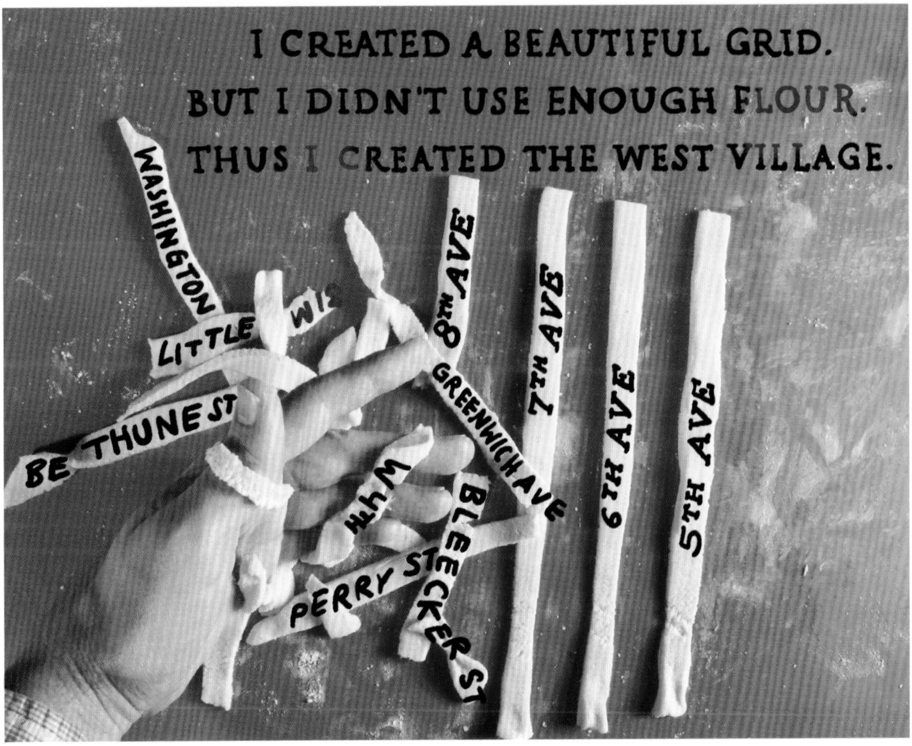
I CREATED A BEAUTIFUL GRID.
BUT I DIDN'T USE ENOUGH FLOUR.
THUS I CREATED THE WEST VILLAGE.
WASHINGTON
LITTLE
8TH AVE
7TH AVE
6TH AVE
5TH AVE
GREENWICH AVE
BETHUNE ST
W 4TH
BLEECKER ST
PERRY ST

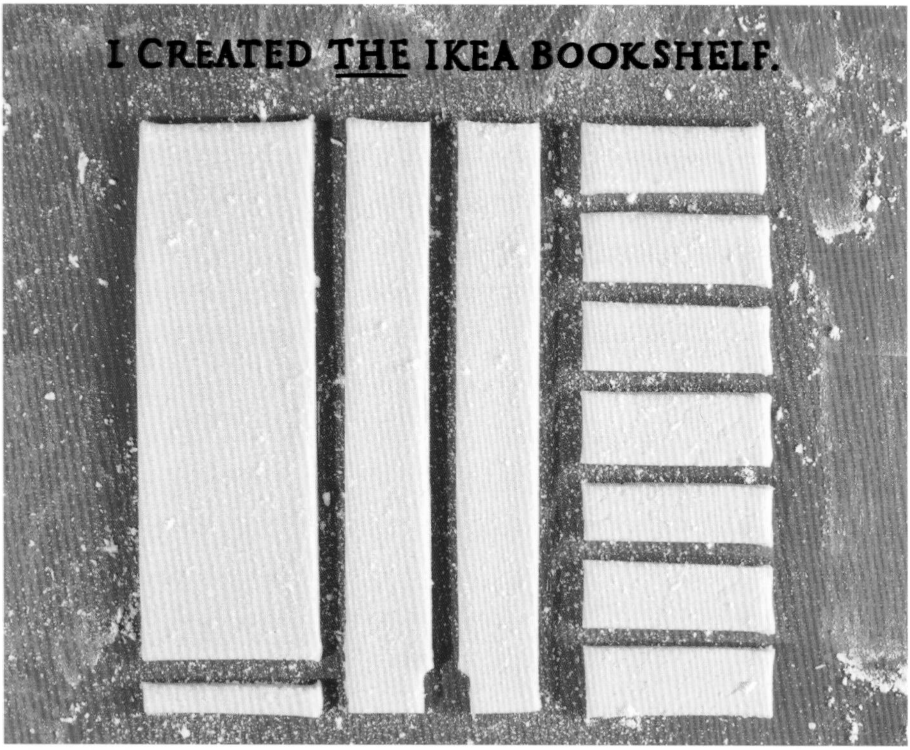
I CREATED THE IKEA BOOKSHELF.

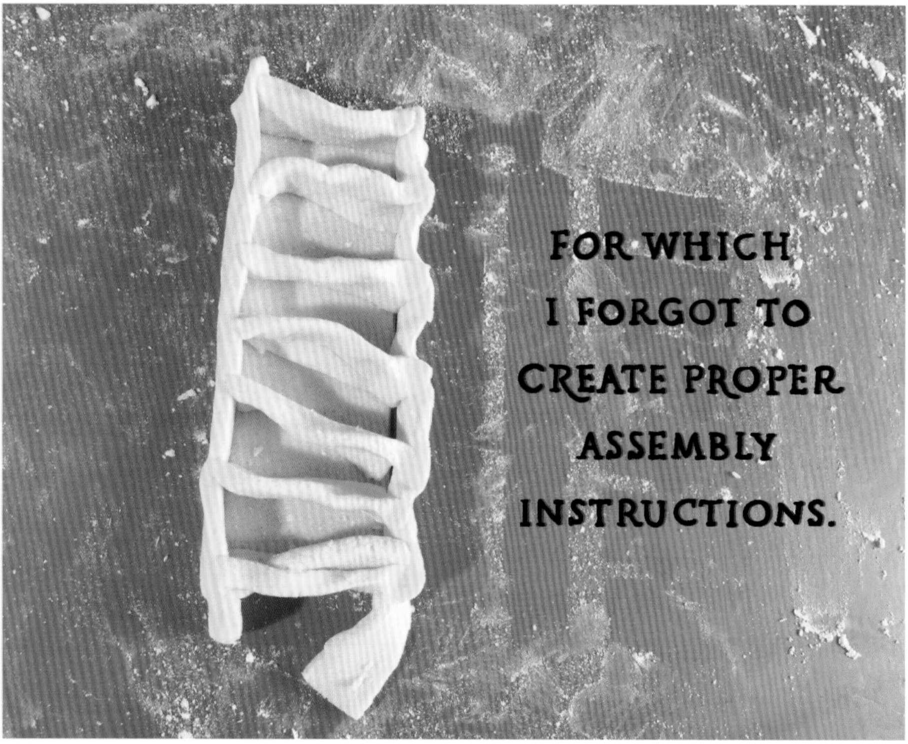
FOR WHICH
I FORGOT TO
CREATE PROPER
ASSEMBLY
INSTRUCTIONS.

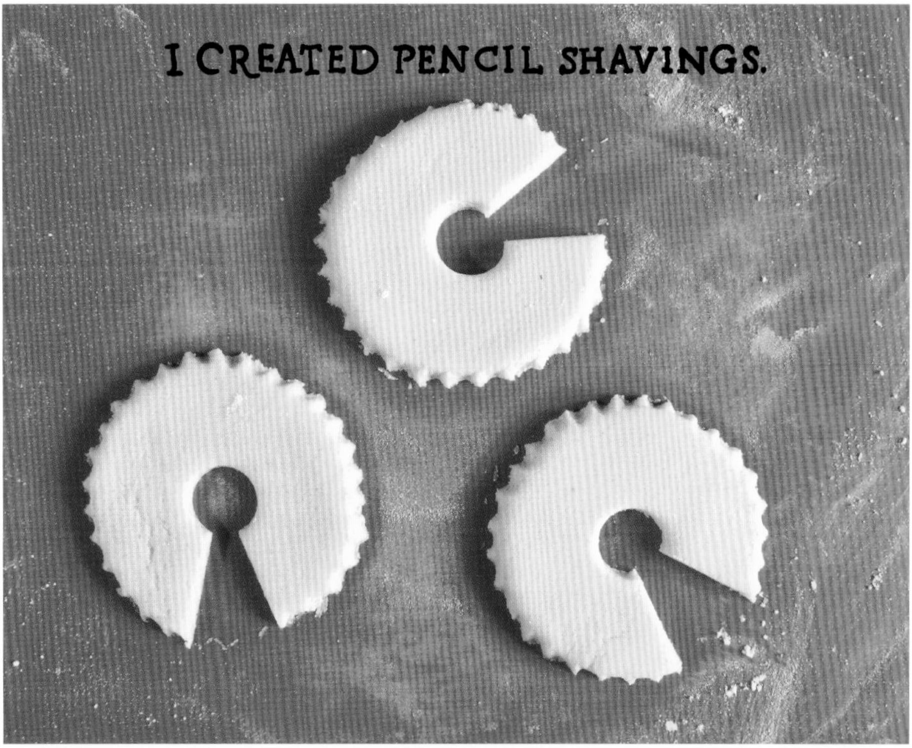
I CREATED PENCIL SHAVINGS.

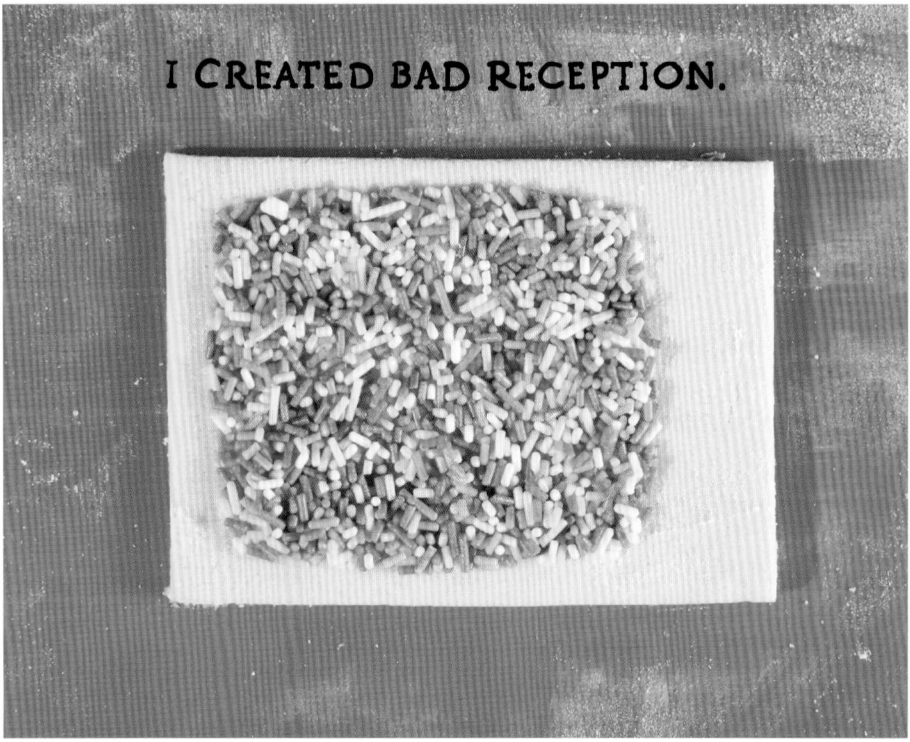
I CREATED BAD RECEPTION.

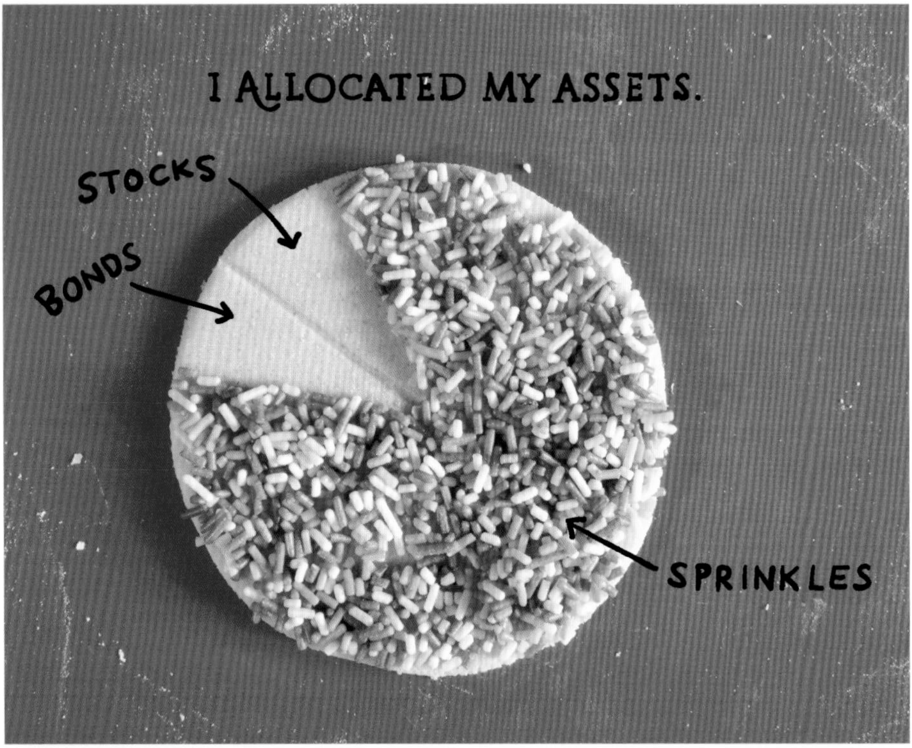
I ALLOCATED MY ASSETS.
STOCKS
BONDS
SPRINKLES

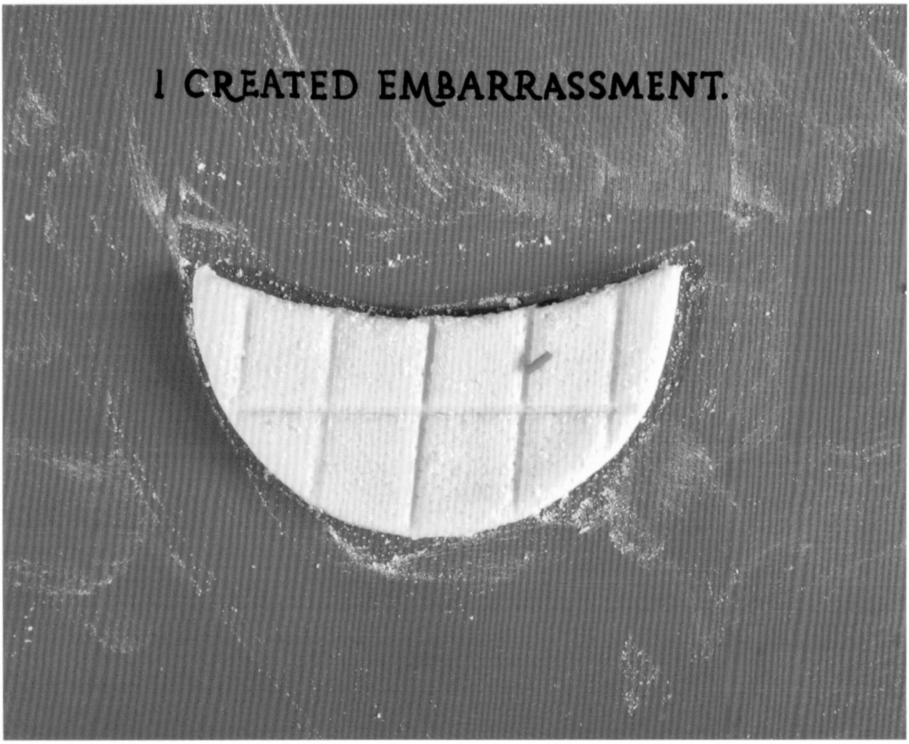
I CREATED EMBARRASSMENT.

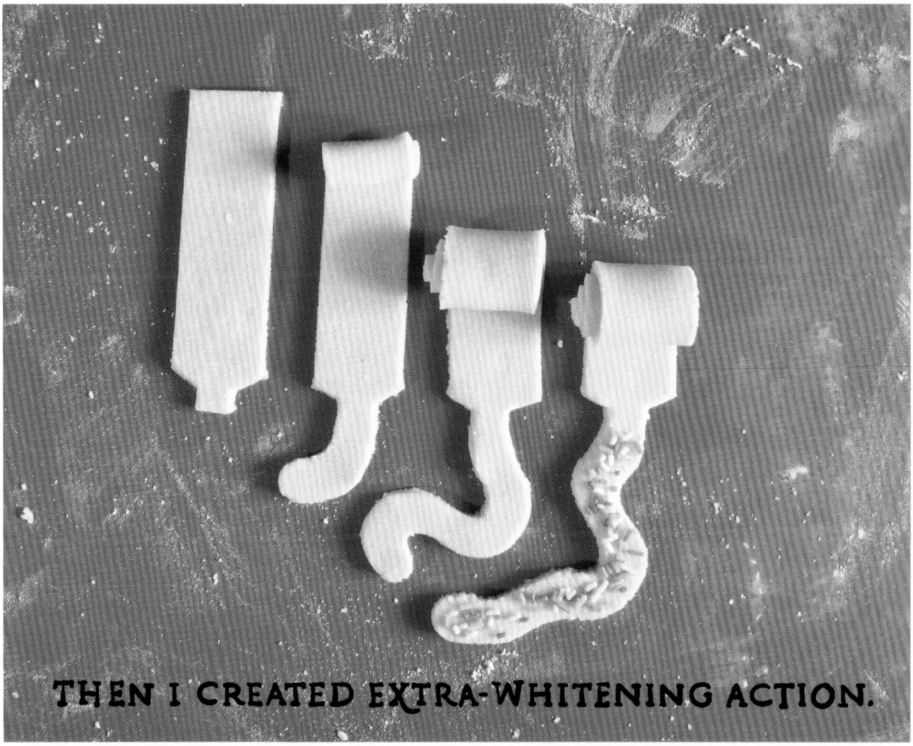
THEN I CREATED EXTRA-WHITENING ACTION.

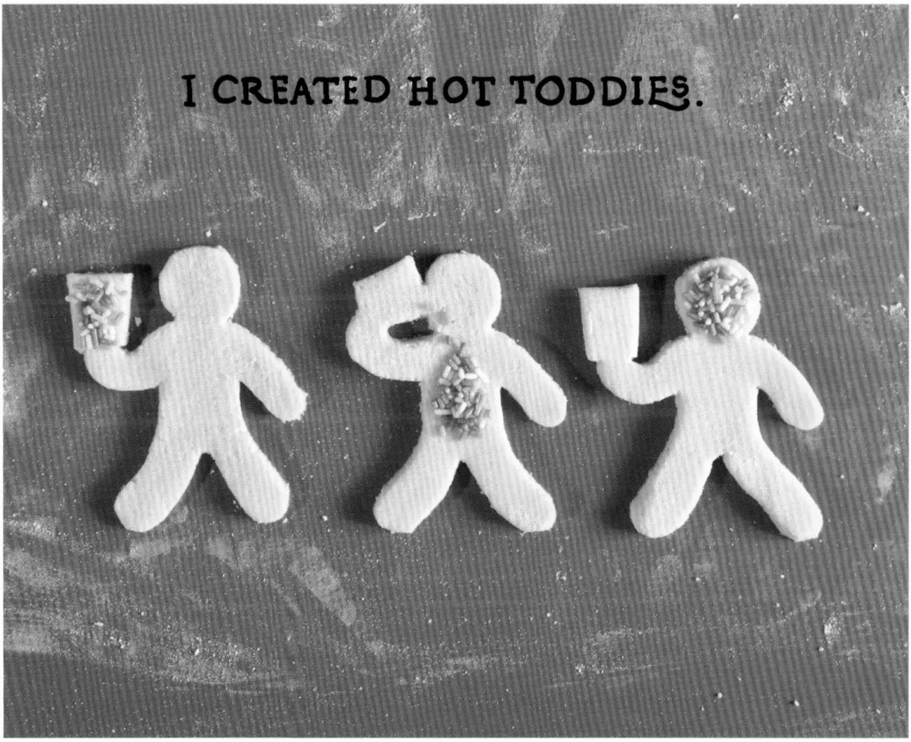
I CREATED HOT TODDIES.

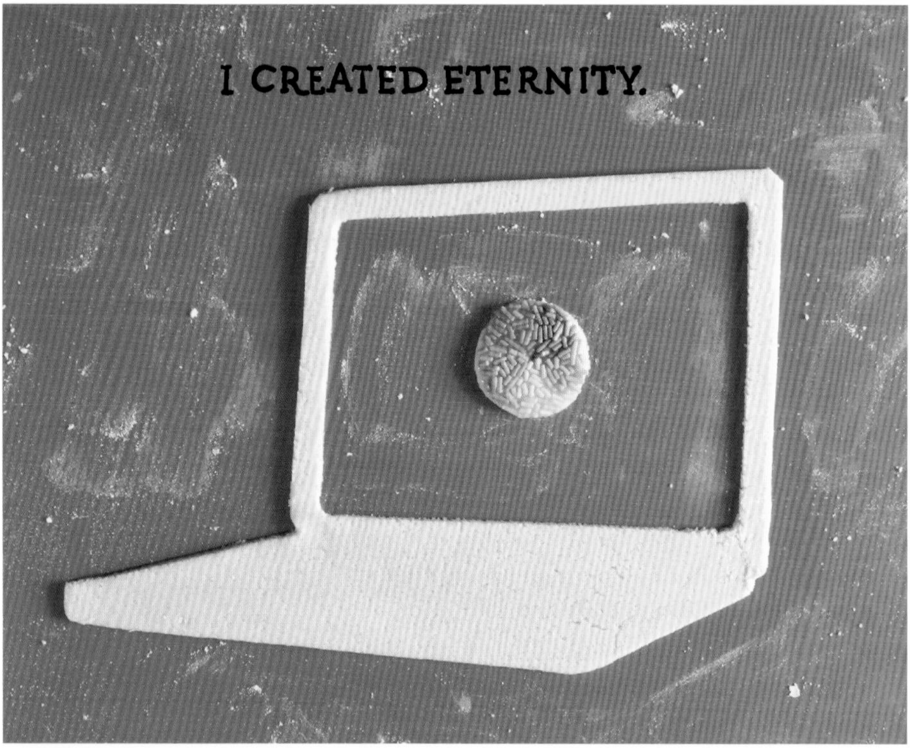
I CREATED ETERNITY.

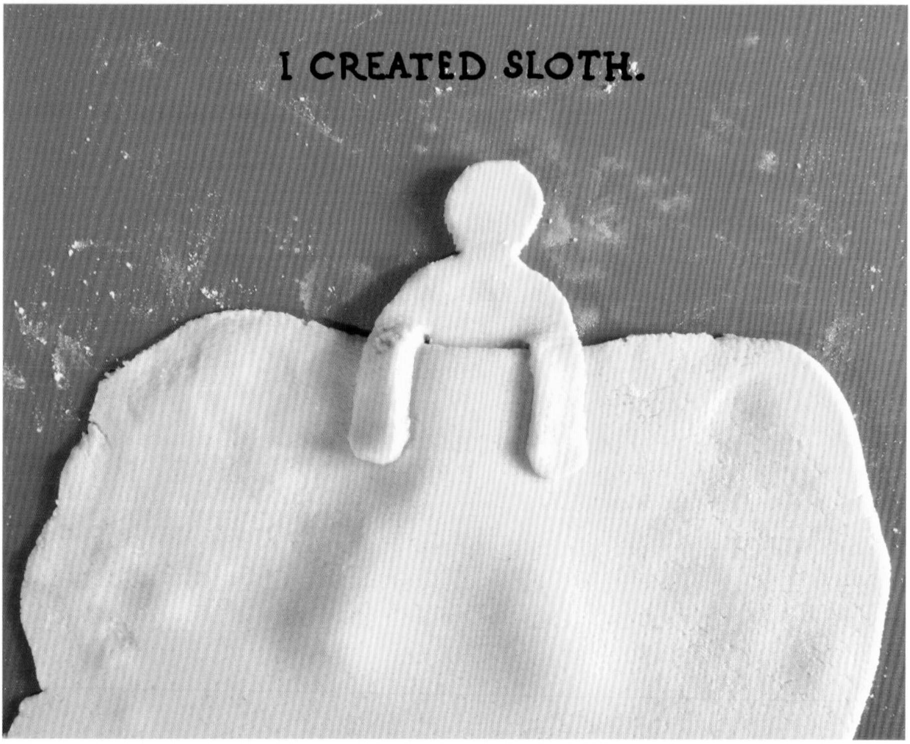
I CREATED SLOTH.

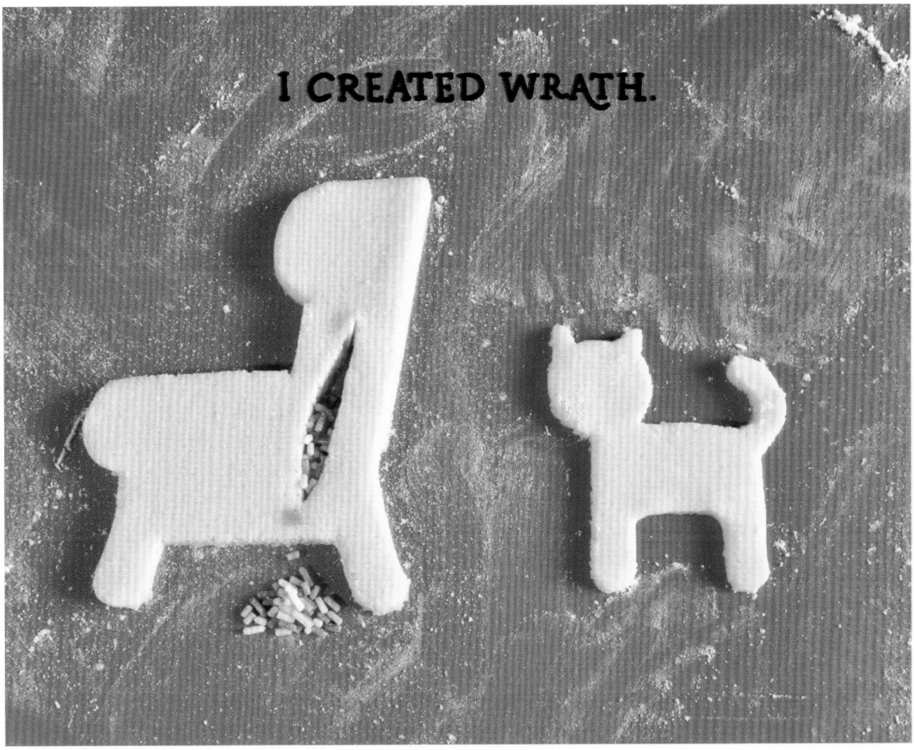
I CREATED WRATH.

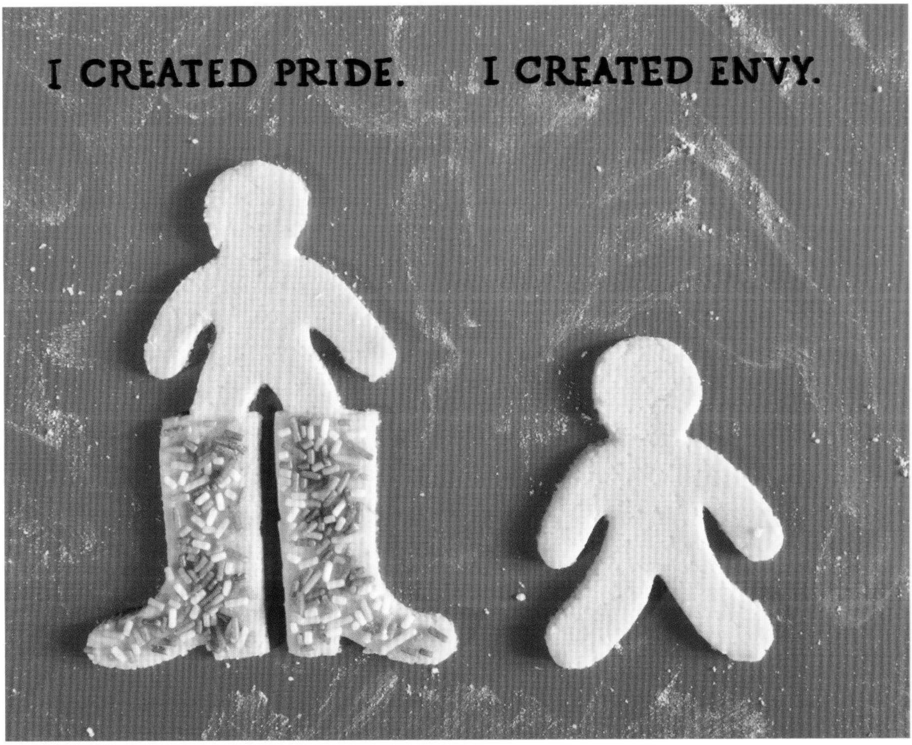
I CREATED PRIDE.
I CREATED ENVY.

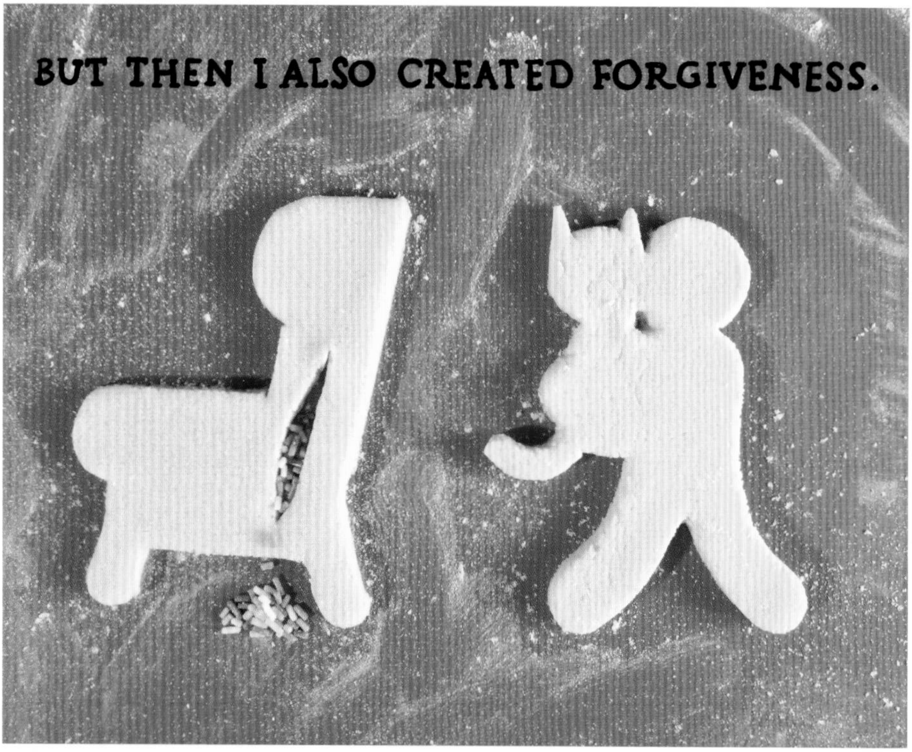
BUT THEN I ALSO CREATED FORGIVENESS.

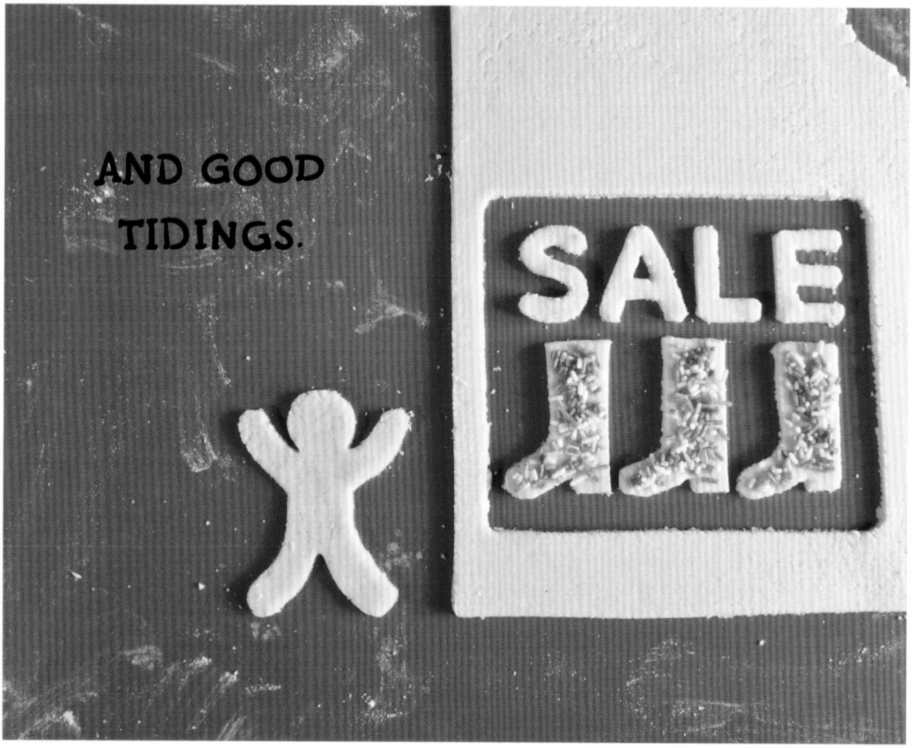
AND GOOD
TIDINGS.
SALE

AND A HAPPY NEW YEAR.

17. Afterword

"I always thought that inspiration is for amateurs—the rest of us just show up and get to work."
—Chuck Close

I go to the studio at 8:45 in the morning. I leave at 5:45 in the evening.

In the meantime, I go through what is often referred to as the "creative process."

Sadly, it looks like this:

8:45 A.M. to 5:45 P.M. That's roughly nine hours.

1h
ADMINISTRATION
4h
CREATIVE
4h
EXECUTION

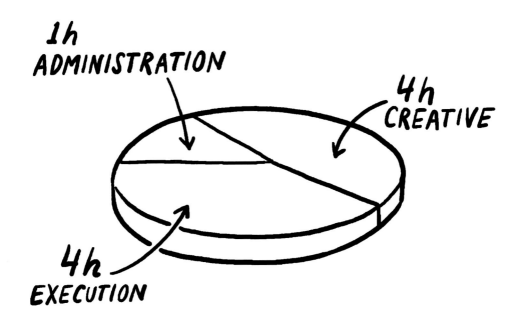

Fun fact:

If I reconfigured my workday and devoted three hours each to administration, creative, and execution, I wouldn't get my work done. The above chart, however, would very closely resemble the Mercedes Benz Logo.

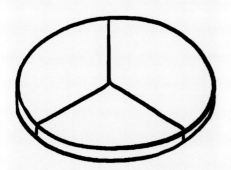

Fun fact encore:

If I stopped working altogether and instead devoted two hours and fifteen minutes each to artichokes, mushrooms, ham, and olives, my workday would perfectly emulate a pizza quattro stagioni. But since somebody has to actually order and pay for the pizza, I suppose I would have to reinstate the administration part, which I would take out of the olive portion since that always feels like a waste anyway.

MUSHROOM
ARTICHOKE
OLIVES
ADMINI-
STRATION
HAM

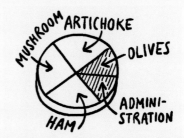

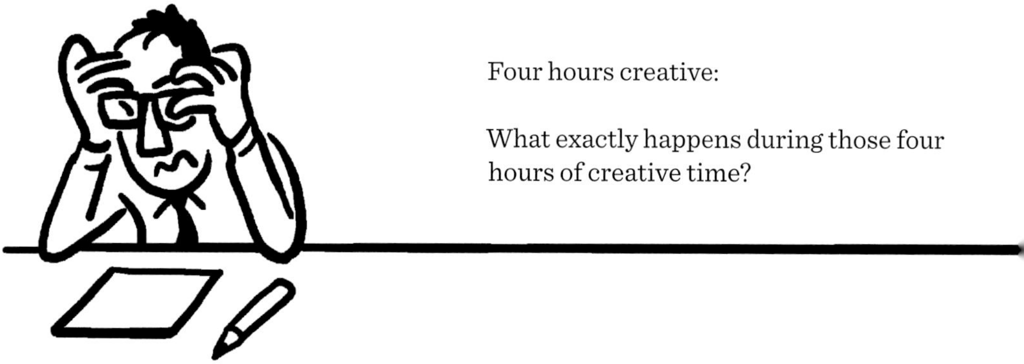

Four hours creative:

What exactly happens during those four hours of creative time?

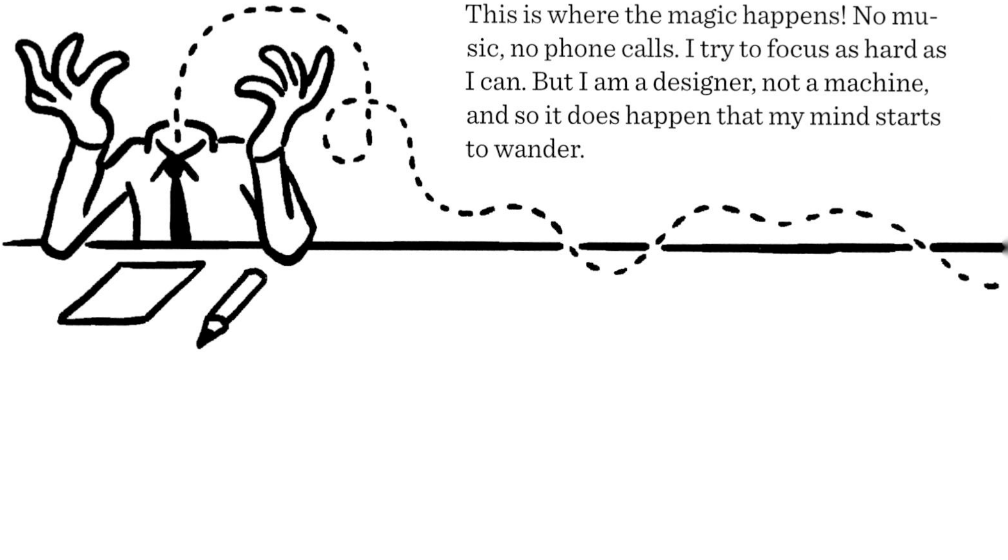

This is where the magic happens! No music, no phone calls. I try to focus as hard as I can. But I am a designer, not a machine, and so it does happen that my mind starts to wander.

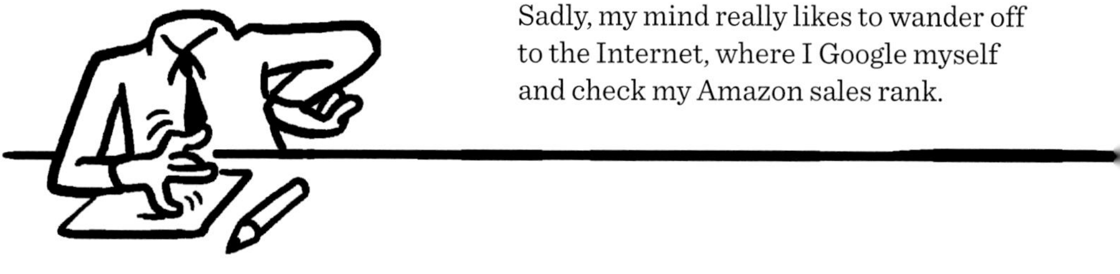

Sadly, my mind really likes to wander off to the Internet, where I Google myself and check my Amazon sales rank.

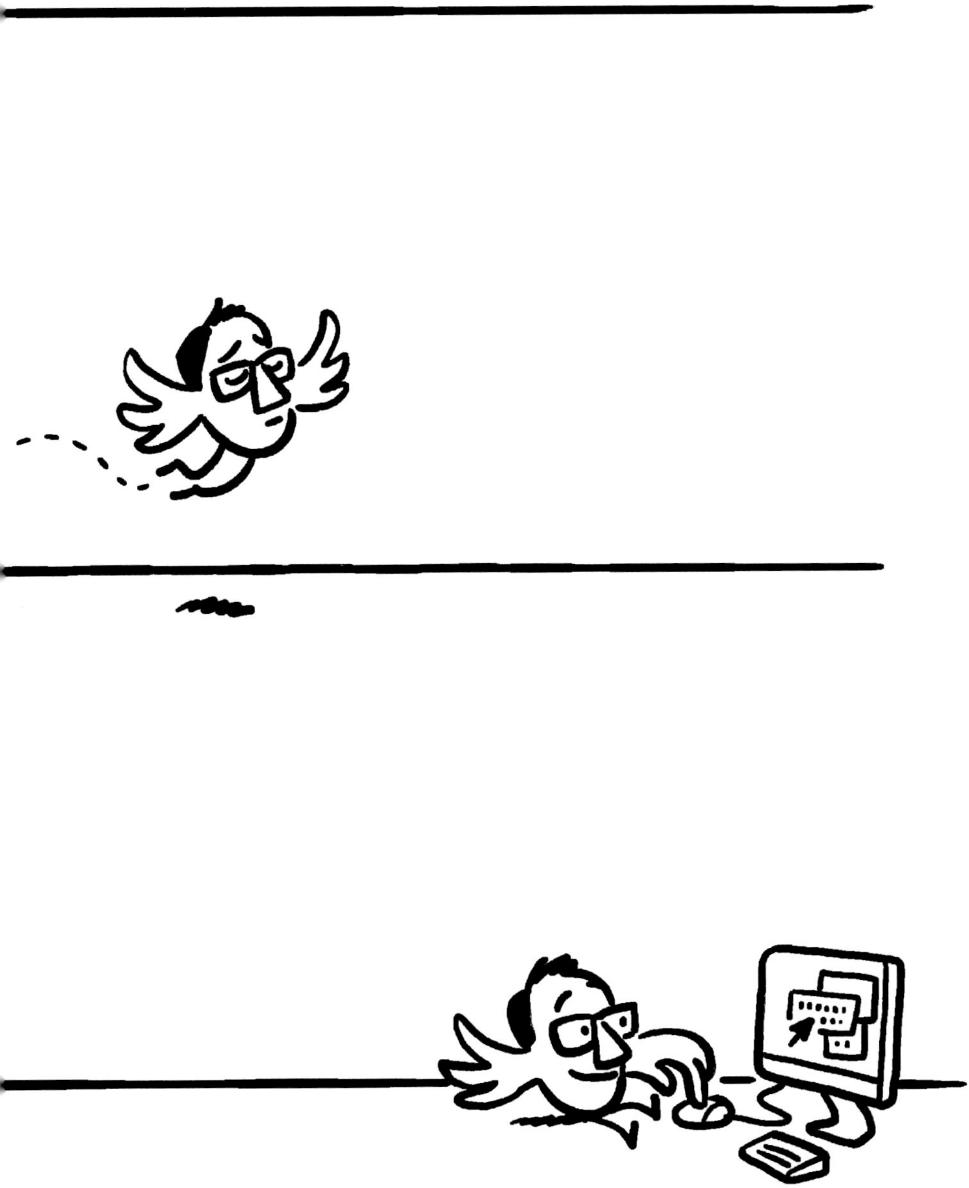

When we had our first child, I made a resolution to always be home by six in the evening. I was afraid that this would lead to a big drop in my productivity, but I was surprised to find that it didn't and that working steadily for eight or nine hours was much more productive in the long run than working well into the night.

I realized that I have a finite amount of creative energy and concentration in me. I can't give you the precise math, but, for conceptual work, I cannot really go more than four hours in a given twenty-four-hour time period. If I push myself to work beyond that threshold, all I produce is garbage.

When it comes to drawing or designing on the computer I can go longer, but there is a time when my mind just goes numb. Even worse, if I try to extend the workday to ten or fourteen or eighteen hours, I will be punished with two subpar days after that.

This means there are four hours for turning the ideas I generate into actual illustrations.

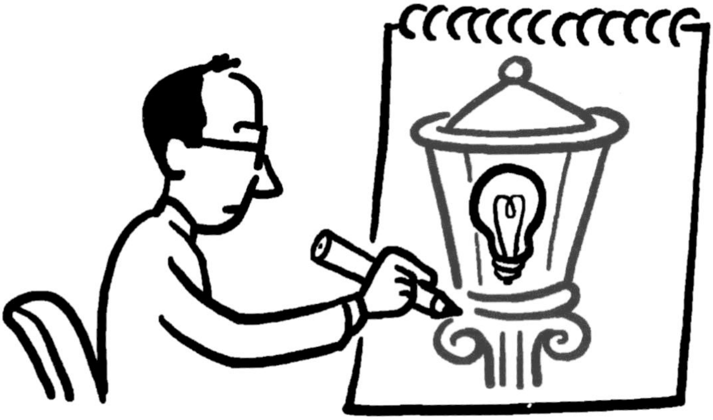

Two of those hours for drawing and designing . . .

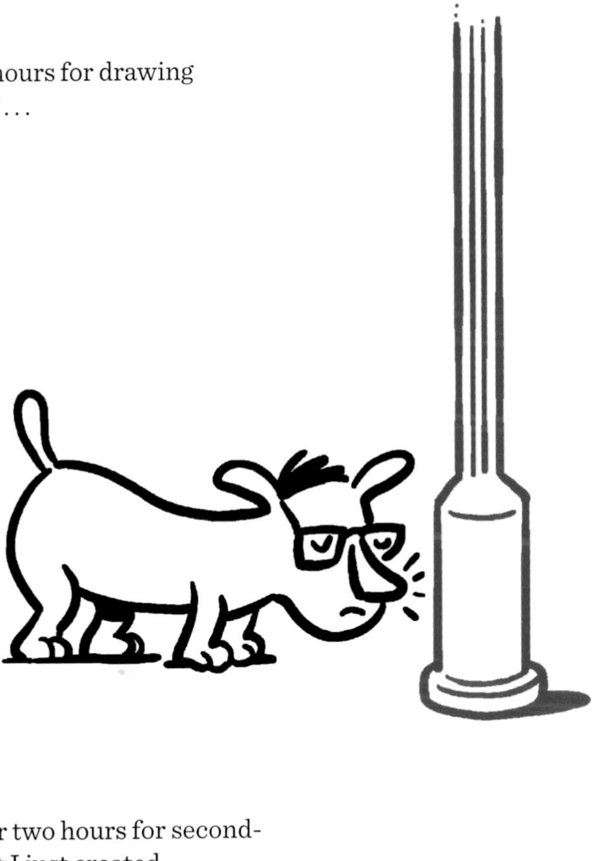

. . . and another two hours for second-guessing what I just created.

Quickly going back to the creative part:

WHAT DOES IT TAKE TO COME UP WITH A REALLY GREAT IDEA?
87% EFFORT
7.5% LUCK
0.5% TALENT + DIVINE INSPIRATION
5% STAYING OFF INTERNET FOR CONSECUTIVE 90 MINUTES!

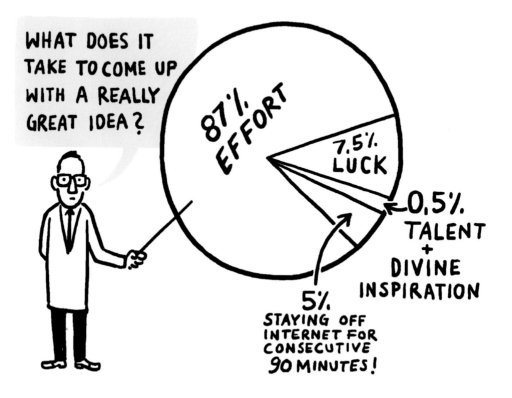

Some of my friends in the creative industry are different, of course.

They tell me that for them it's all about relaxing, maybe taking an inspiring stroll through the park to get their creative juices flowing, and then the ideas just appear naturally once they sit down at their desk.

For my "normal" work, illustrating articles for magazines and newspapers, I am presented with a problem for which I have to find a solution. This can be very difficult. Over the years, however, I have gotten so used to this process that I actually find it strangely rewarding to operate within such a tight set of restrictions.

PROBLEM
SOLUTION

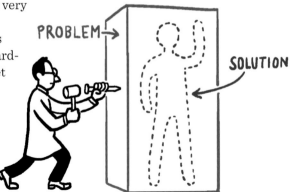

In the last few years, I began working on self-generated projects, such as children's books and visual essays. The biggest challenge here is that before I can even begin to think about a solution, I have to first create the problem to be solved.

B
R
O
E
P
L
M

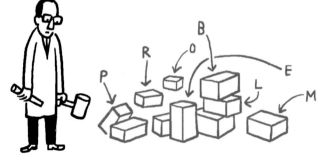

And as I struggle with an interesting solution, I constantly worry whether I should have started with a different problem.

WRONG PROBLEM
HENCE DEFICIENT SOLUTION

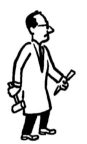

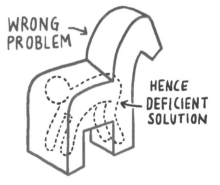

I hate it when people tell me, "You are talented." The word "talent" implies a natural gift. As if there is a miraculous superpower that helps an artist produce decent work.

Some people probably do have an aptitude for drawing or writing, and that makes it easier for them to create, but even this is worthless if you don't hone your skills through years of practice. If there is any kind of talent I would consider relevant, it would be natural enthusiasm, which keeps you going despite the difficulties and frustrations that are inevitably part of creative work.

But if natural ability doesn't matter that much, why do some of us choose a creative profession to begin with? Here's my theory:

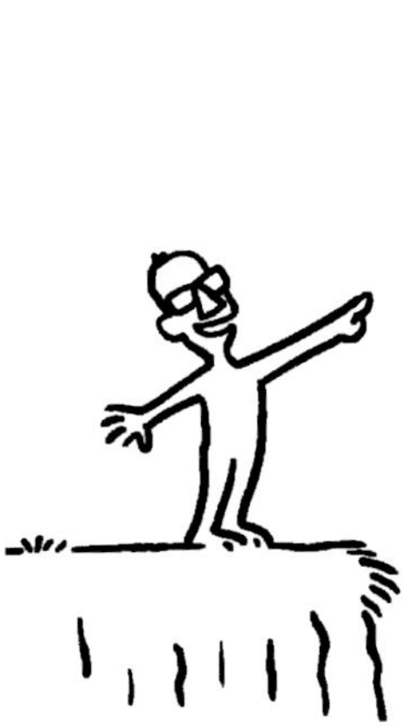

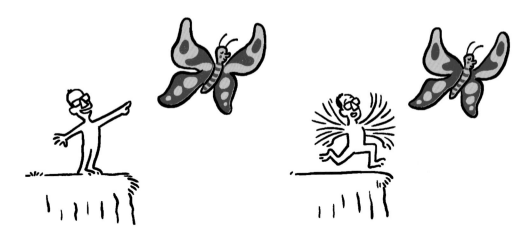

When you're young you see a special work of art—a painting, a book, a movie—that touches something inside you.

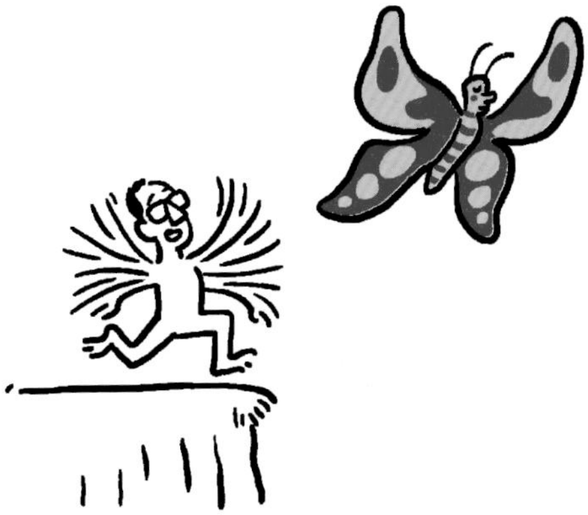

This is such an intoxicating experience that it stirs within you the deep desire to create something as thrilling and powerful.

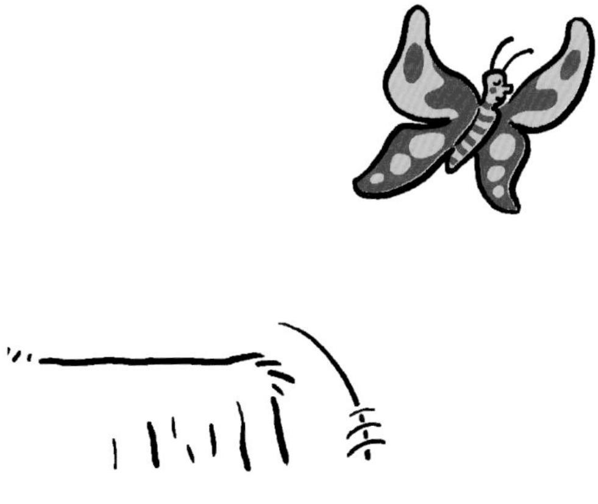

Next up is the painful realization that your heartfelt desire to make something special does not equal your actual ability to do so. For most, this constitutes the end of a creative career.

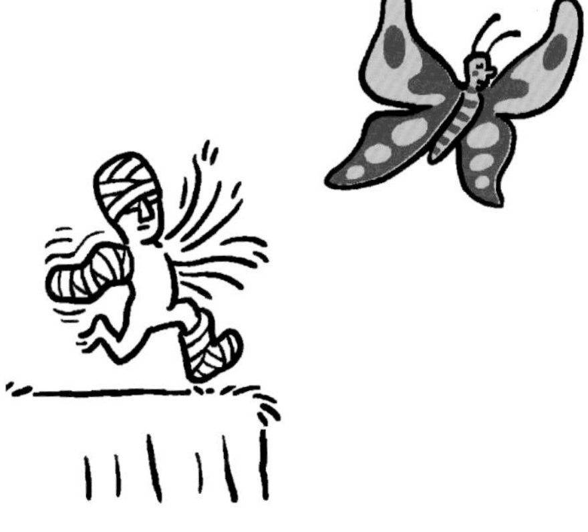

A few others keep on trying.

There is one annoying question people ask me:

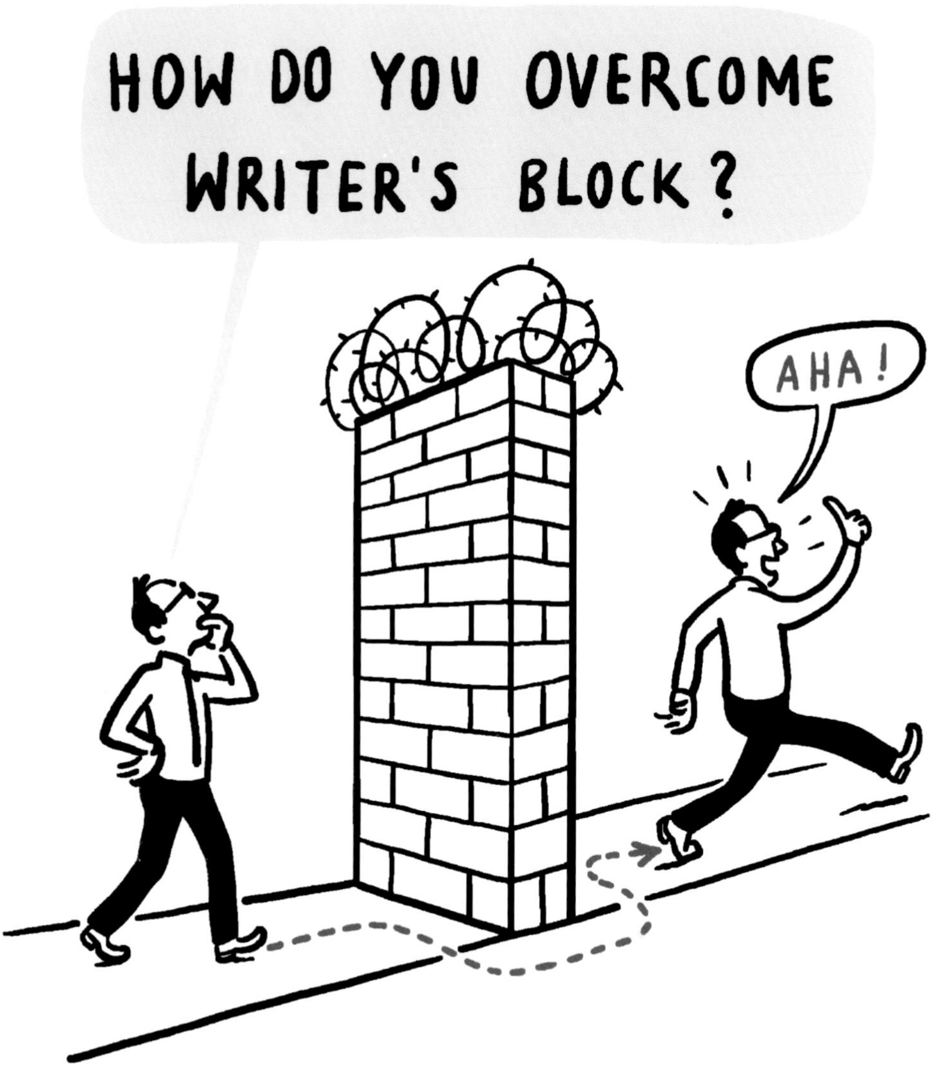
HOW DO YOU OVERCOME WRITER'S BLOCK?
AHA!

This makes it sound as though writer's block is something that (a) you encounter infrequently and for which (b) there is some sort of remedy. Like a skin rash.

The truth is that

MY ENTIRE PROFESSIONAL LIFE IS ONE BIG FAT WRITER'S BLOCK.

Trying to overcome this is exactly what I do from the second I enter my studio to the time I clean up my desk at night.*

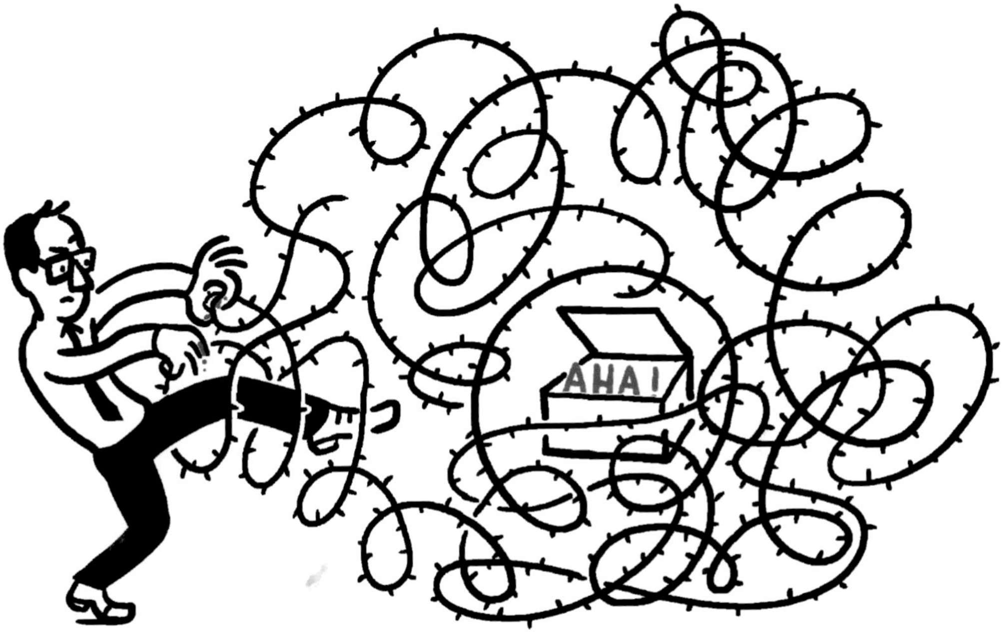
AHA!

*This is, of course, just a figure of speech. I never clean up my desk at night.

As you can see here, I spend my workdays in a state of almost perpetual grumpiness:

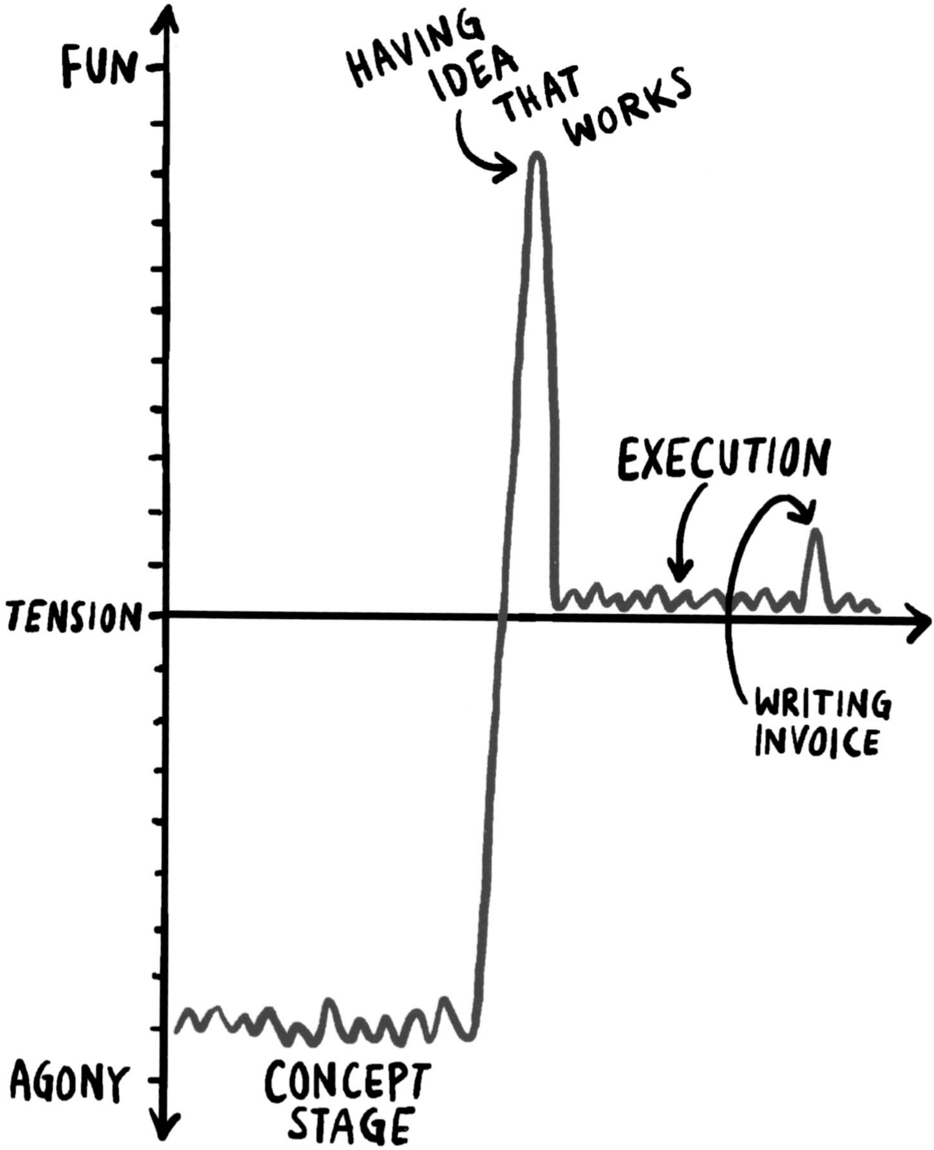
FUN
TENSION
AGONY
HAVING IDEA THAT WORKS
EXECUTION
WRITING INVOICE
CONCEPT STAGE

Over the years, I have developed a remarkable ability to hide my mood when I am on the phone with clients.

My non-designer friends envy me for my job. They think it must be fun to sit around all day, doodling away, and thinking of funny ideas.

I try to tell them that it's quite the opposite and that I often feel that I am spending all day trying to catch chickens with my bare hands.

You know, like Sylvester Stallone in that great scene from *Rocky*.

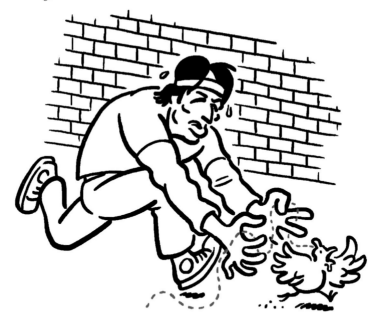

It seems so simple at first glance, but it turns out to be all but impossible and also highly unglamorous.

Also, contrary to what one would hope, a half-assed effort will not yield half a chicken.

REWARD
1 CHICKEN (MAYBE)
1/2 CHICKEN
NO CHICKEN
FULL EFFORT
1/2 ASS EFFORT

Fun fact:

The lowercase version of the Greek letter μ (mu) looks just like half an ass:

μ → μ

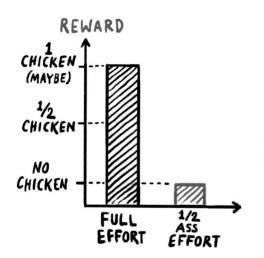

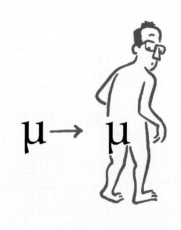

A LITTLE CAUTIONARY TALE...

A few years ago I had some issues with back pain and I started doing yoga. I would go to Chelsea Piers two or three times a week for a class at lunchtime. Although it worked wonders for my body, it also made me calmer and more relaxed. I started feeling this sense of inner peace and harmony. So I would come back from class, go back to work, and I would look at some drawing I had done that just wasn't quite there, and instead of thinking "I have to redo it!! Somebody may hate it," I was completely calm and thought, "It's not perfect, but aren't there more important things in life?"

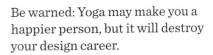

Be warned: Yoga may make you a happier person, but it will destroy your design career.

QUALITY OF WORK
INNER PEACE

As I grow older, I hope to become a more confident and well balanced human being. But as far as my creative work goes, I have realized that self consciousness and tensity are actually professional assets.

If I continue to carefully nurture them, they will help me to sustain a long and prolific career.

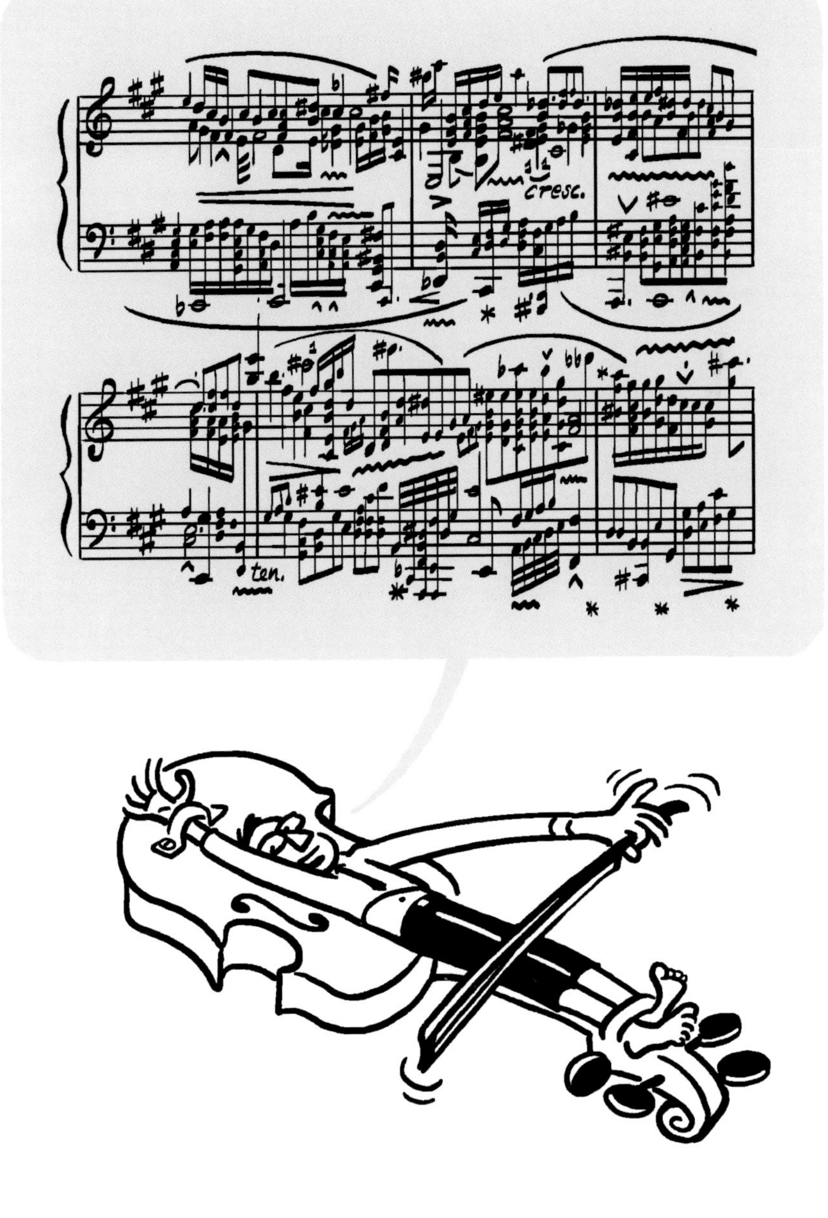
cresc.
ten.

This book would not have been possible without the wisdom and support of the following people: Deborah Aaronson, Nicholas Blechman, Caitlin Kenney, Brian Rea, David Shipley, and Jeremy Zilar.

Special thanks to: Paul Sahre and his assistants Ramona Heiligensetzer, Santiago Carrasquilla, and Alex Stikeleather for the beautiful book design, George Kalagorakis for being a wonderful editor, and Lisa Zeitz for being my smartest critic, greatest inspiration, and fact-checking goddess.